Plan A. Work hard at school, secure a
your sights on promotion, climb the corporate ladder,
live happily ever after.

Reality check for Plan A. Work longer and longer
hours just to make ends meet, being condemned to a
life of wage slavery, drowning in a sea of debt, a
poverty of mind and spirit, existing only to work.

Plan B. A simple yet revolutionary idea . . .

GET OUT WHILE YOU CAN

by George Marshall

Geronimo Books
www.geronimobooks.co.uk

Get Out While You Can - (Pbk)

© George Marshall, 2011

ISBN 978-0-9535932-1-7

Also available in Kindle format

Published by Geronimo Books, Scotland
Printed by CPI Antony Rowe, England

Oi! Oi! The title of this book was taken from the song, Get Out While You Can, by street punk legends, The Business.

Get Out While You Can
www.gowyc.co.uk

Introduction

"There's no secret. You just press the accelerator to the floor and steer left."

Bill Vukovich on how he won the Indianapolis 500

Let me begin this book by asking you something that you probably haven't been asked before.

Why do you go to work?

It's a strange question because most people think that the answer is as plain as the nose on their face. You go to work to earn money to pay your bills and to provide all the good things in life for you and your family.

That's the obvious answer, but it's not the real reason.

You go to work because that's what is expected of you.

It's as simple as that. It's what has been expected of you and me since we were knee high to a grasshopper.

Your family expects you to go to work, your friends expect you to go to work, the people you work with expect you to go to work, your neighbours expect you to go to work, society in general expects you to go to work. In today's society, we are conditioned - brainwashed even - into accepting a life of employment without question.

When you grow up you get a job. Everybody knows that.

I call this Plan A.

In theory it sounds great. If you work hard at school, secure a good job, set your sights on promotion, climb the corporate ladder, you will live happily ever after.

The reality unfortunately is often somewhat different.

For far too many people, Plan A means working longer and longer hours just to make ends meet, being condemned to a life of wage slavery, drowning in a sea of debt, blighted by poverty of mind and spirit, and existing merely to work.

Unfortunately, so ingrained is the work ethic in our belief system, that when Plan A starts to go wrong – as it inevitably does for the vast majority of us - we blame ourselves. We blame ourselves for being inadequate and we try to make amends by working harder, longer and faster. People would rather suffer sleepless nights, a nervous breakdown, even a heart attack, than stop working because, according to Plan A, work is what we do. In fact, as any doctor will tell you, some people would rather die than face the fact that their job is killing them.

Others run up massive debts so that they can maintain a standard of living that their wage packets simply cannot sustain without the help of loans, credit cards and overdrafts. UK consumer debt as of August, 2009, stood at a mind-numbing 1.457 trillion pounds. According to the money education charity, Credit Action, average household debt as of September, 2009, was £58,280, and, together, we pay £181 million in interest payments alone every single day.

The UK is one of the richest countries in the world. Why would we need to be in such collective debt if Plan A worked?

Let me ask you another question. Is Plan A really all that the miracle of creation had in store for you when you first entered this world? A life of drudgery and mediocrity? From cradle to school to work to bus pass to grave? Because from where I'm standing, it looks like a lot of very good people are giving their lives to wage slavery and getting very little back in return.

Plan A is simply not delivering the goods for an increasing number of people, not only in the UK, but throughout the world. And yet society continues to conveyor belt us towards accepting Plan A as if it is the only game in town. And I suppose it is if you want to play by the rules.

But why play by the rules in a game you cannot win?

If Plan A isn't working for you, I want you to urgently consider my Plan B. It's a simple and yet revolutionary idea. And it's this.

Get out while you can.

Get out of a system that values you less than the share price of any PLC you care to name. Get out of the rat race that sees you working longer hours and still unable to make ends meet. Get out of the debt that is like a yoke around your neck. Get out of the madness that has become our daily lives.

Job insecurity and rising unemployment, unsustainable levels of both consumer and government debt, an ageing population and the tsunami-like pension crisis that will inevitably accompany it, spiralling health care costs, turmoil on the world's financial markets, peak oil, global terrorism - these and other problems are creating cracks in a system that increasing numbers of people are falling through. In times like these Plan A should be shoved to the back of the queue and relabelled Plan Z.

As worrying to those who value freedom, the huge and increasing costs associated with our failing system mean that escaping the rat race is going to become increasingly difficult. Someone has to pay for the decades of mistakes and missed opportunity, and if you are not careful that someone will be you.

It might not be a bad idea to have an escape route ready should that day come and that means being able to earn money wherever you happen to be, whether that's Grimsby or Grenada.

The fact that all is not well is not telling you anything you don't already know. To paraphrase Warren Buffet, I don't just want to tell you that it's raining and that it's going to keep on raining. I want to show you how to build an ark. My hope is that this book will provide a blueprint for you to start doing just that. At its heart is my Plan B, my get out of jail card.

Probably like yourself, I have read more books and listened to more motivational speakers than I care to remember, all vowing to improve my life or income by one means or another. All promised so much, but few were really talking to me. In fact when I look along the bookshelves that now house this collection, it's easy to see why. Most are little more than unwitting tools of the wage slave system.

For the most part they aren't trying to set you and me free from a life of wage slavery. They simply want to make us better wage slaves. How to climb the corporate ladder, how to succeed in the stock market, how to get 25 hours out of every day, how to get a five star credit rating. Blah, blah, blah. Each and every one a temporary fix to mask the symptoms of the wage slave disease that is wrecking your life, leaving you out of pocket, breaking up families, and perhaps even sending you on your way to an early grave.

For the duration of this book, all I ask is that you open your mind and eyes to the possibilities it contains. This is far from your typical business book aimed at middle management or stock market investors, and it isn't your typical motivational book, promising immense riches in return for sitting in front of a lighted candle in a dark room for ten minutes every morning.

Neither does it even begin to provide all of the answers, but hopefully it will offer you at least a glimpse of a brave new world beyond wage slavery. The more you think about it, why would anyone in their right mind actually want to work for a living anyway? Why would anyone want to go to work?

For wage slavery to survive, its backers have to ridicule any serious thought of an alternative. So I will be asking you, urging you, begging you, to challenge many of your deepest held beliefs about work, money, and life in general.

There is nothing fundamentally wrong with working for someone else, but equally you should be fully aware of what economists call the opportunity cost of doing so. Put simply, what could you do if you weren't a slave to a wage packet that doesn't even begin to deliver the life you crave for yourself and your loved ones?

Imagine working less hours. A lot less hours.

Imagine working only those hours that fit in with what you really want to do every day - instead of your life having to fit around your work.

Imagine being able to work from anywhere you choose. Anywhere in the world.

And imagine making money whether you're working or not. Even while you're sleeping!

But then again why imagine anything when it can be reality.

There's only one thing to do when Plan A no longer makes sense. Urgently consider Plan B. And then get out while you can.

George Marshall
Costa Blanca, October, 2009

Keeping up with the Beckhams

"Each player must accept the cards life deals him or her: but once they are in hand, he or she alone must decide how to play the cards in order to win the game."
Voltaire

In September, 2008, Manchester City shocked the footballing world when they paid a British record transfer fee of £32.5 million for Robson de Souza (you can call him Robinho). Not only that, but they immediately made the Brazilian striker the best paid player in the English Premier League thanks to a wage packet reportedly worth £160,000 a week.

One hundred and sixty thousand pounds a week! Every week! Can you imagine earning that sort of money?! That's an incredible £8.32 million a year and doesn't even include the money that Robinho earns in sponsorship deals and the other nice little earners that seem to fall at the feet of top footballers as readily as the ball does.

There are plenty of people – not least in the red half of Manchester – who will tell you that Robinho was a waste of money. Whatever your opinion, the fact that he moved to Brazilian side, Santos, on a six month loan deal in January, 2010, tells me that Man City didn't need him quite as much as the money spent signing him would suggest.

Of course there are plenty of other Premier League footballers who are paid fortunes every year. Chelsea's Frank Lampard is said to be on £150,000 a week while the likes of teammate, John Terry, and Liverpool's Steven Gerrard earn around £135,000 every week. There's a certain irony in the fact that when England take to the pitch to play "the people's game", they are represented by eleven millionaires.

And as with Robinho, being paid to play football is only part of the story. Wayne Rooney was sold by Everton to Manchester United for over £25 million in 2004 when he was just 18 years old. He currently earns £100,000 a week in wages, while endorsement deals from the likes of Nike, Coca-Cola, Mercedes and EA Sports bring in another £6 million a year. Celebrity magazine, *OK!*, paid Wayne and his wife to be, Coleen, a whopping £3.2 million for the exclusive rights to cover their wedding. Harper Collins chipped in with five million pounds for a five book deal. Whether Wayne, who left school without getting a GCSE in English, will actually write any of those books remains to be seen. His first, *My Story So Far*, was ghostwritten by journalist and author, Hunter Davies, and his second, *The Official Wayne Rooney Annual*, was edited by football journalist, Chris Hunt.

There's Only One David Beckham

According to accountancy firm Deloitte's *Annual Review Of Football Finance*, the Premier League's wage bill for the 2007-2008 season topped a billion pounds, with your average Premier League footballer now earning more than a million pounds a year. David Beckham is of course far from average as far as footballers go. The 33 year old no longer plays his football in the Premier League, having signed a five year deal with LA Galaxy in 2007 worth over £25 million a year (subject to appearances and increased attendances at the team's Home Depot Center stadium in Carson, California).

Nice work if you can get it.

That is only part of the story though because, just like Wayne Rooney, David Beckham more than trebles his on the field earnings thanks to his ability to exploit his "brand name" off of it. Adidas paid Beckham around £1.25 million during 2001 for the player's endorsement – a year after the company was dragged in front of the European Parliament to face allegations that it was paying factory workers in the Far East literally pennies an hour to manufacture its sporting goods. Giorgio Armani paid him a reputed US$20 million to be a global ambassador for the company in 2007. Other deals with the likes of Pepsi, Sony, Brylcreem, Motorola, Marks & Spencer, and Police sunglasses (to name but a few), have swollen the Beckham coffers further still over recent years.

His wife, Victoria, is no slouch in the earning stakes either. Tesco paid her and each of the other Spice Girls a million pounds each to appear in their 2007 Christmas television commercials, and Victoria followed in husband David's footsteps by becoming the face and body of Armani's ladies underwear, earning around £12 million in the process.

Not bad going for someone who kicks a ball about a park while his wife does a bit of singing. Put into some sort of perspective, an entry level midwife working shifts in a Manchester hospital earns around £20,000 a year and would have to work for 600 years to earn what Victoria was paid just by Armani. Sadder still, the midwife might not be able to curl a ball like David can in his trademark Adidas Predator football boots, but she can probably hold a note just as well as his missus. Only joking, Victoria.

They think it's all over

Footballers aren't the only sportsmen on big money.

When Lennox Lewis fought Mike Tyson in June, 2002, he earned around £14 million for one night's work. Fourteen million pounds for a fight that didn't even go the distance. And let's not forget the US$335,000 (just over £200,000) Tyson had to pay Lewis out of his purse for biting him at a pre-fight news conference. I might even let Iron Mike bite me for that sort of money.

Then there's Tiger Woods. *Forbes* magazine reported that the golfer earned US$115 million in 2007 alone and it expects him to pass the one billion dollar mark in lifetime earnings by the end of 2010. Infidelities permitting of course.

And Formula 1's Lewis Hamilton is expected to earn tens of millions of pounds a year in wages and endorsements after becoming the world's youngest ever F1 World Champion in 2008. He now lives in Switzerland, incidentally, where he pays far less tax on his earnings than he would if he remained in the UK. Mind you, he's still got some way to go to catch the latest F1 success story to hail from these shores. According to *The Sunday Times Rich List*, Jensen Button is already worth an estimated £40 million and his stock is set to soar now that he is 2009's World Champion.

Motor racing is a dangerous sport granted, but as dangerous as serving Queen and country in the likes of Iraq and Afghanistan where we pay a private in a British infantry regiment around £16,000 a year? Arguably not.

What a waste of money?

What do you think an alien would think of our "civilisation" if it landed on Earth and discovered that we place a higher monetary value on someone who can punch a head or who can kick a ball than we do on someone who saves lives or who is prepared to give his or her life?

What does that say about the world we live in?

Of course, most of us would like to be rich. Everything else being equal, it is better to be rich than poor, even if for no better reason than the good that you can do with money. That's why thousands upon thousands of people have phoned the premium rate telephone number to take part in TV's *Who Wants To Be A Millionaire?*, but as each series airs there is only ever one guaranteed millionaire on the show, and that's the host, Chris Tarrant, who earns over three million pounds a year.

That's chicken feed though compared to what the cast of *Friends* earned when they made the tenth and final series of the American sitcom. The six stars of the TV show were each paid an incredible £700,000 per half hour episode. That means that Joey, Chandler, Ross, Rachel, Monica, and Phoebe, each made the UK's average yearly wage in about 60 seconds flat. Incidentally, more than 60% of workers in the UK earn less than that so-called "average wage".

I could go on and on about the crazy mixed up world we live in. For many people, the mere mention of the names Posh and Becks are like a red rag to a bull when it comes to money, and that's why I've used them as my prime example.

In just over a decade the high profile celebrity couple have amassed a huge fortune - and they know how to spend it too. The couple famously splashed out £48,000 on a scaled down Ferrari complete with leather seats and DVD player for their son, Brooklyn, when he was just nine months old. And whereas Mr and Mrs First Time Buyer might struggle to borrow £70,000 to buy a house, Mr & Mrs Beckham are said to have spent that much on a barbecue for their Hertfordshire mansion.

"Nobody's worth that sort of money," is a common complaint whenever you mention the name David Beckham, no doubt fuelled by more than a pinch of jealousy. I've echoed that sentiment too in the past, and no doubt you have too.

But never again.

Because the truth is that David Beckham is worth every dime, nickel and cent he earns, and not just because he generates far more for his football clubs and his other benefactors than what he is himself paid (sales of Police sunglasses for example doubled during the first year of his promotional contract and they did the same again the following year). Other footballers, TV personalities, movie stars, and anyone else you care to mention on huge wages, yes even bankers with their bonuses, are worth every penny too.

And by the time you finish this book you will realise that not only are the David Beckhams of this world worth every penny, but that you are too.

Comfort zone? How about discomfort zone?

Our problem is that we tend to live in a comfort zone. Reality, like beauty, is in the eye of the beholder, and from the safety of our personal comfort zones we can pass judgement on the world at large.

We don't have anywhere near the money that David Beckham has and so we retreat into our comfort zone and console ourselves by saying that he is vastly overpaid for what he does, that it's a disgrace that footballers earn so much, no wonder match ticket prices are so high, the man's an idiot, his wife's a . . . you get the picture.

The first task of this book is to drag you, kicking and screaming if necessary, out of that comfort zone of yours because unless you have everything you want in life (in which case this book would hardly have been at the top of your reading list), that comfort zone of yours is nothing of the sort. It's a discomfort zone.

The real problem isn't that the likes of David Beckham are massively overpaid. The true source of your discomfort is that you are severely underpaid.

Start spreading the news

Okay, so you're not 100% convinced. That's fine by me. We're only a few pages into a new book, and for what is probably the first time in your life, someone is telling you that David Beckham is worth every penny he earns. And this someone isn't pulling your leg either.

It's a lot to swallow I know, but by the time we're finished, you'll be writing apology letters to the man for all the bad things you've ever said about him.

Here's something else that might surprise you.

When the Dutch West India Company purchased Manhattan Island from the native American Indians in 1626, the history books tell us that they did so with trinkets and beads worth a mere US$24. You read right. Twenty four dollars! If they'd paid in pounds sterling, they would have got change out of a £20 note for the entire island of Manhattan!

Of course, in 1626 there was no Wall Street, no Empire State Building, no Fifth Avenue with its designer shops, and no bright lights of Broadway. In fact there were no American dollars either. But even so, the purchase of what is now the bustling commercial and business heart of New York remains one of the biggest bargains in American real estate history.

It's also a story that has more than a touch of the Hollywoods about it. Although there is no doubt that the Dutch West India Company paid only a paltry sum for the island, there are in fact no historical documents or contemporary accounts that mention trinkets or beads being used as payment. Only money.

What's more, no matter what was handed over to the Indians, it would not have been accepted as payment for the ownership of what has become the heart of the Big Apple. You see, the locals believed that all land was sacred and belonged to a Creator. Owning it and trading it was as alien to them as the idea that you could buy and sell the air that we breathe.

Paradise lost

When the native Americans first made contact with European settlers they could never have imagined that a way of life that had served them so well for thousands of years would be virtually destroyed within two centuries. "Civilisation" had arrived in North America and the freedom of the plains was eventually to be replaced by the chains of the reservations.

Before Christopher Columbus "discovered" the New World, the indigenous people of North America were doing very nicely for themselves thank you very much. Deeply held spiritual beliefs meant that they were as one with Mother Nature, living for the most part as nomadic hunter-gatherers and subsistence farmers. Everything they needed was made from local materials (horses were only introduced to North America by the Spanish at the start of the 17th century so means of transport before then were extremely limited).

The simplicity of their lifestyle meant that beyond finding enough food to eat, and the making and maintenance of what few possessions they owned, they had no need to labour from morning to night - unlike their European contemporaries. They also had no taxes, duties or tithes to pay, so there was even less need to produce a surplus beyond what might be needed for the limited trade that would have gone on between tribes in neighbouring areas. A typical "working week" would have been ten to 15 hours long, no more.

In short, the very same people who the missionaries and settlers described as "savages" and "heathens" were actually living the life that the Bible itself says God had provided for Adam and Eve in the Garden of Eden. That is until the good people of Europe dropped in uninvited.

With the benefit of hindsight, it's unlikely that the native Americans would have made the same choices when confronted by pale faced visitors to their shores. Indeed, if the settlers had been driven from the New World at the outset, the world we live in today might be a very different one.

Beads and trinkets

Every day of our lives we make choices, just like the native Americans did, all of which have a bearing on the rest of our journey through life. Whatever position you find yourself in today is the sum total of all the choices, big and small, you have made during your life to date.

We've all made our fair share of mistakes, but by learning from our own mistakes and from the mistakes of others, we hope to make better choices in the future. We can look back through the centuries with a wry smile at the trusting naivety of the "red injuns". And naturally enough, we would all like to think that if we ever had something as valuable as Manhattan Island that we would not repeat such a momentous mistake.

And yet do you know what? You do have a birthright that is every bit as valuable as the whole of Manhattan plus the other boroughs of New York put together. And then some. In fact, go to the top of the Empire State Building on a clear day, and even if you owned and sold everything that the eye could see from its 102nd floor observatory, you still would not be able to afford your birthright.

And the saddest thing of all? The chances are that, just like the Indians supposedly did back in the Seventeenth Century, you unwittingly trade that birthright each and every day of your life for little more than a handful of beads and trinkets.

The birthright in question? Your time.

Did you know that you can literally buy time?

There is only one thing in life that we can all be certain of and that is that one day we will die. You and me both. Death comes to us all sooner or later, and when you are dead, so the saying goes, you are dead a very long time. Our time on this

Earth is very limited. True, our life expectancy is becoming greater, but in the grand scheme of things, 80, 90, 100, or even the 140 years that some optimistic scientists believe will soon be within our reach, is but a blink of an eye when compared to the hundreds, thousands, millions, billions, zillions of years that we will be dead.

The very fact that we are dead a very long time should bring home to us that while we have the gift of life we should make the most of it. The reality is that very few of us do. Our time on Earth might be very limited, but we squander it like we had forever and a day left to live. Before we know it, another day has passed us by and we have little if anything to show for the most priceless gift of all.

Imagine for a moment though that you could buy time.

How much would you be willing to pay for it?

Imagine that you are on your deathbed, about to breathe your last breath, and you are given the chance to buy some extra time by an obliging angel.

How much would you pay to turn the clock back to when your children were young so that you could spend a few extra hours playing with them?

If you have children you will know only too well the feeling of guilt associated with the fact that you can never spend enough time with them because of work and other commitments. Even when you are at home with them, you're just too tired, the lawn needs mowing, that report needs finished by tomorrow morning, your favourite programme is about to start on TV.

Thanks to our obliging angel, you now have an opportunity to buy some of that missed time back.

How much would you be willing to pay for it?

How much would you pay to go back in time so that you could tell your partner, your mother and father, your brothers and sisters, your friends, just how much you loved them at times in their lives when they needed to hear you say those words most?

How much would you be willing to pay to be ten years old again, playing in the late evening warmth of a Summer's day?

And how much would you pay to have your time over again so that you could pursue that dream that eluded you your entire lifetime?

You can't take it with you is a common enough expression. If I set up a stall at the pearly gates selling time, I know I could make more in a day than anyone could spend in a lifetime, including the Beckhams.

It's worth thinking about because when you do think of time in these terms you quickly realise that it is something so precious and priceless that you can't even begin to put a price on it. And yet that's precisely what you are doing day in and day out.

What's even more startling is the fact that you don't need divine intervention to buy time. You even know people who are literally buying time. You know these incredibly lucky people because it is YOUR time that they are buying. In exchange for a pay cheque, you sell your time to someone who is buying it. And probably at a ridiculously low price too.

Time isn't money

From an early age, we are told that time is money. It's the catchphrase of a society that knows the price of everything and the value of very little. The truth is that time isn't money.

The phrase "time is money" first appeared in Benjamin Franklin's book, *Advice To A Young Tradesman*. Mr Franklin is famous for a number of discoveries and inventions, and not least for his work with electricity and thunder and lightning. During his lifetime he was also a statesman, a diplomat, and an entrepreneur, making a great deal of money as a printer, publisher and writer. And all this from very humble beginnings. Born in 1706, he was the 15th of 17 children, and at the age of 12 he was already working as an apprentice printer.

His most successful publishing venture was *Poor Richard's Almanack*, a collection of articles on a wide range of subjects, "conveying instruction among the common people". It proved very popular and made Franklin a small fortune. *Advice To A Young Tradesman* was in a similar vein.

His "time is money" phrase underlined the point that both are limited resources, but it was never meant to be taken literally. As Benjamin Franklin knew all too well, time is not money. Indeed, his true thoughts on time were summed up when he wrote, "Do you love life? Then do not squander time, for that is the stuff life is made of."

Time isn't money because you can't put a value on time. I know people try to, but whether it's ten pounds an hour or £10,000 an hour, those who value their time only in terms of money will always undersell it. My time, your time, everyone's time, is priceless. Once a day has gone, it has gone forever, and all the money in the world can't change that.

The first step towards a better life for you and your family is to realise the true value of your time and the folly of giving up your most precious possession, day after day, for little more than a handful of trinkets. You choose how you spend your time and those choices determine your life's path. If you want to walk a different path, it's as simple as making different choices.

You can fly

Another amazing fact. You can fly. You and me both. All we need is a plane ticket and away we go. In fact air travel, particularly on certain routes, has never been cheaper. So-called budget airlines such as Ryanair, Easyjet and Jet2, have sprung up to take on the traditional airlines, with the result being lower airfares. For some anyway.

The reason I say for some is that even people on the same flight, sitting in neighbouring seats, may have paid different amounts for their tickets. And it's all down to what the business schools call revenue management.

Basically, every flight has so many seats available. Every seat sold means money in the airline's bank account, but every empty seat is an opportunity to make money lost forever. Once that plane leaves the tarmac an unsold seat is worthless.

Not surprisingly, airlines don't like flights leaving with empty seats so they employ complicated formulas to maximise their revenue by literally putting bums on seats. They know for example that a certain percentage of their customers will pay top dollar to sit in the luxury of first class. They also know that the majority of passengers are happy enough to sit in the more spartan and cramped conditions of economy class if it means cheap air travel. There are also those who will travel by plane instead of say train on domestic routes if they get a very cheap seat, and some of these people don't mind booking far in advance or indeed waiting until the last minute. And then there are others who need a flight at very short notice, someone travelling on business for example, who will be willing to pay anything within reason just to get on the plane.

If the airline gets it right, the flight will leave with a combination of passengers paying varying amounts for their tickets, resulting in the airline maximising its income for that particular flight.

Airlines aren't the only businesses employing revenue management techniques. Hotels do it, theatres do it, restaurants do it, even your local hairdresser probably does it. Ever seen those signs that offer old age pensioners half price perms if they have it done on a Wednesday afternoon? That's revenue management in action.

Wanna buy a ticket, mister?

Revenue management has much to offer a wide range of businesses and is something you may be able to employ in any current or future enterprise. During the 1990s, large companies spent millions implementing revenue management programmes in a bid to maximise their profits and it quickly became the latest management fad. These fads come and go with alarmingly regularity, but few if any offer anything particularly new.

For example, while Harvard and other business schools spent months teaching their students the latest revenue management techniques, a lot of time and effort could have been saved by sending each student out for a week's work experience with their local friendly ticket tout.

Ticket touts have been employing revenue management techniques for years now. Touts make money by selling tickets to events such as football matches, pop concerts and the theatre. Wherever demand is likely to exceed the supply of tickets available, chances are you'll find a tout willing to sell you a ticket - at a price. If demand is massive, the tout knows that he can charge high prices because there will always be those willing to pay virtually anything for one. And yet if he is left with any tickets once the event starts, they become worthless.

And so the clever tout knows instinctively what he will get for any ticket at any given time. I've seen touts holding out for ridiculous sums of money - and getting them - with only ten minutes to go before a football game kicks off. Five minutes later, I've seen the same touts in pubs virtually giving away any tickets they have left.

The tout is only interested in the total amount he can get for any number of tickets. If he has more money in his pocket at the end of the day than he originally paid out, then he'll go home a happy man. A small entrepreneur who could run circles around some of the best revenue management brains in the country.

Candy from a baby

We were talking about time, and revenue management has a very important lesson for us all. Every working day, we each have so many hours to trade for money and we generally receive the same amount for each hour of every day. In management circles it's called a pittance.

At certain times though, you may be able to earn more money in return for one or more of your working hours. Working unsociable hours for example (nights, weekends, holidays) can lead to extra money in your pay packet. It can come at a cost too though. According to sleep expert and co-author of *Rhythms of Life*, Leon Kreitzman, working nights for a long period of time has the same impact on your health as smoking 20 cigarettes a day. How many non-smokers would work for a few extra pounds if it meant having to smoke a packet of fags a day? Not many I'd wager. You'll find plenty working at night though.

That said, as we go further and further down the road to a 24 hour society, what were once thought of as unsociable hours are quickly becoming the norm, and basic pay rates are becoming the order of the day (only a third of workers in the UK today work "normal" hours). In fact, countless people work extra hours for nothing just so that they can hold onto their jobs and hopefully look good when the crumbs of promotion are next handed out.

At those times when you are paid more money for your time at work, you are being offered a glimpse of a better world. Even bosses are willing to pay their workers that little bit extra to work hours that will add even more money to the employers' coffers. They know only too well that once that hour has passed, so too has the opportunity to make money during that hour. If it means paying you that little bit extra to make that money, then so be it.

That tiny glimpse of a better world should open your eyes to your full potential. At certain times of the day even your employer is forced to admit that you are worth more than they are generally paying you. What they don't want you to know is that you are actually worth far more than they will ever pay you.

Every waking hour you possess can only be used once and then it is gone forever. Time is the most precious resource you possess bar none. Revenue management can teach you that at certain times you can earn more money by trading that working hour than at other times. Common sense must tell you that, since your time is priceless, you are currently underselling yourself hour after hour, day after day, year after year.

You are in effect a tout selling tickets for the biggest event imaginable (living and breathing) for the price of the paper the tickets are printed on. No wonder your employers are taking 40 or more of them off you every week. It's like taking candy from a baby.

That David Beckham's a decent bloke

David Beckham's worth every penny he earns. So's his wife Victoria. Whether they realise it or not, they are selling their most precious asset - time - and being handsomely rewarded for doing so. The only tickets they'll be giving away are complimentary ones for football matches and fashion shows.

You start every day with exactly the same quantity of time as do the Beckhams of this world - 24 hours, 1,440 minutes, 86,400 seconds - and yet you choose to give it away for peanuts. As I said a little earlier, it isn't that the likes of David Beckham are being paid too much for their time. It's that you and countless others further down the food chain are being paid far too little.

David Beckham must wake up every morning thinking he is one of the luckiest men alive. He is paid a fortune to do something that he loves doing. You on the other hand are paid next to nothing in comparison and may even hate what you are doing. If your lottery numbers came up, chances are you would be out of the office door faster than a greyhound out of a trap.

Beckham meanwhile gets the equivalent of a lottery win in earnings every year and could walk away from the game tomorrow, but chooses not to because playing professional football with the biggest clubs on the planet is a dream come true for him. How good must that feel?

It isn't David Beckham's fault that you're not in a dream job earning your dream income. There's no point having a go at him every time his name is mentioned in conversation or on the box. It isn't anybody's fault but your own.

Plan A sucks. And it sucks big time. Working for a living, and being paid a measly sum by the hour, is robbing you blind of your most valuable asset. Value your time, and I mean REALLY value your time, from this moment onwards and you will have all the riches that life can offer. And I'm including all the riches of life that money can't buy too.

Even if you still think it's outrageous that footballers get paid as much as they do, answer me this one question before we close this chapter. Can you honestly say, hand on heart, that if someone offered you the opportunity to earn vast sums of money to do whatever gives you the most pleasure in life, that you would decline that offer?

I hope not because I'm about to do just that.

Footnote: We all have dreams and there can surely be no better way to spend your life than making those dreams come true. Supposing though your dream is to be the next David Beckham and things don't work out as you would like them to. What next? Pick yourself up, dust yourself down, and set your sights on another dream. That's what. Do something else that rings your bell and gets the adrenaline pumping through that body of yours. Just like Gordon Ramsay did. Gordon was a promising 19 year old footballer with his boyhood heroes, Glasgow Rangers, when a string of injuries cut his career short. So he decided to train as a chef on a day release course. He could easily have settled for a life of Sunday league football and cooking food at his nearest Berni Inn, but instead he pursued a different dream and became the first Scottish chef to be awarded the highly coveted three Michelin stars. He now runs his own restaurants including a flagship eatery in London, as well as having a 25 year lease on the restaurant at top London store, Claridge's. He serves food to the likes of Madonna and Robert De Niro, has a string of books to his name, and has his own television shows. He even gets to swear as much as he wants to.

Work is a four letter word

"The man who trades freedom for security usually ends up with neither."
Benjamin Franklin

Imagine for a moment that you find a magic lamp, and after giving it a rub, a genie appears before you. Ecstatic at being freed for the first time since the days of Aladdin, the genie is only too willing to grant you not just three, but as many wishes as your heart desires. And not just for today, but for the rest of your life!

Is this your lucky day or what?!

So what would you wish for?

Actually, that's a silly question because I probably already know the answer.

If you are like most people you would wish for a demanding job or maybe even a dead-end job, a nice enough house with a nice enough mortgage to match, a car that gets you from A to B but doesn't exactly turn heads along the way, a couple of credit cards and as much overtime as you can get to pay for them, two weeks in the sun every year (even if the sun is in Blackpool and not Barbados), maybe a few hundred pounds tucked away for a rainy day, that sort of thing.

Basically, wherever your life is at now, that's what you would wish for. Day after day after day.

Am I right? Or am I right?

First off, you've got someone you hardly know (that's me) telling you that David Beckham's a decent bloke. Now he's trying to tell you that if an accommodating genie walked into your life today that you wouldn't even ask for so much as a packet of crisps more than what you've already got on your plate.

Is he bonkers or what? Well, you tell me. Because you already have a magic lamp and a genie. The magic lamp represents your life and the genie represents your time.

Where's the magic gone?

Take a typical Monday morning. You wake up bright and early with a brand new day ahead of you. You're definitely still alive and you have the remainder of 24 hours at your disposal. Your genie is stood by your bedside offering you the most precious resource of all - time. What's more, not even the richest man in the whole world is being offered more of it than you are.

So, what is it that you wish for?

How you choose to spend your time is no different to how you would use your wishes, and from where I'm standing it looks like you're saying to your genie, "Nothing amazing today thank you very much – just more of the same please."

Just consider the language that we use to describe our lives.

We work so that we can earn a living.

Earn a living? Is working 40 or more hours a week really living? And I mean REALLY living because to earn that living we spend our priceless time at work. Most of our waking hours in fact. You spend your priceless time earning £5, £10, £20, £50 an hour, for the best part of your life and we call that "a living". A magic lamp and a genie at our disposable every day of our lives and we settle for "a living". Not living life to the full. Just "a living".

My name's Bob and I'm a builder

Such is our dependency on this "living" that we even define ourselves in terms of the job that we do - when a job description tells us almost nothing about who we really are. In fact what we do for "a living" matters very little. If you lose your job, sure it's disappointing. But you don't cease to exist just because you've lost your job title.

There is no reason why you should do tomorrow what you did today just because it is expected of you. No reason at all. Indeed, the most important thing you can be doesn't have a job title. It's simply to be yourself.

If you want to know about the potential of human life, talk to a child under the age of five. They believe anything is possible. When they grow up, they'll own their own zoo. They'll fly aeroplanes. They'll picnic on the moon. And who's to say they won't do all that and then some?

If you have children of your own, you will remember that magical moment when they first came into this world and you were in total awe of the incredible potential that each newborn child has. Anything is possible for a five year old and it's a flame that all parents should keep burning in their children forever.

Barely a day goes by without me instilling in my children that they can do whatever they want with their future as long as they never stop believing, and I'm maybe the only parent that you know who doesn't want their kids to grow up and get a "good" job. I don't want them to "earn a living". As long as they live their lives chasing their dreams, that's all that matters to me, and I'll remain the proudest father alive.

So where does the magic go? At what age do most of us stop believing in the limitless potential of the human spirit (you know, the one that invented the wheel, landed on the moon, discovered penicillin, built the pyramids, opened our eyes to the wonders of Pot Noodles), and settle for "a living"?

Certainly by the time we leave school most of us find our ambitions are far more mundane. Instead of owning a zoo, we settle for visiting one. Instead of flying our own plane we're grateful for a seat on a train. And instead of picnicking on the moon, we grab a burger at McDonald's. For the most part, we are extraordinary human beings leading incredibly ordinary lives.

We gotta get out of this place

The history books tell us that slavery was abolished throughout the British Empire in 1833 with the passing of the Slavery Abolition Act, and yet nearly two centuries later a different form of slavery is still thriving. Wage slavery.

My dictionary defines slavery as being under the control of another person, work done under harsh conditions for little or no pay, exhausting labour or restricted freedom.

Exhausting labour for little or no pay? How often have you arrived home at the end of a working day cream crackered? How many people have no choice but to work 40, 50, 60 hours a week just to make ends meet? How many people work extra hours without pay?

And as for being under the control of another person and restricted freedom, you are at the beck and call of your employer for five or more days a week for the most productive years of your life, are you not?

Our entire economy is based on wage slavery. Just because we get to vote in elections, drink Coca Cola, and tie our own shoe laces, we are fooled into believing that we are somehow free spirits in control of our own destiny when, for most of us, nothing could be further from the truth.

The latest offering from Michael Moore, *Capitalism: A Love Story*, includes reference to a Citigroup Equity Strategy newsletter that argues that rather than democracies, the USA and the UK are actually plutonomies – societies "where the majority of the wealth is controlled by an ever-shrinking minority". I actually like Michael Moore and his work a lot, but despite presenting the report as if it was somehow the mask being pulled away from the dreaded New World Order, Citigroup wasn't telling us anything we didn't really already know. By claiming that the UK is a plutonomy, the report's authors openly state that they are going against conventional thinking, but from my vantage point they were doing no more than stating the obvious. Wealth equals power in good old Blighty. You don't need Citigroup or Michael Moore to tell you that.

If you think the politicians are going to remedy the above any time soon, you'll need to think again. I don't believe there is a political solution. Only an individual one. Successive generations of politicians have shown themselves incapable of rising to the immense challenges we face. You have to wake up and smell the coffee for yourself. Maybe start by questioning the path that you've been put on towards wage slavery.

From before you were even walking, you have been conditioned for a life of wage slavery. It pervades the very fabric of our society so deeply that we are virtually blinkered to any other outcome for ourselves and our loved ones.

As I've said before, when you grow up, you get a job. Everybody and his dog knows that. It's the oldest trick in the book and yet we fall for it time after time. And we haven't even mentioned the long stressful hours many people endure commuting to and from work, or the work that they take home, or the sleepless nights spent worrying about issues relating to work. That's why more often than not a wage packet is fool's gold. A handful of trinkets in exchange for the best years of your life.

Fool's gold?

Hit the pause button. You're quite attached to that wage packet of yours aren't you? And you probably don't take too kindly to having it described as fool's gold either.

That's perfectly natural. Up until now you've played the game by the rules because as far as you were aware it was the only game in town. Not for the likes of David Beckham obviously, but for a mere mortal like yourself. The problem is that you are playing a game that you lose every single time that you clock in.

We spend our childhood and early adulthood going to school not to get a real education, not to develop our true potential, but to be prepared for "the real world" and a lifetime of wage slavery. We then spend the next four decades (give or take a few years) going to work, assuming of course that we manage to stay in employment or don't have a nervous breakdown or a heart attack along the way. Come retirement age, when the wage slave system has no further use for you, it's goodnight Vienna and you are put out to pasture. It's as if you never existed.

We can kid ourselves that once we retire we will be able to do all those things we never could while working, but reality begs to differ for far too many on reaching retirement. Planning to spend the winter in the sun every year? Let's hope you're not one of the estimated two and a half million older households left at home living in fuel poverty then.

You are a POW – a Prisoner Of Work

Do you ever wish you could escape from the trials and tribulations of every day life? I suppose we all do at one time or another, but to escape you must first be held captive. If you think about it, you are a prisoner for most of your life. You are a POW. A Prisoner Of Work. That's what a life of wage slavery does for you. That's what your wage packet buys you. That's why it's fool's gold.

You set your alarm clock so that you get up in time for work. You get the kids off to school so that you can go to work. You fight your way through the rush hour so that you can get to work. You spend most of your waking hours at work. You miss lunch because you've a lot on at work. You take work home so that you can catch up on your work. You brave the rush hour again so that you can get home from work. You snap at your family because you've had a hard day at work. You need an early night because you're exhausted after work. You can't get to sleep because you're thinking about work. You set your alarm clock so that you get up in time for work . . .

Most of your life will be devoted to work. Not to yourself or your family or your dreams, but to work. It's a 40 year sentence that most people would rather not do, but as a POW they have little choice.

Safety in numbers

Lemmings don't really kill themselves by throwing themselves off of cliffs. This urban myth dates back to a 1958 nature film made by Walt Disney entitled, *White Wilderness,* in which several dozen of the Arctic rodents are seen plummeting to their deaths over a cliff. In fact the film crew staged this apparent mass suicide by stampeding the poor animals to their doom so that they could capture a migration sequence. Lemmings aren't even native to Alberta, Canada, where the filming took place - they had to be imported by the film-makers!

As humans, we are more than happy to adopt the lemming-like qualities of legend. We accept our fate of having to go to work to earn a living almost without question. In fact most of us can't wait to leave school so that we can get a job and start earning a living. It's what our great grandparents did, it's what our grandparents did, it's what our parents did, it's what we do, and it's what we expect our kids to do.

We all fall victim to that other urban myth that might as well have come straight out of a Hollywood film script too. Going to work pays the bills and provides for our family's needs.

Working for the rat race

Scratch away at the gloss that we so carefully paint our lives with, and just below the surface you will find the stuff of nightmares. Nightmares that can all too easily make your life a living hell.

According to Oxfam, almost a quarter of the UK's population - more than 13 million people - live below the poverty line, and this despite the fact that the UK is the fourth largest economy in the world. As a nation we create incredible wealth and a quarter of our people live in poverty. Go figure.

Of course, if you happen to be rich, life has probably never been better. Just ask David Beckham or indeed the United Nations. In 1996, the UN Human Development Report showed that the gap between the rich and the poor in Britain was twice as big as it was in Third World countries like Ethiopia and Sri Lanka. Today, the gap between the richest and poorest members of our society is greater than ever. And that's after 13 years of having a Labour Government. The rich are getting richer and the poor are getting poorer, and those in the middle are finding that they need more and more money just to keep their heads above water.

And yet, compared to the lives of our forefathers, the vast majority of us have apparently never had it so good. In a report published to coincide with Queen Elizabeth II's Golden Jubilee, the National Statistics Office found that we are twice as well off as we were 50 years ago and can now spend far more on luxuries than was ever possible before. What it failed to point out is that, as a nation, we are only able to do that because we are also slowly drowning in a sea of debt. Debt that 50 years ago would have been totally unimaginable. The NSO's findings must also be cold comfort to the millions of the Queen's subjects struggling to put food on the table in 2010.

Does your job really pay?

All the pretty clothes and fancy goods that fill our lives are masking a horrendous truth. Most of us just don't earn enough money to support even our current existence, let alone the lifestyles we perhaps dream of. If we did we wouldn't need overdraft facilities and pieces of plastic to see us from pay day to pay day.

A frightening number of people count the days to pay day, and many don't even know if cash machines will give them any money towards the end of the month. What's more, 20% of the working population regularly end the month overdrawn. In the UK, there are over 60 million credit cards in use. France with a similar population can boast less than three million. That tells you all you need to know about how too many of us finance our lives.

We live in a society where far too many people have little or no control over their finances and where most of us just aren't earning enough money to make ends meet in today's materialistic world. The former should be a matter of basic school education and it's a disgrace that financial management isn't taught to our children. The latter requires a radical overhaul of how we choose to spend our lives.

We are working longer and longer hours as a nation, apparently earning more and more money, and still the debts pile up. And the stresses and strains resulting from this madness are there for all too see. Being afraid to open the post in the morning is just the thin end of the wedge. Just wait until they are repossessing your house or your marriage ends up in the divorce courts. Maybe you've already been there and got the t-shirt to prove it.

Job for life?

What amazes me most though is the fact that most people are willing to accept this situation as if it was somehow inevitable. Tattoo this on your brain. Wage slavery is anything but inevitable. Nobody forces you to go into work every morning. You choose to do so. And you can choose not to do so too.

One reason we take so readily to employment is the sense of security it gives us. We know that come the end of the month, we'll get a wage packet. Or at least that's what we used to know.

There was a time when jobs were like buses. Even if you didn't like the one you had, you knew that there was going to be another one coming along any minute.

But the world of today is very different. Our world is changing and changing fast. And nowhere is that more evident than the work place. In our national psyche, job security was virtually the be all and end all, irrespective of how good the job actually was for you (financially, physically and mentally). And then, boom! Or rather bust. Changes in technology and the creation of a truly global economy have changed everything. The days when a job was yours for as long as you wanted it have vanished.

Traditional industries have disappeared, laying off hundreds of thousands of people in the process. Nearly one and a half million manufacturing jobs have been lost in the UK during the last decade alone and it's a slice of the job market that is still shrinking by the day. The simple truth is that labour and production costs are just too high in the UK when the business game is being played on a world stage. Why pay factory workers in Sheffield pounds an hour when you can pay factory workers in Indonesia pennies? Or why pay computer programmers high wages in London when equally skilled people are available at a fraction of the cost in India?

Even companies that you think of as British through and through, more often than not have production plants abroad. Hornby, the makers of model railways and Scalextric car sets, shifted all of their manufacturing to China in 2001. As recently as 1999, about half of all the clothing sold by Marks & Spencer was made in Britain. Today most of it comes from Eastern Europe and North Africa. And even Dyson, makers of bagless vacuum cleaners, has shifted its manufacturing overseas.

Manufacturing today makes up less than 20% of the UK's Gross Domestic Product (GDP), the total value of goods and services we produce as a nation, so when economists talk about GDP nowadays, they may as well be discussing Gross Domestic

Services. Not that very long ago, over a million people in the UK worked in the coal industry. Today three times as many people work for the BBC than do in mining.

A nation of shopworkers

The city of my birth, Glasgow, was once known throughout the world for its shipbuilding, locomotive works and engineering. A quarter of all the large ships in the world were built on the banks of the Clyde once upon a time. Today, over 80% of all jobs in the city are provided by service industries. Shipbuilding has virtually become a museum curiosity. According to a piece in the *Scotsman* newspaper in 2006, more than 100,000 Scots now work in telephone call centres – far more than are employed in the Scottish fishing, oil and gas industries put together.

You can't really blame big business. You shop with your feet if you think there's a bargain to be had across town, so why should we expect businesses to act any differently? And as politicians are quick to tell you, over the last 50 years, manufacturing jobs in the UK may have more than halved, but over the same period the number of people in employment has actually increased by 20%.

More people do indeed have jobs than ever before, but often the quality of those jobs leaves a great deal to be desired. Countless people are on short-term contracts, casual contracts or they work part-time. Almost two million people in the UK today are employed as temps, temporary workers who are often paid less than permanent staff and who miss out on a range of other benefits, such as pensions. It's a sign of the times that the biggest employer in countries from the USA to Holland is now Manpower, the temporary staff agency.

In today's climate of job insecurity though, the terms "temporary" and "permanent" are virtually redundant. In the cold light of day, everyone who works for a wage could lose their job tomorrow. Nobody knows if their job is safe anymore. Contracts can be terminated in the wink of an eye after years of loyal service. Just ask the workers at BMW's Mini plant at Cowley, some of whom had worked there for four years straight without being offered permanent contracts. 850 of them lost their jobs with immediate effect in February, 2009. As agency workers they had few rights, especially when it came to redundancy payments.

Face facts. The only jobs available today are temporary ones. And don't think just because you have a job in a service industry that you are safe. There is a myth that jobs in services are not as badly affected as those in manufacturing during times of recession or adverse economic conditions. When the job axe starts swinging, the people who find themselves out of work are hardly going to be first in the queue for a table in a fancy restaurant to celebrate (although that may well change if enough people read this book).

In the wage slave economy, you are nothing more than a tiny cog in the gigantic wheel of fortune. It doesn't matter how good you are at your job, how long you've been doing it, or how hard you work. You are at the total mercy of the wheel's turning for your very existence, and yet to the owners of the wheel you are as disposable as a Bic razor.

The easy way to full employment

It's estimated that every day more than a quarter of a million people take time off work for stress-related illness. Okay, so some of them are at it, but stress is a genuine problem for many, and absenteeism costs the UK economy £13 billion every year. More of us might have jobs, but a happy contented workforce we are not.

Ironically, a great deal of stress-related illness comes from job insecurity. According to research published in 2002 by the Organisation for Economic Co-operation and Development (OECD), out of the 24 developed nations surveyed, only workers in South Korea have higher levels of job insecurity than their British counterparts.

Why the worry? Despite the job loss announcements that litter news bulletins with increasing regularity these days, unemployment in the UK is still relatively low when compared with the far higher figures found in neighbouring European countries such as Germany, France and Spain.

And yet, as you've probably already guessed, the UK unemployment figures don't tell the whole story. They are based on the number of people out of work AND claiming benefit - and in recent years it has become increasingly difficult to be doing both. There are at least half a million other people out there who are looking for work, but who are not claiming benefit. Two million in part-time work want to be working full-time. Millions of others have been forced back into education or are on the sick. Over two and a half million adults in the UK today receive the Employment and Support Allowance, the new name for incapacity benefit. 16 and 17 year olds have ceased to exist. In fact, nowadays if you don't have a job and are claiming benefits, you're not even technically unemployed. You're a job seeker. All we need to do now is reclassify "job seekers" as "job centre temps" and we will be well on our way to that economic goal of old, full employment.

Two weeks in the sun? Why not 52 weeks?

We devote not only the best years of our life, but also most of our waking hours to work. And for what? Counting the days until Friday? An Employee Of The Month certificate? A couple of week's holiday a year? The hope that when retirement comes, we will be able to heat our homes in the winter?

There are people who are happy in their job, who enjoy going into work every day, and who are well rewarded for their time and effort. It may even be one of their dreams to land the job they have. Good luck to them, but they aren't likely to be the ones reading this book.

For decades now we have been force fed a system that gives us bread and water when we could be dining out on milk and honey. Every day that you do a job that you hate, that neither pays you enough to fully enjoy life or allows you to pursue the dreams that lie at the soul of your very being, you are a prisoner of that system. A Prisoner Of Work.

Some of us seek to escape from wage slavery, and the debt, insecurity and unhappiness that comes with it, by living for the weekends. Some pretend everything is hunky dory and have multiple credit cards and mounting debts to prove it. Others seek comfort in drink, drugs and other vices.

What we are attempting to escape from is the lives we lead - not the lives we were born to lead. We are so blinkered from any other options that we just assume that they are one and the same when they most definitely are not. In its own way, work itself is addictive. You become dependent on that wage packet whether or not it's in your best interests to be going into work every day.

A pay slip says you exist, but surely you want so much more than mere existence. When our time is no longer our own there is every chance that it will end up in the wrong hands. Someone else will decide how you spend your most precious resource and you then cease to be the master of your own destiny.

Somewhere along the line we have come to accept "a living" as the norm, a norm that is only challenged by "special" people, be they footballers, actors or successful entrepreneurs. But the only difference between you and them is how you choose to spend your time. We are all special in lots of different ways - it's just the way of life we choose that can make us feel so very ordinary.

Children are always being asked what they want to be when they grow up. At an early age the possibilities seem limitless, but as we are railroaded through the education system, our choices are slowly by surely focused to the point where, on the day that we finally leave school, we are pressured into choosing a career path. It's at this point that so many of us say goodbye to our dreams and settle for a life of wage slavery.

And yet as human beings we keep on growing throughout our lives. There is no magical age at which you have to decide your entire future based on what the job section of your local newspaper has to offer. If there was it certainly wouldn't be in your late teens.

The billion dollar question

Is a 40 hour plus working week for the best part of our lives the best human ingenuity can come up with?

If there was a competition, with a billion dollars in prize money, to find an alternative way of allowing each and every one of us to fulfil our genuine potential, do you think the wage slavery system would come out on top? I doubt it very much.

Incredibly, we entrust our governments with billions of pounds of our money every year and the best they can come up with is you having to work 40 hours or more a week. The European Working Time Directive was supposedly designed to protect workers from exploitation by employers and in particular to ensure that no employee is obliged to work more than an average of 48 hours a week. When a typical working week for someone in the UK is 42 hours, setting the limit at 48 hours can hardly be considered ambitious, but incredibly our Government fought tooth and nail to be excluded from this clause so that employees can work longer than 48 hours if they choose to do so. I'm all for freedom of choice, but any government that truly valued you or your time would not want you working anything like 48 hours a week.

So what's the alternative? For the vast majority of people I don't have an answer, but I do know of an escape route that could be used by tens of thousands of individuals to get out of the rat race. If you are serious about breaking free from the chains of wage slavery, I am more than willing to share the tools, plans and strategies that have allowed me to declare financial independence and live free from the chains of wage slavery.

Escape from Colditz

Colditz Castle near Leipzig was thought to be escape-proof by the Germans and was an ideal choice to house important prisoners of war - mainly officers and those who had escaped from less secure camps during World War Two. Despite the maximum security conditions and the very real risk of death, the British, French, Polish, Dutch and Belgian prisoners in Colditz saw it as their duty to escape. There were an incredible 300 escape attempts between the start of 1941 and liberation in 1945, and 130 POWs managed to get out. Given the courage and bravery involved in planning and executing each escape attempt, it's little wonder that these men are admired for the heroes they undoubtedly were.

Every family needs a hero. Someone who will guide them to that better life you know they deserve. And that hero is you. I don't care whether you are a father, a mother, a brother, a sister, a daughter or a son. You might even be the family dog for all it matters. Part of the deal you make with yourself when you read this book is that you are going to become a hero for the ones you love the most. A knight in shining armour (if you're of the fairer sex think Joan of Arc) who rescues your loved ones and leads them to the promised land.

Just for a moment imagine a life where you worked less hours than you do today. Probably a lot less hours. Imagine making more money than you do today working those fewer hours. Imagine being able to do this wherever in the world you want to live and wherever you happen to be.

We are living in times of incredible change and for the first time in the history of mankind, the likes of you and me have the opportunity to break free from the chains of wage slavery. It may all sound too good to be true, but all I ask is that you read the remainder of this book and then consider joining me on the other side.

Three ways to make more money

"We ask ourselves, who am I to be brilliant, gorgeous, talented and fabulous? Actually, who are you not to be?"
Marianne Williamson

Monster change that turns the human world inside out and upside down tends to happen every 500 years or so. During the transition between what has gone before and what is about to replace it, major upheaval is inevitable. Casualties are inevitable. We live in such times.

Just as the printing press heralded the beginning of the end for feudalism and a largely agricultural economy, so the computer chip proudly trumpets the arrival of a new technological or information age. What we have always thought of as the modern world is no longer modern. The 1970s might as well be the 1870s such is the frantic pace of change, and those born in what will come to be seen as the last decades of the industrial age are in real danger of being left behind.

So what?

And yet, despite all the talk of our changing world, life goes on. You still walk your dog along the same streets. You still get your bread from the same shops. You still watch United on a Saturday afternoon. The sun still rises in the morning and sets in the evening. It's a bit like elections. No matter who you vote for, the government always gets in. So let the geeks, the great and the good worry about the future. You've got a life to get on with.

And that's exactly my point. You do have a life to get on with, but the chances are that like nearly every other sucker who has bought into the get a job culture of the industrial age, you're not leading your life. In fact, you're barely going through the motions.

You have been hoodwinked by a system that uses and abuses you for the best years of your life and then spits you out when you're past your sell-by date. Then it's off to join the queue at the Post Office on Thursday morning with your pension book in hand. That's if you are lucky enough to still have a Post Office within walking distance. Over 4,000 have closed over the last ten years. More evidence of our rapidly changing world.

The Chinese word for change is made up of two symbols. One means danger and the other means opportunity. Our changing world offers both by the bucketful. Indeed, opportunity isn't only knocking on your door as you read these words, it's ready to kick it in. The danger is that you won't be home to embrace it as it does so. You'll be at work.

The bad news in these changing times is that the days when you worked hard at school to secure a good job that would take you through to retirement are, by and large, over.

That's the good news too. The days when you worked hard at school to secure a good job that would take you through to retirement are, by and large, over. Thank goodness. We should never have allowed our lives to be defined by work in the first place.

Only time will tell whether the monster changes in the way we live mean good news or bad for you personally, but either way, those at the helm of our economy couldn't care less. You're just a statistic. A national insurance number.

Chances are that if you are in work at the moment, you are relatively cash rich and time poor. That's relative to someone who is unemployed and who is cash poor and time rich that is, and not relative to the likes of David Beckham. In an ideal world you want to be both cash rich and time rich. In short we need to get you working less hours while earning you more money.

The really interesting thing is that despite the current worldwide economic turmoil, the possibilities to break away from wage slavery and to do just that have never been greater. Ask Mr Beckham if you don't believe me (if he's still talking to you after everything you've ever called him). You'll no doubt be pleased to hear that he's making more money than ever. And so is Victoria.

Money money money

It's worth taking the time to analyse exactly how the likes of David Beckham make so much money (particularly if you don't) because despite the quality of some of his free kicks, the man is only human after all. Just like you. What's more, because there are only three ways for mere mortals to make more money than they currently earn, it shouldn't be that difficult to arrive at the answer.

You and David Beckham have at least two things in common. The amount of time you have every day and those three ways of making more money. And as you've probably gathered by now, it's how you choose to use your most precious resource that is key to the gulf between what the likes of David Beckham earn and what you earn (if you haven't grasped this, go back to the start of this book and stop skipping pages).

The first way for you or David to make more money is to work longer hours.

It stands to reason that if you are paid by the hour, you will make more money by working more hours. A lot of us try this, but quickly come unstuck when we realise that there are only 24 hours in any one day. Not that it's possible to work every hour God sends - although by the looks of it, a few of us are doing our best to do just that. In fact, Brits in general already work longer hours than anyone else in Western Europe.

Do you think David Beckham works more hours than you do? Probably not.

Even if you do work extra hours, you are hardly going to turbo charge your earnings unless you are on an enormous hourly rate in the first place. The sad reality is that millionaire status is not likely to be waiting around the corner just because you've put in extra hours as a wage slave. And anyway, who wants to work more hours? We want to work LESS hours.

The second way to make more money is to earn more money per hour. Again, a lot of us try this. Promotion, wage rises, changing jobs, all offer us the opportunity to add pounds to our wage slip, but chances are you will still have a long way to go before you can describe your pay packet as obese.

Do you think David Beckham spends any time wondering about how he can increase his hourly wage rate? I don't think he's losing any sleep over it anyway.

Longer hours, more money per hour, both offer only tiny crumbs of comfort to a wage slave. Of course, we all need money to pay for all the things that we want out of life that have price tags slapped on them. A few of us are born with money or inherit it, others seem to make incredible amounts of money doing very little (pop stars, footballers, celebrities, fat cat bosses), but the vast majority of us have to work hard for it.

In fact wage slaves are working so damn hard that they rarely have time to even consider the third and final way of making more money. And yet it holds the key to the secret of David Beckham's success, Bill Gates' success, Warren Buffet's success, in fact the financial success of virtually anyone you care to mention who earns serious money. And naturally enough it is the key to your future success too.

And the winner is . . .

The third way to make more money is to develop what I call multiple revenue streams.

Multiple revenue streams.

Sounds like business speak I know, but you'll soon get the hang of it.

Take those three words in turn. Multiple simply means more than one. Revenue means income. Streams in this instance refers to money that will flow towards you.

You must develop multiple revenue streams if you are ever going to break away from wage slavery.

Some people hold down two or more jobs in the wage slave economy. That's both an example of working longer hours and having more than one stream of revenue. Two or more employers pay you, but that's the lowest form of developing multiple revenue streams. Indeed, it's little different to working longer hours for the one employer. Developing multiple revenue streams offers you so much more than this as the likes of David Beckham know only too well.

Third time lucky

Chances are you may already have multiple revenue streams at work for you, but perhaps don't fully realise their significance in demonstrating just how much you would earn if you developed others.

If you have savings in an ISA, a bank account or a building society account for example, you may well earn interest on those savings. That interest represents a stream of income, albeit a rapidly shrinking one in today's economic climate thanks to record (artificially) low interest rates. Indeed, a lot of pensioners, who until recently relied on interest payments to supplement their income, are now having to dig into their capital to make ends meet - and that's particularly true of those who have retired to say France or Spain where the pound is worth far less than it was a year or two ago. Nevertheless, interest from savings is a good example of a revenue stream that earns you money.

Similarly if you have ever invested in stocks and shares they too can provide you with a revenue stream. Apparently, 12 million of us in the UK own shares, although an increasing number probably wish they didn't given the recent fortunes of the stock market. The FTSE 100 had its worst year on record in 2008, losing 31% of its value in just 12 months. It's risen since – one daily newspaper even called it a "new boom" - but it still finished 2009 lower than it was a decade ago.

I've never actually invested in the stock market myself. Having studied Economics at University, I fully appreciate the stock market's pivotal role in raising capital for business, but it is a market that is all too often driven by sentiment. Sentiment that usually takes the form of either greed or fear, two traits that aren't particularly attractive to me.

It is possible to make a great deal of money from the stock market, even when the market generally is falling, but I'm not the person to tell you how unfortunately. There are those who will tell you that anyone can make money from stocks and shares providing they take a "long term" approach. This is evident nonsense. There is a risk attached to investing in shares, hence the potentially higher rewards when compared to less risky investments such as bonds or bank accounts. If we can all agree that this risk exists in the short term, then what alchemy is at work that evaporates that risk over time or "the long term"? In fact there is no reason why investing in stocks and shares should be less risky over time. The risk doesn't diminish at all. Indeed, if anything, risk gives way to uncertainty and when that happens we're talking lucky dip.

And what exactly does "long term" mean anyway? Does it mean five years, ten years or even longer? Taking the last decade as an example, the FTSE 100 reached a record high in December, 1999, of 6,950. Looking ahead to December, 2010, it doesn't look particularly likely that the FTSE 100 will come even close to that figure. Warren Buffet came closest to the truth when he said, "Our favourite holding period is forever".

For me, Fred Schwed Jr's classic book, *Where Are The Customers' Yachts?*, paints a perfect picture of who is really making money out of the stock market. The title comes from an old story about a visitor to New York who is shown all the yachts in the harbour owned by brokers and bankers. Naively, the visitor asks where the customers' yachts were. Of course there were none.

Another example of a revenue stream that we are all familiar with is property, whether from rental income or capital gain, although it too is not without its risks. If you have ever bought and sold a house for a profit, you'll know how good it feels though. The downside of course is that any profit from property caused by a rising market is tempered by the fact that when you come to buy again, you soon discover that the price of the property you want has also risen. If you are able to move to a part of the UK where property prices are lower, or indeed you can move abroad to a country where property speculation isn't a national obsession, you can end up quids in (some good news – the opportunities presented in this book mean you can live virtually anywhere in the world you want to).

Property isn't the one way bet we are all too often led to believe, however, and in the current climate it's not a potential revenue stream that I would recommend. Indeed, a great deal of the media hype that has surrounded property speculation in recent years has been little short of irresponsible, with most of the talking heads wheeled out to big up the market having vested interests in doing so. Whoever coined the phrase "property porn" hit the nail firmly on the head. I know plenty of people in Spain, for example, who now rue the day that they ever watched *A Place In The Sun*.

In any case, to make big money from property, stocks, or indeed savings, you need to be willing to invest (and therefore risk) substantial sums of money. Sums of money that most of us don't have - or if we do, can ill-afford to lose.

The real problem with being a wage slave isn't a lack of money to invest in developing new revenue streams though. That's because it doesn't have to cost very much to get new revenue streams up and running. I will shortly be showing you how to start the ball rolling for less than £50, money that you can quickly rustle up by spending an afternoon selling unwanted clutter at a car boot sale or from the comfort of your own home via eBay. So you don't need vast sums of money. The real issue is one of time and how you spend your time. You've probably been too busy working to give alternative multiple revenue streams more than a passing thought.

What is interesting about the examples above is that you don't make that money by actually working. You don't work to earn interest from a bank account. You don't work to collect dividends from shares. You don't work to enjoy the benefits of a rising property market. Those revenue streams work for you.

Water water everywhere

If you think of money as water, a wage slave's income trickles out of one tap in a house with low water pressure. For the sake of argument, let's pretend it's the cold water tap in the kitchen. Meanwhile David Beckham is running around his house (and it's a big house) turning on taps (gold taps at that) like there is no tomorrow. Water is gushing out of them in the kitchen, in the utility room, in the bathrooms, and even out of his designer shower heads. There are fountains and water features in the gardens, his swimming pool is full to the brim, and he's taking delivery of lorry loads of Perrier. All because he knows the secret of multiple revenue streams.

That's why he plays football for LA Galaxy and Inter Milan. That's why you can buy David Beckham calendars, David Beckham books, David Beckham DVDs, David Beckham posters, David Beckham computer games, David Beckham pyjamas, David Beckham football scarves. That's why he appears in television commercials both here and abroad. That's why he does photo shoots for glossy magazines. That's why he appears on billboards in Japan. That's why he wears Adidas football boots and Police sunglasses. That's why he's opening football training schools for kids.

Each and every one of the above represents a revenue stream for David Beckham. Even when he is sleeping, these multiple revenue streams are earning him money, all over the world. 24 hours a day, 365 days a year. How good must that be?

Isn't it just the case that David Beckham "works" just like the rest of us, but just gets paid more? No, not at all. Look closely and you'll see that the work that David does in any one hour more often than not continues to make him money long after that hour has past. That's why developing multiple revenue streams that do exactly the same can totally transform the way you earn money and live your life.

The big mistake we make is to sell our time by the hour. Instead we should be doing what Mr Beckham does. Do an hour's work and then allow that hour's work to make us money for days, weeks, months, years even, to come. We can't all be top footballers unfortunately, but thanks to the information age, anyone who can turn on a computer can put their time to work for them just like David Beckham does.

Food for thought

Here's someone else you might know. Jamie Oliver. Jamie was living in a tiny flat and working as a chef at The River Cafe in Hammersmith, London, when a television crew arrived to make a documentary about the Italian restaurant. At the time, Jamie was like anyone else who works in a kitchen. Paid by the hour to feed faces.

When the documentary was aired in 1999, it changed Jamie's life completely. He was a natural in front of the cameras and the following day he received phone calls from five television production companies interested in working with him. It wasn't long before he was on the box again in his own *Naked Chef* series.

As a chef in a kitchen he can cook for a limited number of people during any shift. He could be the best chef in the world and that wouldn't change. His income would then be dependent on a wage, if he was employed, or a cut of the profits if he had a stake in the restaurant. That was Jamie's lot before he became a celebrity chef.

Since then of course, Jamie has discovered the magic of multiple revenue streams. Jamie now has his own restaurants like Fifteen in London which was featured in the Channel 4 television series, *Jamie's Kitchen*, and then *Return To Jamie's Kitchen*. Books by the same name are available, as are a dozen or more others for which Jamie will receive royalties (*Happy Days With The Naked Chef* sold more than half a million copies in 2001 alone).

Despite being born and bred in Essex, his love of Italian food has led to the launch of a new chain of eateries called Jamie's Italian. The first one opened in Oxford in 2008 and there is now a Jamie's Italian in Bath, Kingston, Brighton, Cardiff and one at London's Canary Wharf too.

If you go along to Jamie's restaurant on Westland Place, London, N1, and he happens to be there, he might even cook you some of his pukka tukka. If he does you will eat it and the time that went into preparing that meal will be gone forever. But imagine you could cook a meal that could be enjoyed by not just one person, but by thousands of people. And not just within minutes of it being served, but for years to come. And not just at a table in a restaurant, but in homes throughout the world. That one meal would be worth a small fortune to you. A hugely successful spin on any revenue stream is to be able to do just that. Buy one of Jamie's DVDs and you'll see exactly how that's done too. Jamie isn't working every time someone buys and watches his DVD, but he is earning money.

Feed the world

In fact Jamie took this concept one step further by cooking live on stage in front of an appreciative paying audience during his Happy Days Tour - a tour that was filmed for subsequent release. Not only that, you can guarantee that there was also a stall in the foyer selling Jamie Oliver merchandise, adding yet another revenue stream to that particular project and earning the main man even more money. Not only did Jamie make a DVD, people paid to watch him make it!

What Jamie is effectively doing with a project like the Happy Days Tour is selling one hour of his time, not just once to an employer like a wage slave does, but to thousands of people all over the world. And that one hour of work will be earning him money for many months if not years to come because the *Happy Days Tour* DVD and related products can be reproduced and sold for as long as there is a demand for them. Jamie doesn't have to lift a finger beyond opening the envelopes with the big fat royalty cheques inside.

Jamie also writes regular articles for magazines for which he will be paid, and then there's the consultant chef work he does for Monte's restaurant in London, not to mention the money-spinning trips to Japan and the USA. You can even buy Jamie Oliver aprons and tea towels, and there's the Jme range of kitchenwear too. He's also the face of the Sainsbury's supermarket chain and has played a big part in increasing the company's turnover. Sainsbury's themselves have said that he is responsible for generating 20% of their profits and his current deal with them is said to be worth more than a million pounds a year to Mr Oliver.

Want to know what Jamie listens to while dicing carrots and peeling spuds? Look no further than the compilation CD, *Cookin'*, a collection of Jamie's favourite songs (with something like this, he'll pick up regular royalty payments simply by putting his name to the finished product).

Not bad going for a 35 year old who left school at 16 with little in the way of qualifications. You need to be thinking along similar lines. Develop multiple revenue streams and get the most out of at least some of your time by selling it over and over again. That's how the likes of David Beckham and Jamie Oliver are making more money in a year than most people make in a lifetime. Selling the time that they spend working over and over again.

Celebrity squares

Hold on a minute though. Developing multiple revenue streams is fine and dandy when you're David Beckham and Jamie Oliver because they are celebrities. You're just a mere mortal, and the last time you checked, Tesco and Asda weren't in a bidding war to use your ugly mug in their forthcoming marketing campaigns. But the truth is you don't need celebrity status to develop multiple revenue streams.

Do you know Greg from Devon? Or his mates Swift, Gail and Ernie? Probably not. Greg, Swift, Gail and Ernie are sheepdogs. Their owner, David Kennard, runs a farm near Woolacombe in the West Country. You've probably never heard of David either.

Like a lot of farmers, David was struggling to make ends meet and there were no more hours in the day to work. His wife was a part-time nurse, but even with this extra source of income, it was proving financially difficult down on the farm.

Then David hit on an idea involving Greg, Swift, Gail and Ernie. He decided to film his day to day work and the result was a video entitled *A Year In The Life Of A Sheepdog*. It cost £15,000 to make the finished video and David then needed to sell 3,000 copies to recover those costs. He ended up selling 20,000 copies in the West Country alone before a distributor stepped in to offer national distribution.

David had to work on the farm anyway, but the video gave him the opportunity to sell those working hours over and over again. I don't know what other plans he has, but his success to date readily lends itself to developing related opportunities such as a book, a calendar, sheepdog cuddly toys, a follow up DVD, or even running weekend shepherding courses.

As you will discover later in this book, you definitely don't need celebrity status to develop multiple revenue schemes. And before you ask, no ,you don't need a sheepdog either. Or £15,000 to splash out on a video.

Even when you know about multiple revenue streams, the temptation is to continue doing what you've always been told to do and serve your life sentence as a wage slave. Everyone and his dog is in the same boat so why should you be any different? But as David and Greg have just shown you, everyone (and his dog) is not prepared to stay aboard a vessel that's looking increasingly like the Titanic. Opportunities are there for the taking and now is the time to grab a lifejacket and jump overboard. That's when you'll discover that the water isn't quite as deep as you'd always imagined it to be, and that land - paradise in fact - is only a short swim away.

Forget about working longer hours and forget about dreaming of a pay rise. If you've already got savings, stocks and shares or have invested in property, forget about those too for the moment. It's time to do something outrageous for once in your life. Invest in yourself.

Invest in yourself, develop multiple revenue streams, and you will be a slave no more.

Time management made easy - just say no

"Welcome to Hollywood. What's your dream?"
Happy man on Sunset Boulevard in Pretty Woman

Fans of *Only Fools And Horses* will remember this particular episode well. Del Boy Trotter, market trader and millionaire (this time next year), has become a yuppie. And so it is that he finds himself in a trendy London bar - white wine spritzer in one hand, black leather Filofax in the other - talking to his friend, Trigger.

Two attractive and smartly dressed women walk into the hostelry and Del's eyes are quickly drawn to them. "I think we're on a winner here, Trig," says Del as he leans against the bar. "Play it nice and cool, son, play it nice and cool."

Unfortunately, our hero fails to notice that the barman has lifted the flap on the bar close to where he is standing, and when he goes to lean back against it, Del falls right over!

"Come on Trigger, we're leaving," says a flustered and embarrassed Del Boy as he picks himself up off the floor.

The Eighties was the decade in which the Filofax personal organiser truly came of age and it was up there with the mobile phone (remember when they were the size of bricks?) as an icon of the young upwardly mobile city types who typified that get-rich-quick decade.

Today, Filofaxes and their kin, be they paper based or electronic, are an essential part of many people's lives. If you're like me, you might even have a collection of them. Hands up who still gets an imitation leather personal organiser from a well-meaning relative every other Christmas?

The history of the Filofax actually dates back as far as 1921 when a company was set up in London to sell personal organisation systems, and the trademark Filofax (a corruption of "file of facts") was first registered in 1930. Interestingly, it wasn't a multi-national conglomeration that made Filofax a household name in the Eighties, but two Filofax devotees, David and Lesley Collischon. The couple set up a mail order business in 1972 to market Filofax and related products from their home. Such was their success and belief in Filofax that in 1980 they bought both the company and the trademark, and then set about developing what is now a brand name recognised throughout the world.

It must have been a dream come true for the Collischons when their relatively obscure product became such a roaring success. Of course we all have dreams, mental images of things that we aspire to or hope to achieve in our lifetimes, but despite the wide range of page inserts that are available to Filofax customers, it's always struck me as odd that there has never been one for you to list your dreams.

A life of wage slavery doesn't usually encourage this, but it's my honest and total belief that all of our time and energy should be devoted to pursuing and achieving our dreams. Any time management system or personal organiser that does not recognise this is selling you short. Looking at the huge array of time management books, organisers, systems and seminars currently on the market, it's not only Filofax who seem to be missing the point.

The only explanation for such a monster oversight is this. Although they value both your patronage and the money that comes with it, the vast majority of time management systems simply do not value your time. It sounds crazy, but it comes down to the fact that they fall victim to the same lie that most of us do. The all pervasive belief that somehow our time is not our own and that it is somehow the property of others.

Just say no

Here's an example of what I mean. How many times have you been asked to do something that you really didn't want to do and yet you agreed to do it? Countless times I'd wager. Someone makes a demand on your time and although your brain says no, your mouth opens and the word that comes out is, "Yes."

It's as if our time is not really our own and is constantly at the disposal of others.

Here's another one for you. How many fingers do you need to count the times you have spent an entire day that was exclusively devoted to just you, without a single demand on your time from someone or something else? One hand is usually more than ample when answering that one. Try it tomorrow. See how far you get into the day without someone imposing on your time, be it welcome or otherwise.

It's inevitable that this will happen because we are constantly interacting with other people and all relationships require the giving and taking of time to be successful. But what we're talking about here runs far deeper than that. We are so conditioned to giving our time to others that we would much rather agree to do so than risk upset or offence by saying no.

Virtually all time management systems are happy to go along with this by offering tips, tricks and lists aimed at allowing others to get the most out of our waking hours. It's a frightening thought that while thousands of us strive to become more organised, we do so not really for ourselves, but so that others can make better use of our time! Hence most time management systems are aimed at employees and the hours that they spend at work - and most time management courses are paid for by employers.

It's as if the only important hours in your day are the ones you spend at work when nothing could be further from the truth for most of us. There's a book currently available called *Time Management For Dummies*. Most time management books and tools seem to have dummies in mind too. That's why if you were thinking here comes the bog standard time management chapter that virtually every self-improvement book contains, you'll have to think again.

By far the best time management system I know is simply this. Just say no.

Back to school

I've been helping my son, Scott, revise for his forthcoming Scottish Higher exam in Business Management and part of the course deals with business objectives. So for example, the business objectives of a sole trader might include business survival, to maximise profits, to improve the owner's personal status, and to have a good image in the community. The same might be true for a partnership whereas possible objectives of a public limited company might include maximising profits and dominating a market. All of the above objectives are straight out of the textbook.

I'm in business too, but my main objective isn't anywhere to be seen. Indeed, I doubt you'd find it in any business textbook used in school to teach kids. That's because my objective involves time, the most precious resource of all that somehow gets totally overlooked. Specifically, I aim to make as much money as possible in as little time as possible. That's it. I'm not interested in dominating markets, maximising profits, or in having the highest possible sales revenue. I just want to make the money I need as quickly as possible and then I'm out the door spending something far more valuable than money. My time.

I'm not advocating life as a selfish arsehole. It's good to give your time to others. There's nothing more precious you can give someone than your time. Just don't keep giving away so much of it for beads and trinkets if it means that you don't have the time to do what you really want with your life.

Satisfaction guaranteed

In the 1950s, a brilliant motivational psychologist by the name of Abraham Maslow developed a pyramid shaped ladder of human needs. He called it the Hierarchy Of Needs and his work is as relevant today as it was when first published.

At the bottom rungs of the ladder are the most basic of needs, physiological needs. Then comes our need for security and safety, followed by our social needs. Further up the pyramid are our needs relating to esteem and recognition and then at the very top comes our need for self-fulfilment.

To progress up the ladder, Maslow argued that we need to first satisfy our needs at every level below the one we are reaching for. This makes perfect sense when you consider the categories of needs in more detail. Physiological needs are needs that must be satisfied for us to function properly and include our need for water, food, shelter, warmth, even sex (biologically speaking, our big role on planet Earth is the creation of a new generation of our species).

Unless our physiological needs are satisfied, they are likely to dominate our thoughts and actions. Fortunately, the vast majority of people living in the developed world can take such things for granted. You want a drink, you turn on a tap. You want something to eat, you phone for a pizza. You want shelter, you go home. You want warmth, you turn on the heating. You want sex . . .

Once those basic needs have been satisfied, the next steps up the ladder deal with safety and security. Again, in a modern developed society we often take our safety for granted except during times of war or civil unrest, but our often irrational fear of being victims of violent crime is one example of a primeval need to feel safe.

Beyond those first rungs of Maslow's Hierarchy Of Needs comes what are called social needs - our need to be loved, our need for affection, acceptance, the need to feel that we belong, and our need of recognition. Loneliness and rejection are unfortunately increasingly common symptoms of modern life and many of us find ourselves dealing with needs at this level at some point in our lives.

For those who have satisfied their physiological, safety and social needs, the next rungs up the ladder deal with higher needs relating to personal esteem and self-respect. We all like to think that we have value and deserve recognition for what we do and who we are. If these higher personal needs go unfulfilled we can be left feeling inferior or even worthless and our self-confidence will plummet, thereby preventing us from reaching the top rungs of the ladder and what Maslow saw as the zenith of human existence – self-fulfilment.

According to Maslow, it doesn't get any better than when you are satisfying your needs for self-fulfilment, the desire to push the boundaries of your own potential. It is on this frontier that people are driven onwards in pursuit of what they really want out of life and towards realising their full potential. Your life's vocation, your calling if you like. What I call the pursuit of dreams.

Maslow surmised that most of us would want to continue climbing the ladder of needs throughout our lifetimes so that we could fulfil our potential as individuals - unless of course we were prevented from doing so.

When you think about it, that's exactly what's happening to millions upon millions of people who have signed on the dotted line for a lifetime of wage slavery. They are being prevented from doing so. Instead of pursuing dreams and striving for self-fulfilment, they spend their time clinging on to the bottom rungs for dear life. The likes of David Beckham aren't any different to the rest of us. They just spend most of their time at the top of Maslow's ladder.

Going up?

Think about how the wage slave system manipulates your needs instead of satisfying them. The shelter we need usually takes the shape of a home, be it a semi in suburbia or a castle in the country. We fill that home with all our possessions, and naturally enough, we want to protect ourselves and our family, our homes and our property. Hence the need for both the emergency services and the armed forces which we pay for collectively through taxation.

To pay for our homes, and all the things we put in them, we need money. And to pay for security and protection (as well as the myriad of other functions, good and bad, that our government performs), we need even more money. That's where the wage slavery part of the equation kicks in because, for most of us, the need for money means we get a job. For most of us it also means the end of our dreams.

Why should this be? Simple. In the vast majority of cases, the wage slave system does not supply us with enough money to pay for the material things we fill our lives with and so we end up borrowing money to make ends meet. And with debt comes insecurity. We then cling to our jobs for dear life in the hope that our efforts will be rewarded with a regular pay packet to fend off this insecurity - when the reality is that jobs today, as we've already discussed, are as temporary as a blue sky on a Summer's day in Scotland. The result? More insecurity.

We might not be chased down the road by sabre-tooth tigers anymore, but today's work-related fears are just as real. That's why we do jobs we hate, that's why we try to save for a rainy day, that's why they can sell us often pointless insurance policies for everything and anything. If your daily focus is on satisfying needs at the bottom of the pyramid, it's not actually that surprising that you don't make it to the top.

Another aspect of man's need to feel safe and secure is the fact that we don't like change. We cling to a wage slave system that doesn't deliver the goods because to venture from the beaten path would mean embracing change. The ship's sinking, we can see everyone aboard reaching for the lifejackets, and yet we still clamber on board because it's simply not British to rock the boat.

Who wants to be Employee Of The Month anyway?

If we can see any truth in Maslow's theory of human needs, it's pretty obvious that the wage slave system is not designed to help you climb the ladder. Quite the opposite in fact. By denying you security, both mentally and physically, it is very difficult for you to progress onto the next level. In fact it plays on our fears to such an extent that we demand very little from wage slavery in return for our time. If we ask for too much, we may end up losing what little we already have, so we keep quiet.

We're actually pretty good at the social needs side of things - humans by their very nature are gregarious. But again the wage slave system, with its increasing demands on our time, hardly gives us a moment to ourselves. "Career orientated" people often sacrifice family life in a bid to achieve success in the workplace. Dad or Mum leave the house so early and come home so late they barely see their kids during the working week. In terms of interaction, think guests in a hotel rather than family.

Even when we do get recognition for a job well done (fancy job title, a clock when you retire, Employee Of The Month t-shirt, a lucky bag at Christmas), we are often left with a nagging feeling that there must be more to life than work. That's because there is!

We have a built-in desire to satisfy our potential and to climb Maslow's ladder, a desire that is denied us by the chains of wage slavery and a society that is built upon it. When you are prevented from climbing to the higher rungs of Maslow's ladder, it's no wonder your dreams seem such a distant goal. By removing the chains of wage slavery you will be freeing yourself from its constraints and will be answering only to your higher calling. The pursuit of dreams.

I know phrases like "the pursuit of dreams" have an unfortunate New Age air to them, part fantasy part wishful thinking, but believe me, I'm no hippy. For me, it's the ones who see nothing wrong with a wage slave society who are away with the fairies, not those who seek to fulfil their potential.

Let's rekindle the magic

The dilemma for most people is this. When you are working, you might have the money to do some or all of the things you'd like to do, but you simply don't have the time. And if you aren't in employment, then the chances are that you have all the time in the world to do exactly what you want, but you don't have the necessary money to do so.

If we are to spend our lives pursuing and fulfilling dreams, then we need to be both cash rich and time rich at the same time. We need to spend as little time as possible earning the money we require to pursue our dreams.

I watched a television documentary a few weeks ago called *Fat Man Slim*. It was about a 40 year old man called Paul Jeffries who apparently had it all. After moving from England to New Zealand in 1986, he forged a successful career in advertising, becoming the Managing Director of M&C Saatchi in Auckland.

On paper, Paul was incredibly successful. Three houses, a sports car, a wine collection, a big salary and the lifestyle to match it. The truth was though that his job was killing him. He was morbidly obese and behind the facade of success was a man who hated himself.

Paul's solution was as radical as it was necessary. He got out while he could. He gave up his job and dedicated the next year of his life to his health. Weighing in at over 26 stones (168kg) at the start of the year, the man they called Squeeze embarked on an exercise program and a new diet regime that would see him transform himself over the coming months. At the end of the year he had lost just over ten stones (64kg) and had regained his health.

It was also during this year that Paul discovered multiple revenue streams as a way of making money while doing what he wanted to do with his life. As well as making the documentary, Paul wrote a book entitled *Diary Of A Fat Man* which was published in 2003 and was followed by another book, *Fat Man Cooks*. He also wrote newspaper columns, made television appearances, and was employed as a public speaker to motivate others.

Lots of us would like to lose weight and improve our health, but what should be a big priority in our lives is relegated to trying to squeeze in a few gym sessions around our already busy schedules or attempting to avoid comfort eating when we return home from a knackering day's work. No wonder so many people fail to lose weight.

Paul on the other hand was always more likely to succeed because he took an entire year of his life and dedicated it to himself and his dream of losing weight and regaining his health. And when you think about it, shouldn't we all be dedicating large chunks of our life to our well-being?

It all comes back to time and how we use every 24 hours that our life affords us. When people moan that they don't have enough hours in the day to do what they really need or want to do, it's because they are giving away most of their time to an employer. And for buttons too.

Faking It

If you're anything like me, you probably watch more television than is good for you. According to the book *UK 2002*, women watch an average of 27 hours of television each week - three hours more than men. That means that if you live to be 75, you'll have probably spent an entire decade of your life with your eyes glued to a TV screen. There's ten years right there for starters that you could dedicate to pursuing your dreams.

As the children's television programme, *Why Don't You?*, was fond of telling you during the school holidays, "Just turn off the television set and go and do something less boring instead". Or in your case, something more rewarding (in every sense of the word) instead. Not before you've seen at least one or two episodes of the excellent documentary series, *Faking It*, though.

The premise of *Faking It* is simple. Take ordinary people and completely change their identity within three to six weeks. At the end of the allotted time period the transformation has to be so complete that a panel of experts will be convinced that the subjects of the experiment are in fact the real deal.

So you have a man who runs a burger stall being transformed into a top chef in just four weeks before entering a cooking competition against genuine chefs from top London hotels - and winning! You have a sheep shearer who becomes a hair stylist in barely a month. A diminutive gay public schoolboy who has four weeks to learn the ropes in the East End of London before working the door as a bouncer at Stringfellows like an old pro. A singer with a punk band conducting the London Philharmonic Orchestra. And a bicycle riding country vicar, with no knowledge of the motor trade, who manages to convince seasoned dealers that he is in fact a secondhand car salesman from Essex.

As each episode begins, there doesn't look like the remotest chance of the subject being transformed into somebody he or she so obviously isn't. And yet, as the series demonstrates time after time, anyone can be anything they want to be if they will only dare seize the opportunity. Obviously the lad who sells hamburgers isn't a cordon bleu chef after those four weeks, but there's certainly no doubt left in anybody's mind that he could be one if he wanted to be. Which begs the question, why is he flipping burgers into the early hours when he could be doing so much more with his time?

The reason for these successful transformations is simple. All of us are capable of doing so much more with our lives. Average Joe doesn't exist because none of us are average. Each and every one of us is incredible. Truly incredible, with the potential to do great things with our lives. And yet your typical person escapes from every day life by watching a box in the corner of a room that displays moving pictures for ten whole years. You can commit murder these days and do less time.

What could you achieve if you claimed back just four weeks of those ten years to realise some of your potential? Four weeks devoted to nothing except developing a new skill, learning a new language, launching a part-time business.

And why stop at four weeks? How much more could you achieve in six weeks, eight weeks, ten weeks, ten months or even ten years? How much could you achieve by devoting your entire life to doing exactly what you want to do?

"20 years from now you will be more disappointed by the things you didn't do than by the ones you did do," Mark Twain once said. "So throw off the bowlines. Sail away from the safe harbour. Catch the trade winds in your sails. Explore. Dream. Discover."

That's exactly what you need to do right now. Catch the trade winds in your sails and dare to explore, dream, discover . . .

The magic of numbers

"The greatest mathematical discovery of all time."
Albert Einstein on compounding

To be a success in life means different things to different people. In a material world, it's always tempting to measure your success in financial terms, but as we've already discovered there is something far more valuable than money. And that's time.

We all have exactly the same amount of time at our disposable on any given day so the potential for success is there for anyone to grab with both hands. If you are in a position to do whatever you want with your time each and every day, then as far as I'm concerned, you are as successful as you can be. That said, unless you want to live as a hermit in a cave half way up a mountain, you're still going to need money to be in that position.

Money gives us the power to make choices concerning what we do with our lives. The more money we have, the more choices we have. A self-made millionaire once told me that the most important thing money can buy you is power. Power over your own life. The very rich can spend their days doing whatever they want because they have the money to finance such a lifestyle. In contrast, the not so very rich often find their choices limited because of a lack of money or the need to devote precious time to earning it. All the time that you spend at work is time you are not spending sipping cocktails by the pool at the Grand-Hôtel du Cap-Ferrat on the French Riviera.

The brightest bulbs in the factory

Be careful what you wish for though. It is all too easy to become obsessed by how much money we earn and what we term our "standard of living". Whether we like it or not, the Western world is primarily a material world. We try to keep up with the Joneses by buying the biggest cars we can afford, adding conservatories to our houses, wearing designer label clothes, watching ever bigger flat screen televisions; and this level of material comfort we call our standard of living.

Don't get me wrong because I like some of the finer things in life too, but how much money you earn is of little importance when compared to what you do with it, and it is of limited value if the demands on your time are so great that you barely have the time to enjoy your success.

Again, it's back to the words we use to describe our lives, but why would anyone who has seen through wage slavery for what it really is be any more interested in a "standard of living" than they are in "earning a living"? How many flash cars sit in company car parks all day every day? How many 50" TV screens entertain our kids because we are still at work?

Your own standard of living, paid for by the hectic commuting, the long hours at work, and the other sacrifices you make to bring home the bacon, pales into insignificance when compared to the quality of life you enjoy - or don't as the case may be.

Quality of life is a very personal issue, but don't confuse it with your standard of living. You may have a good standard of living, but stress at work, job insecurity, traffic congestion, lack of time spent with your family, and a hundred and one other things, may be affecting your quality of life.

Not that a lifetime of wage slavery is likely to make you rich beyond your wildest dreams anyway. The vast majority of people work from Monday to Friday and still don't have the money they want to pursue their dreams.

Just take a look at those who follow Plan A to the letter. Those who spend three, four, five or more years in further education are, generally speaking, better paid than those with little in the way of a formal education. They are the success stories of the wage economy, with Universities UK estimating that university graduates earn, on average, about a quarter more than young people who leave school after their A-levels. Whoopee doo. Hardly lavish rewards for being among the brightest bulbs in the factory.

A study by Warwick University in 2009 found that the "graduate premium" in earnings was shrinking anyway, with students who attend less prestigious universities or who only get a mediocre degree, seeing only a "marginal" earnings premium over non-graduates. The Government's wheeze of increasing the number of university graduates, simply by rebranding higher education establishments as universities, means that in years to come there will be plenty of graduates not even seeing a marginal benefit, particularly if they are still paying off student debts which are currently running at around £20,000 per graduate (as an aside, it is blatantly wrong for someone to start their working life with that amount of debt, but somehow we have come to see it as acceptable. Debt has become the new black).

Even as better paid wage slaves, how many graduates can say they live the life of their dreams? How many are free to do as they choose each and every waking hour? Our education system condemns the vast majority of even the brightest students to a life of underachievement (there's no other word for it given the vast potential of every human being) simply because they are bound by the shackles and chains of the wage system. As Albert

Einstein said, "It is a miracle that curiosity survives formal education."

Why are a million or so people working for the minimum wage?

That said, all else being equal, I'd rather be a graduate in employment than someone further down the food chain working for the minimum wage.

When you grow up you get a job. Everyone knows that. When wages and conditions are poor, people still cling to the belief that they are one of the lucky ones. At least they have a job. Even if that means working for the minimum wage.

When introduced in April, 1999, the national minimum wage stood at just £3.60 an hour - or £144 for a 40 hour week. That's £7,488.00 for a year of your life. At the time of writing, it has increased to £5.80 an hour if you are over 22 years of age, a smidgen over £12,000 a year.

No matter how you look at it, £5.80 an hour is not a living wage, it's an insult. The powers that be spend almost three times that keeping someone in prison. According to the Scottish Prison Service for example, the average cost per prisoner place in 2007-2008 was £32,358.

When 40 hours a week of wage slavery pays you little more than doing no work at all, it simply underlines what a bad deal working for a living can be. And as far too many people in the UK today are all too well aware, you are often better off not working. According to figures delivered to Parliament in November, 2009, by Jim Knight, the Minister of State for Employment and Welfare Reform, 300,000 households receive £20,000 a year or more in benefit payments. At the same time, 40% of all those in work earn less than £18,000 a year – and that's before income tax and national insurance contributions are deducted.

Living on state hand-outs was once seen as a last resort, but when you are able to get more money signing on than you can earn by working, you can see the attraction - and why it is that generations of the same family have never had a job in their lives.

Perhaps surprisingly, the UK Statistics Authority doesn't publish figures for the number of people who earn the national minimum wage, but from various press reports it's safe to assume that at least a million people in the UK take home no more than the national minimum wage every week.

Why are a million or so people working for the minimum wage in this day and age? Is that truly the limit of their individual and collective potential? Why don't we as a society make better use of the incredible pool of knowledge, wisdom and ability that rests in each and every one of us?

I know not everyone that reads this book will turn their back on a life of wage slavery, but if you are going to work for someone else, at least make damn sure that they are paying you well. After all, chances are that they will want you to give them the best years of your life so you deserve to be well rewarded. If you're not being well rewarded, look elsewhere.

Grab a granny

Here's another example of how our wage slave society undervalues people. While parked at a motorway service station a few days ago, a coach full of old age pensioners pulled up beside my car. There must have been 50 or so men and women on that coach and every single one of them had at least 60 years of life experience to draw upon. Incredibly, their combined age of 3,000 plus years would have stretched back hundreds of years before the birth of Christ, before the rise and fall of the Roman Empire, before even the birth of Rome itself. An amazing thought. And all that experience, wisdom and knowledge, aboard just one coach.

Even in their twilight years, just imagine what 3,000 years of experience could be worth if put to good use. Even more amazing is how Western society virtually writes off a life's worth of knowledge and experience as soon as you qualify for a bus pass and half price perms on a Wednesday afternoon. Indeed, today things are far more desperate than that. Men and women in their forties are being made unemployed and told they will never work again.

Financial security? How about financial insecurity?

We are brainwashed from an early age into accepting the wage culture as the only way of providing an income in adult life and yet it fails to deliver for millions of us. Too many of us are too busy working to realise that the very financial security that we seek by getting a job is being denied us because we accept beads and trinkets in return for our time.

Financial security is just one of a whole host of needs we have as human beings. Most of our needs are what Abraham Maslow, the psychologist we met earlier, described as "deficit needs" - needs that only motivate you when you don't have enough of something. When you are hungry you feel the need to eat. But once you have satisfied your hunger, that particular need is no longer a concern to you. It's like a car and petrol. You can only get so much in its tank.

At the top of Maslow's hierarchy, you find what are known as "being needs". Being needs - the pursuit of dreams, the desire to fulfil your potential, self-fulfilment - know no bounds. When you have a full tank of petrol, the open road is yours for the taking.

Life being what it is, deficit needs in one form or another usually take centre stage, and so only a small minority of us are in a position to truly pursue our being needs. Maslow himself put the figure at just 2% - meaning that a whopping 98% of people are tending to their deficit needs rather than their being needs.

The way we live our lives, and our dependence on a wage and benefits culture, means that the vast majority of people in one of the richest countries in the world don't even come close to fulfilling their potential or their dreams. There has to be something fundamentally wrong with an apparently wealthy society in which only two out of every hundred people are fulfilling their potential.

There may have been a time (although I seriously doubt it) when working for a wage was a better option than pursuing alternatives, but that time isn't now. We are at the dawning of a new era for the entrepreneurial spirit. Technological advances in the last decade have catapulted the opportunities available to radically change our lives to incredible new heights. It's now perfectly possible for you to earn more money than you currently do (or are likely to do in the foreseeable future even with promotion) while working less hours.

No more rush hour traffic. No more crowded trains. No more deadlines and targets to be met so that you can line the pockets of your boss. Indeed, no more boss! And more time with the family, more money in your pocket, and most importantly, more leisure time to enjoy it.

So the challenge for you has to be this. Make more money working less hours so that you can devote your life to pursuing the dreams you have for you and your family. By declaring financial independence from wage slavery and by developing multiple revenue streams (including some that make you money whether you work, rest or play) that's exactly what's going to happen.

Were you born to be an entrepreneur?

Are people born to be successful entrepreneurs or is it something that can be learned? It's an interesting question because many people believe that they simply don't have what it takes to be enterprising enough to develop multiple revenue streams.

Entrepreneurs are often depicted as super human whirlwinds who are destined to succeed from birth. The Richard Bransons and Duncan Bannatynes of this world. Scary dragon types. You've either got entrepreneurial flair or you haven't. Or so we're told. It's therefore not surprising that most people think that they fall short of this image - and of course it suits society to foster such a belief so that most people accept their role in life as a wage slave.

The truth is that not only are some people born to be successful entrepreneurs, we all are. Human beings are the most enterprising creatures on this Earth and we dominate this planet thanks to the enterprise we have shown over thousands and thousands of years. Indeed without enterprise, there would be no progress and we'd still be living in a Stone Age world.

Life for most people in the Western World today is so safe, so comfortable, and so bland, that there is little need to show any enterprise. That's not true for everyone on Planet Earth. In many Third World countries, for example, spare parts for vehicles are often in very short supply or too expensive for many people to afford, and yet vehicles keep on running thanks to the incredible enterprise and ingenuity of backstreet mechanics, many of whom have had no formal education whatsoever. Nothing is wasted and even the most unlikely of objects is recycled to provide the part or tool required to get the vehicle back on the road.

We are all born to be entrepreneurs, we all have the potential to achieve amazing things, but that flame that burns so brightly inside each and every one of us at birth is all but extinguished by the society we live in as we get older.

Our education system for example - where we spend ten or more years of our childhood - does little to nourish our entrepreneurial spirit. It's main aim is to produce wage slaves, people who will go from cradle to school to work to bus pass to grave without rocking the boat, without bucking the system. Education without knowledge as it has been described.

Interestingly, those who cannot or do not conform while at school often don't have the entrepreneurial spirit knocked out of them. It's not really surprising to hear that the likes of Richard Branson did not do well at school or that Bill Gates dropped out of Harvard. Just like Mark Twain, they never let schooling get in the way of their education.

By the time most of us leave formal education, however, we are conditioned to accepting our role in life as a wage slave. And of course once we sign up for a mortgage, credit cards, a car loan and all the other trappings of "success", we cling on to our wage packets for all we are worth.

The pressure on us to conform - even from well meaning friends and family members - means that even the thought of an alternative way of life can seem daunting, but that does not alter the fact that we were all born to be entrepreneurs.

The amazing amounts of money "ordinary" people raise for charity is a good example of this simple truth. There are countless individuals who will rise to the challenge of raising thousands of pounds each year for any given charity. They will stand out in the cold with collection tins or make fools of themselves in silly costumes while running marathons, and yet very few of them feel able to rise to the challenge of raising say an extra ten thousand pounds for themselves and their family. Charity begins at home is a saying we would do well to heed.

The machine that makes pound coins

I have in my possession a machine that makes one pound coins. I have two of them in fact, but don't worry, neither came out of the back door of the Royal Mint. My two machines make badges and because badges sell for a pound a pop, every time I make one it is the equivalent of minting a one pound coin.

Making badges is child's play once you get the hang of it. The badge machine company supplies everything except the artwork which today can very easily be produced on a computer. The machine itself acts as a press and basically "squashes" the components together. All you have to do is put them in the machine and pull down the press - twice in the case of most badge making machines - and then you simply add the pin to the back. The cost of manufacturing a button badge using a home-based set-up is between 5p and 10p. People expect to pay up to £1 for a badge so that is why I like to call my button badge machine, "the machine that makes pound coins".

I strongly believe that entrepreneurship should be part and parcel of every child's education and I would love the opportunity to take "the machine that makes pound coins" into schools. What kid wouldn't like to get their hands on such a machine? Over a period of weeks you could introduce different aspects of running your own business. The kids could design the badges themselves, set the price, do the marketing, sell them at school, produce basic accounts, and eventually share the spoils.

Risking it all

One of the biggest obstacles to us escaping the rat race is our inherent fear of failure. No matter how much you want a better life, the security blanket that is wage slavery is hard to let go of.

There was an interesting documentary on the BBC a while back which sought to support the myth that entrepreneurs are somehow different to "ordinary" people. One way used to demonstrate this was based on a psychological experiment of old whereby people are asked to throw a ball into a bucket from one of three positions.

From the nearest position success at this task is very likely, but the rewards are very small. From the second nearest position, success is less likely, but the rewards are higher. And from the furthest position, success is highly unlikely but the rewards are very high.

Where do you think an entrepreneur would stand?

Most people think that those who stand furthest away are the ones most likely to be entrepreneurs. After all, they are willing to take the biggest risk to get the biggest rewards. Indeed, those entrepreneurs featured on the BBC programme chose to stand furthest away, but the experiment was flawed. The entrepreneurs who stood furthest away had nothing to lose by doing so (it was only a game) and everything to gain in terms of their reputation as risk takers, but it was more likely a sign of bravado than a real demonstration of their entrepreneurial spirit. For the cameras they wanted to be seen as the big risk takers they were billed as.

In similar experiments conducted under more scientific circumstances, people who showed entrepreneurial characteristics in other experiments - psychological profiling for example - were not the ones who stood furthest away. They were the ones who stood in the middle, close enough to be in with a chance of succeeding and yet far enough away to claim a big enough reward for their success. That's because successful entrepreneurs don't just take risks. They take calculated risks. And that's what I ask anyone looking to escape the rat race to do. Take calculated risks.

Being a successful entrepreneur isn't about wheeling and dealing. It's not about ruthlessly pushing others aside to grab a larger slice of the cake. It's not about selling sand to the Arabs. It's about realising your potential and it's about making the most of the countless opportunities that are out there waiting for you.

You were born to be a successful entrepreneur. Don't let society, your school, well meaning friends, your family, or anyone else for that matter, tell you otherwise. Instead make a commitment that will relight that flame. Before you know it you will be the beacon of enterprise that is your birthright.

The magic of numbers

Remember that coachload of old age pensioners? Chances are that what you will remember most is their combined age. 50 men and women with an average age of 60 have a combined age of 3,000 years. It never fails to amaze people that the combined age of so few people can add up to three millennia. That, my friend, is the magic of numbers. And since we count money in numbers, that's also the magic of money too.

Take the month of February. Unless it is a leap year, it has only 28 days, making it the shortest month of the year. Imagine that I started saving money on the 1st of February by placing a single penny into my piggy bank. I then agree to save twice as much money on each subsequent day until the end of the month. So on the 2nd of February, I place two pennies in my bank, and on the 3rd of February I put in twice as much again, four pence. On the 4th, I save twice as much again, eight pence. And so on, right up until the 28th of February.

If I doubled the money I was putting into the bank every day for the entire month, how much would I be putting into the piggy bank on February the 28th? A few pounds? A few hundred pounds? A few thousand pounds even?

You'd better sit down for this one. Starting with just a penny on day one, I would be putting 64p into the bank on the 7th of February. On the 14th of February, Valentine's Day, the princely sum of £81.92 would be going into the piggy bank. By the end of the third week, on the 21st of February, I would have to find £10,485.76 to put into the bank (this is one very large piggy bank remember). That's right. Over £10,000 just 21 days after starting with a single penny! Surprising really.

But the most incredible sum of all is the amount of money I would be forcing into the piggy bank on the 28th of February. Believe it or not, an eye-popping £1,342,177.28! Well over a million pounds!

At this point, readers generally start reaching for their calculators to see if this can possibly be true, but it is true. Starting with a penny, you can have well over a million pounds simply by doubling your investment every day for just 28 days. In fact the grand total of the 28 days' worth of saving actually comes to £2,684,354.55.

Looking at it another way, if I offered you a sure-fire business plan that involved an initial investment of just one pence and I promised to double that investment every year on the condition that you reinvested the new sum year on year, you would be a multi-millionaire within 28 years. Just 28 years to go from a penny to over two and a half million pounds!

If at first you don't succeed . . .

The magic of numbers is certainly something we want to put to work for us because it alone will allow you to make the quantum leap from pauper to prince (or princess) as you develop multiple revenue streams. Before we get carried away with ourselves though, there's another very important lesson to learn from the above. Don't throw in the towel simply because you don't see immediate results from your Plan B.

Too many people fall by the wayside as they walk the often treacherous road between their starting point and their ultimate goal. Halfway into the journey from the 1st of February to the 28th of February, we have less than two hundred pounds to show for our efforts. Many who don't know what's waiting for them just another 14 days down the road, might decide to quit at this point, believing that despite their best efforts, they are getting nowhere fast. Sadder still are those who go three quarters of the way towards their goal and then settle for just over £20,000 - a large enough sum, but still far short of their hopes and dreams. Only those who go the full distance will hit the jackpot and scoop the two million plus pounds that awaits them on the last day of the month.

Sarah Tremellen is a woman who knows all about staying the distance. In 1995, while pregnant, Sarah was appalled by the lack of choice available to women who needed big size bras. Standard bra sizes came in every colour and design imaginable, but the lingerie industry just didn't cater for "big boobed women" to borrow a phrase from Sarah herself. The only big bras on sale were plain, full cupped, and available in just three colours -

black, white and natural. And the bigger the bra size, the more limited even this choice became.

What made matters worse was that few shops stocked even this limited range, preferring to cater for only the most popular sizes. Everyone in the business knew that there were big breasted women out there, but for some insane reason everyone in the industry also believed that they didn't want either choice or availability.

So Sarah decided to do something about it. She started a mail order business called Bravissimo, working from home in her living room, sending out catalogues and filling orders. Within a year the business had grown too big for her house and it has been growing ever since. Today, Bravissimo is a multi-million pound company with its own warehouse facility and 20 High Street stores. Gone too are the days of limited choice. Bravissimo stocks more than 50 different styles of bra by different manufacturers, most of whom have finally responded to the enormous demand for big bra sizes thanks to the likes of Sarah Tremellen and the 500,000 plus Bravissimo customers.

Way back in 1987, I knew a woman who had exactly the same idea as Sarah and who started a mail order catalogue business selling bigger size bras and lingerie. This woman had spotted the very same gap in the market based on her own experiences of buying bras.

The business got off to a flying start, helped along the way by free publicity courtesy of the national media (big boobs have always sold newspapers in the UK). And yet within six months the business had closed its doors. A national postal strike (the stuff of nightmares for mail order businesses) had caused cash flow problems, but rather than baton down the hatches and weather what was a brief if traumatic storm, she decided to throw in the towel.

I got a phone call from her telling me what had happened and how she was now starting a new venture, a public relations company, based on her (very limited) experience of getting the national press coverage for her bra and lingerie business. Needless to say, the PR idea had an even shorter life span and I never heard any more from her.

If things had been different, there probably wouldn't have been a Bravissimo. Sarah Tremellen would probably have become a happy customer of the lady who had the idea before her. But discovering a niche market with unfulfilled demands is only part of the recipe of success. You have to be prepared to see your idea through to the end.

When times are hard and it looks like your latest idea isn't going to be as successful as you'd hoped, the real danger isn't that you will fail. It is that you won't stay the course to enjoy success. Sarah Tremellen stayed the course. The other woman didn't.

One of the main reasons that I can see for Sarah's success and the other woman's failure is passion - or indeed the lack of it as the case may be. Sarah didn't just want to sell big bras. She wanted to shake up an entire industry. She wanted manufacturers to make bras that women would really want to buy and really want to wear. And she has succeeded in doing just that. If you bring that amount of passion to any poorly served niche market, success is there for the taking. Add staying power, and success is an odds on certainty.

You owe it to yourself to keep striving towards whatever dreams you truly want to reach in your lifetime, because by doing so, spectacular things can be achieved. I think it was the founder of the Ford Motor Company, one Henry Ford, who once said something along the lines of whether you choose to succeed or fail, eventually you will, and he was bang on the money.

The miracle of compounding

The fact that money can grow so quickly from a penny to millions is because of the miracle of what is called compounding. Simply put, compounding money means you add any gains to your initial sum and reinvest the total. It's like a snowball rolling down a hill. As it makes its way down it accumulates more and more snow and the end result can be quite astounding. Just ask any kid. No wonder Albert Einstein called compound interest, "The greatest mathematical discovery of all time".

Compounding is obviously something that we must put to work when developing multiple revenue schemes if we are to see sky rocketing incomes after the initial years of hard work. The key is to get the best return possible, and even a few percentage points can make an incredible difference.

If I put £100 into a bank account on the first day of every year for ten years, without withdrawing a single penny, how much I would have at the end of the period would depend on the interest rate being offered. At 0% interest I would have just the total of my deposits, which would amount to £1,000 (£100 multiplied by ten years).

If I was offered a 5% interest rate every year for ten years I would be a lot better off. At the end of the first year, my £100 would be worth £105, the sum I would carry over to year two to add to my next £100 investment. By the end of the second year, my £205 would have grown into £215.25, the sum I would carry on to year three to add to my next £100 investment. And so on and so on until the end of year ten when my investment of £100 a year would be worth £1,320.68. An extra £320.68.

If I was offered a 10% interest rate, by the end of year ten my investment of £100 a year would be worth £1,865.15. An extra £865.15.

Supposing I struck gold and got a 25% return every year. By the end of year ten my same investment of just £100 a year, £1,000 in total, would be worth £4,156.61. An extra £3,156.61. Not bad going at all.

And a 100% return on your investment every year? By now you'll be wise to the power of compounding your money when it comes to investing. A total investment of just £100 each year for ten years, with every penny earned being reinvested, would be worth £204,600 after the ten years were up. A very tidy nest egg in anybody's book. And stranger things have happened.

It doesn't take a financial whizz-kid to work out that the better the rate of return, the more money you'll end up with, but a lot of people don't look for the best possible return on their money, and even fewer leave the interest intact so that it can create a snowball effect. If you invest your money wisely, even small amounts can grow into huge sums given both the miracle of compounding and the best rate of return you can achieve.

The time to start your snowball rolling is NOW!

There's a further twist in the tale that makes this even more interesting. The sooner you start out on this path, the richer you will be and the less money you will need in the first place to reach your goal.

Look back at the luckiest February on record where we turned 1p into over two million pounds in just 28 days. If you had joined this cash cow on day one, a penny piece would have been the only investment necessary. If you decided to spend your pennies elsewhere for the first week and joined on day eight, you would have needed £1.28 to join in the fun. Put off investing until day 15, and you would be coughing up £163.84. The 20th of February and a whopping £5,242.88 would be needed. In fact, leave it any later and the sums involved would exclude most people from participating.

It's exactly for this reason that those who want a decent pension when they retire are urged to start putting money into one as early as possible. Otherwise the day might come when it becomes just too expensive to join a worthwhile scheme at all. Whether you should even join a pension scheme in the first place is open to debate, but at least the "start early" part of the argument is correct (another aside, multiple revenue streams make excellent "pensions").

It's safe to say then that if we really want to make serious money, we have to start as soon as possible (no matter how old you are, that means today), we have to ensure we get the best return we possibly can on any money we invest, and we have to make sure that year on year we are allowing our pool of money to grow so that the miracle of compounding can take place. In short, we need to make snowballs.

Once again, wage slaves are at a distinct disadvantage here. Most aren't making enough to make ends meet, let alone invest in anything as frivolous as snowballs. The sooner you start building snowballs, however, the better. You know deep down that life's too short to be doing anything else. It might not be the easiest option to start with, there are no guarantees of success and many will mock you as you pick up pennies in those first days of February, but remember, he or she who strives first strives furthest.

The 80/20 Principle

Almost without exception, when it comes to doing business, a small proportion of your customers will be responsible for a larger proportion of your sales, income and profit. For various reasons, some customers will chose to spend more money with you than some other customers.

In fact, although it can vary considerably, generally speaking just 20% of your customers will be responsible for 80% of your business. And this 80-20 ratio holds good no matter your line of business.

Entrepreneur and author, Richard Koch, has taken research into what he calls the 80/20 Principle to new heights, and has discovered that it applies not just to customers. Indeed, he argues (and with a great deal of success) that the 80/20 principle can be applied to virtually every area of life that involves an input and an output. For example, when it comes to the use of our time, 20% of the time spent doing something usually provides 80% of the results. It isn't difficult to see the truth in this. You have a month to complete a project. For the first three weeks it is difficult to get any momentum going, but as the deadline looms you seem to be able to shift up a gear or two so that the project is indeed completed on time.

Here's an example of the 80/20 Principle that I've yet to see in any other book that mentions the subject. How about this. When you work for someone else, no matter what you are being paid, you will only be paid 20% of what your potential dictates possible. And in return, you'll give them 80% of your waking hours. That means that every day you work for someone else, you are being short changed. Not by a few pennies either. Ring any bells?

Talking 'bout a revolution

Throughout this book you'll find me railing against wage slavery, but unfortunately I'm no Che Guevara. My economics and politics owe more to libertarianism than they ever will communism. Why I dismiss working for a living so readily is that it is rarely the best use of your time. It's as simple as that. Once upon a time, religion might have been the opium of the masses, but today work is. And for me, working for yourself isn't necessarily the panacea for all ills either. I know plenty of people who apparently "work for themselves" and who work longer hours for often no more money than they would if they got a job.

What matters is how you spend your incredibly valuable time. Anything that pays you by the hour – unless it's £50, £500 or more – is unlikely to be worth your time. As a quick rule of thumb, £50 an hour equates to about £100,000 a year. £500 an hour equates to a million pounds a year. If we were all earning that sort of money, there would be little need for a Plan B, but we don't.

The reality is that neither capitalism or communism are designed to help the vast majority of people succeed in life because neither truly value your time. To be fair to both, it's probably an impossible ask, given the very limited number of hours you have at your disposal and how much they would have to pay you for them to keep me happy.

If you are lucky enough to live until you're 80, you'll be alive for 29,200 days (ignoring odd days gained by leap years). If you're 20 years of age when you read these words, a quarter of that total has already been spent. If you're 30 years old, you have around 18,250 days left to be alive (still assuming you live to be 80). If you are 40, half of all the days that you will ever live have gone forever. If you are 50, 18,250 days have gone forever and you have just over 10,000 days left to make the most of your life.

Supposing you work 40 hours a week for 40 years of your life. Give or take a few weeks of holidays, Plan A will see you working for 10,000 days of your life. That would be true under any system that saw you going to work.

The stark reality is this. You simply cannot afford to spend anything like 10,000 days of your life going to work. Not if you truly want to make the most of life. Yes, we all need to make money, but to spend virtually half of your adult days at work is a criminal waste of your time – no matter what they are paying you. And when they are paying you barely enough to make ends meet, it makes no sense at all.

Give a dog a bone

There will always be those who are as happy with their nine to five existence as a dog with the postman's leg between its jaws. And there will always be those who can't survive without the oxygen of a regular wage. You on the other hand must think like a five year old. You have to get back out there in the snow and start making those snowballs. Believe once again that anything is possible and you just might surprise yourself.

Everyone knows that it's unlikely that they will ever make a fortune working for someone else. If you genuinely want financial independence and the power to do whatever you want to do with your life, but are content to keep on working in someone else's factory, someone else's office, someone else's goldmine, five or more days a week, then you might as well close this book now. Time waits for no man. The clock is ticking away, and you can't seriously tell me that on one hand you want to earn what you are truly worth and yet at the same time are willing to work for a tiny fraction of that magical figure.

If you want to be rich in the monetary sense you have to earn big money. There's no getting away from that fact. And if you aren't earning big money working for someone else, then you are doing yourself and your family a disservice.

I am totally convinced that if you have even an ounce of enterprise in your body, you owe it to yourself to refuse to be a wage slave for what amounts to the best years of your life, and that you should devote yourself to bucking the system and becoming a real success story instead.

Don't give up your day job. Yet.

On the other hand, if you are currently bringing home a much needed wage then it would be foolish to hand in your notice tomorrow and risk sinking without a trace. Remember, successful entrepreneurs only take calculated risks.It would be easy for me to tell you to give up your job, but it's not me who has to pay your mortgage and your other bills. Walking away from Plan A is easier said than done and yes it can be a frightening prospect. Giving up your wage packet on a whim, without an alternative source of income in place, isn't a risk I want to see you take. Pinning your hopes on one get rich quick scheme after another isn't what I'm talking about either. Both are more often than not routes to failure. We don't like failure and we don't like others to think of us as failures either.

But consider this. What's the alternative? Remaining in a job that you know in your heart of hearts is never going to give you the opportunity to give you the lifestyle you so badly want? How long are you going to stay in that job? Another year? Five years? Ten years? That is the really frightening prospect.

There's no need to give up the day job just yet though. Start building snowballs in the evenings, at weekends, or even when the boss isn't looking. Put part of your wages to good use by building a more secure and fulfilling future.

Feed and water your multiple revenue streams until they are providing you with enough money to jump ship without causing your family to suffer financially. And then it really will be full steam ahead.

Nobody's fool

"Who is more foolish, the child afraid of the dark, or the man afraid of the light?"
Maurice Freehill

There's an old saying that goes something like this. If it sounds too good to be true, then it usually is. In fact when you are wading through the business opportunity minefield, there is no better saying to live by. Ignore it and you might as well give your hard-earned money away to passing strangers in the street.

The problem is that human nature makes us absolute suckers for get-rich-quick schemes. Pick up any business opportunities magazine or visit the equivalent websites and you will be bombarded with ads for all types of weird and wonderful business opportunities, each one promising to make you rich beyond your wildest dreams. And yet despite everything we know about a fool and his money being easily parted, we want to believe every word. It doesn't matter whether it's a one line classified or a sales pitch that fills an entire page, there is something almost hypnotic about such ads, something totally captivating.

As you read through them, you can feel the adrenaline pumping through your body. You want to discover the magic ingredients, the secret money-making formulas, that will transform your life forever. You do, I do, everyone does. The big hope is that the next ad you read will be the big one. The one that is going to send your earnings through the roof! You really want to believe that all that stands between you and incredible success is your credit card details.

They say money can't buy you everything, but it certainly helps, and with everything else being equal, you and I both know we'd rather be rich than poor. It doesn't matter whether we want to be millionaires or simply want to earn a few extra pounds in our spare time, we are all driven by the same burning desire to finance our hopes and dreams.

Smelling of roses

Get-rich-quick schemes are nothing new of course. Way back in the 1630s, Holland was gripped by what has since been called Tulipmania. Tulips, for which Holland is as famous for today as it is for windmills and wooden clogs, were first cultivated in that country during the 16th century. Carolus Clusius, then director of the Royal Medicinal Garden in Vienna, is generally credited as the man who first grew European tulips and then introduced them to Holland.

As horticultural techniques improved, many new breeds of tulips were created and they became much sought after by the rich who spent vast sums of money on flowers to enhance their status. It didn't take long for people to cotton on to the money that could be made from buying and selling tulips, and by the 1630s the Dutch had gone tulip mad.

All you had to do to become rich was to plant some bulbs and wait for them to grow. It really was that easy. Bulbs were sold by weight, and by 1634, tulip bulbs were literally worth more than their weight in gold. In fact, such was the demand that bulbs would be sold to other dealers before they had even left the ground!

People were selling everything they owned to become involved in the trade - and with what looked like very good reason. For minimal work, some traders were making the equivalent of £30,000 in today's money every month, and despite government attempts to make the trade illegal, the tulip frenzy continued unabated. If anything, government interference drove the prices even higher.

And then in 1637, tulip trading mania came to an abrupt halt. Interest in tulips suddenly waned. Dealers were no longer able to get the highly inflated prices for their bulbs and the market came crashing down. Within a couple of months, thousands of traders, including Establishment figures and some of Holland's leading businessmen, were facing ruin.

The Dutch had fallen victim to what is called a speculative bubble. The price the bulbs once fetched bore no relation to their actual worth, a situation that is only sustainable in the short term. The day will always come when reality returns to the market place - and if you don't see that day coming, it can spell financial disaster.

Money for nothing

Here in the UK, we also have a long history of the pursuit of money for nothing. In 1711, Parliament created The South Sea Trading Company and gave it a monopoly on all trade between Great Britain and Ireland and South America and the islands of the South Seas. Shares in this and similar companies were sold by subscription, largely to pay off the nation's debts that had accumulated from the various wars we waged at the time.

In 1718, no less a man than King George I was appointed Governor of the South Sea Trading Company and he issued a proclamation stating that the purchasing of shares in the company would ensure economic stability for the country. With this royal seal of approval, the price of the company's stock soared and kept on climbing. In January, 1720, you could buy stock in the company for £128. By July of that same year that same stock would cost you £1,000.

What people didn't realise was that they were buying stock in a company that was worthless. All of the money invested was being squandered in far away lands or being used to repay the national debt, and when it was subsequently revealed that the South Sea Trading Company shares weren't worth the paper they were printed on, their value dropped like a lead balloon. By September, the stock stood at £150.

By then, people from all walks of life had invested their life savings in the company, believing it would make them rich. Others had borrowed heavily to participate. Many faced ruin. Sir Isaac Newton reportedly made a fortune from buying and selling South Sea Company stocks, but then lost it all again, and then some, when he rejoined the fray just before the price collapse. Very few people walked away with smiles on their faces.

Of course, it's easy for us with hindsight to say that the price of tulip bulbs and worthless stocks couldn't keep rising by ridiculous amounts forever. But swap tulip bulbs for some of the business opportunities currently in circulation and you soon realise that there will always be those willing to suspend reality in their pursuit of easy money.

The Greater Fool Theory

Deep down, most of us know when something sounds too good to be true, but instead of running a mile, we all too often turn to the Greater Fool Theory for help. The Greater Fool Theory is basically this. You are willing to invest your money in property, stocks, whatever, not because you truly believe that they are worth the asking price, but because at some point in the (often very near) future, you believe a greater fool will come along and pay you even more for them.

For example, all pyramid schemes, from the legal network marketing offerings through to illegal money circles, all have a touch of the greater fool about them. As do an increasing number of business opportunities that you'll find littered around the internet. Including some of those being promoted by "gurus" who are making money by exploiting our weakness for what appears to be easy money.

A classic scenario seems to be this. A business or marketing guru has discovered the latest in money making ideas. Not only is it the latest, it's the greatest too. The easiest money you'll ever make. In fact, sit back and relax because you don't even need to do any work. The guru's done it all for you. And either through a seminar, a course, a set of DVDs, an e-book or the like, this guru is willing to share his or her secrets with you. For a price. And this price can sometimes be thousands of pounds.

You're tempted. Of course you're tempted. We're all tempted by thoughts of easy money. And you don't want to miss out. And anyway, how can you lose? Everyone who attends the seminar or buys the e-book or signs on the dotted line gets master resale rights to whatever it is that the guru is championing this time around. So not only can you sell the product yourself, you can sell others the right to do the same too! Making you a sort of son of guru.

And that's when the Greater Fool Theory kicks in. You aren't entirely convinced that the product really is the next big thing, but how can you lose when you've got master resale rights? What you are banking on is being able to shift whatever the product happens to be to enough "greater fools" in the hope that you can make your money back and then some.

Now, if what you are being offered is truly of value, you will have no problems recouping your money, and there are people out there who are genuinely making lots of money and who can help you make money too. But increasingly, I've seen some very big names in the business opportunity field rush an idea to market for what appears to be for one reason and one reason only. To put bums on seats at seminars or to shift DVD sets by the van load. Or in other words, to fill their own pockets.

Increasingly, the products being offered with resale rights as part of big ticket seminars and similar courses are poorly conceived, of little real value, and are untested in the market place. Finding enough greater fools to buy what often amounts to rubbish is easier said than done, but by the time you find this out, the guru has banked your money and moved onto the next "big thing" - which incidentally he will be offering to those who attend his or her next seminar or who order his or her next course.

You're not quite sure whether you've failed because of something you've done or whether you've been had. So you will either give the guru the benefit of the doubt and buy his or her next big thing, or move onto another guru, or bail out all together (you've probably guessed that the word "guru" does nothing for me. It's a bit like that other overused word, "expert". Me, I'd never want to be either).

My advice is this. If the business idea or business opportunity you are presented with depends on you finding greater fools for it to succeed, forget it. Focus instead on building genuine low risk revenue streams. That way you won't make a fool of yourself and you won't have to make a fool of others to earn a living either.

Teenage kicks

Ironically enough, it was while being taken for a greater fool myself, as a teenager back in the late 1970s, that I accidentally discovered something that is at the heart of virtually everything that makes me money today. The value of information. Indeed, for over 30 years now, I have had a love affair with two very cheap raw materials that in the right measures can produce true alchemy. Paper and ink. Add the secret ingredient – information

– and you can transform that paper and ink into pure gold. Of course, now that we live in the information age, and a computer screen can serve up information as readily as a printed page, the opportunities to make money from information have exploded, making this the ideal time to cash in on the value of information.

As a kid I did the usual things to earn money. I had a paper round. I went scrumping and sold apples door to door. I washed cars. I picked strawberries. I walked dogs. Even at primary school, I knew how to spot an opportunity. When I was probably around ten years old, a boy who lived down the road from me was selling a bicycle that was in perfect condition. I asked if I could take it home to show my Mum and to ask if I could buy it. After getting the approval of the boy's father, I wheeled the bike away. However, instead of taking the bike to my house, I took it straight to a neighbour who was something of a secondhand bike dealer. I asked him how much he would give me for it and it transpired that he was willing to pay me £5 more than the original asking price. I accepted his offer, sold the bike there and then, went back and paid the boy, and pocketed the difference.

Unlike most other kids though, I wasn't just interested in making some extra pocket money. I had other plans. Much bigger plans. Plans to be a millionaire. How exactly this was going to happen to a kid in a council house I didn't quite know. What I did know was that one day it was going to happen.

Barely into my teens, and long before the arrival of home computers and the internet, I discovered the business opportunities section of the *Exchange & Mart*, a classified ads newspaper that is still published today. It was packed with small ads promising the secrets of incredible wealth in return for only a few pounds and immediately I thought that I had found page after page of kindred spirits. Fellow travellers, who had not only discovered the golden path to success, but who were only too willing to show others the way - for a small fee of course. It all seemed a little too good to be true, but the seductive quality of being able to buy "hidden secrets of success" and "the key to untold millions" was a lure that I simply could not resist.

One ad in particular caught my eye. Someone was selling a *Hong Kong Trade Directory* and a *World Trade Directory* for £3 each or £5 for them both (quite a lot of money in those days, particularly for a kid like me). Apparently, both contained all the information I would need to become a major player in the world of import-export. I pictured myself arranging shipments from America one day, Hong Kong the next, and all from the comfort of my own home. What exactly would be in those shipments I had no idea, but that's why I desperately needed those trade directories. It was simply an opportunity too good to miss. The only decision I had to make was which directory to buy, and being a true entrepreneur, I opted for both. After all, if I could capture the Hong Kong market, why not the world?

World domination

Now, I like to think I'm nobody's fool. Even at the tender age of 13, I thought I had my wits about me. The only directories I had ever seen were telephone directories. I had visions of two *Yellow Pages* style publications arriving by post, packed to bursting point with the leads, contacts, tips, and secrets, that would act as a blue-print for me to make my fortune. I imagined flicking through page after page of information that would put me in contact with suppliers from around the world, all eager and willing to do business with me.

As the excitement mounted, I prepared a corner of my teenage bedroom with an old desk and a borrowed typewriter. The moment that I had those directories to hand, I wanted to be able to start making money right away.

The day my package arrived, I didn't know whether to laugh or cry. Instead of the bumper directories I had been expecting, the Hong Kong trade directory was nothing more than nine poorly duplicated sheets of coloured paper held together in one corner by a rusty staple. The world directory only stretched to seven sheets. Had I really just spent £5 on this?

To be honest, I felt confused, not to mention conned, but as far as anyone else was concerned I was over the moon. My pride wouldn't allow me to send it back or ask for a refund (something inside told me I wouldn't get one anyway) and so I soldiered on. Maybe everything you needed to know had been condensed into the few spartan pages I had before me. As I kept telling myself, it was the quality not the quantity of information that mattered.

I decided to send letters of introduction to five of the companies listed. My childish naivety meant that I rather excitedly expected to be the main UK source of a wide array of products, ranging from motorised wheelbarrows to Belgian chocolate. Unfortunately, none of the companies I wrote to saw me in quite the same light. Of the five letters I sent, two never replied and two were returned by the Post Office marked "addressee unknown". Not the best of starts, but I did get one reply from the USA. It was a white envelope literally bursting at the seams with circulars and leaflets for various business opportunity manuals. Perhaps the U.S. Postal Service was offering a special deal – something along the lines of as much debris as you can cram into one envelope and mailed anywhere in the world for a dollar. I had to hand it to my new contact. It must have taken the best part of an hour to squeeze so much into such a small envelope.

I was later to learn that I had just received my first "big mail". "Big mail" was one of the terms I'd seen in various ads, but hadn't really known what one was. Now I knew. It was an envelope full of circulars. The more circulars the merrier. A "never mind the quality feel the weight" type of thing that was a stalwart of the mail order bookselling world at the time.

After being mugged into buying the two trade directories, I wasn't exactly champing at the bit to order any of the manuals offered by my American friend. But I did pour over every single piece of paper he sent me, marvelling at the information that each manual supposedly contained. Nowhere did it quite say exactly what the "golden opportunity" or "passport to riches" might be, but the general gist was that any fool could make money from such "goldmines" of information.

And that's when it hit me like a bolt of lighting. I was never going to make my fortune as an import-export agent. Not with the two "directories" I had at my disposal anyway. There was, however, money to be made in selling those directories and similar manuals. How many people, just like me, had sent that guy a fiver in response to that tiny classified ad? Given that duplicated sheets cost pennies to produce at the time, the profit margin must have been huge. My newfound American friend was also presumably making enough money from selling his manuals to send me half a ream of paper by air mail on the off-chance I'd buy something from him.

Not only that, I had received a further dozen or so "big mails" in the weeks that followed. The directory company had not only fleeced me of £5, but had then sold my name and address to other "mail order dealers", each no doubt hoping I'd send them money too in exchange for the assorted manuals, reports and folios that they were offering. I was what was known in the trade as a "hot opportunity seeker" - a less kind mind might say I'd been added to a "suckers list".

Sucker or not, I presumed that these people too were making the vast sums of money claimed in their sales bumf. It stood to reason that if you were selling a manual that told readers how to make thousands of pounds every week from mail order bookselling, you would presumably have read it yourself and would be reaping the rich rewards.

Like printing money

At least I now knew where the money was. Mail order bookselling. Why it was called "bookselling", I've still no idea. Somehow, I don't think Waterstone's would have been the success story it is today had it been selling duplicated sheets of paper for inflated sums of money. I had seen dozens of ads in the *Exchange & Mart*, though, placed by people apparently making big money doing just that. I was now kicking myself that I hadn't ordered a manual about making "mail order millions" instead of buying those worthless trade directories. Suffice to say, my career as an import export agent came to an abrupt end before it had even started and I became a teenage mail order bookseller.

On paper at least, mail order bookselling was the perfect business opportunity for so many reasons. Each page that cost pennies to print might as well have been a pound note spewing out of the duplicator. Even if you wanted to add that little more class and used a photocopier instead, the mark-up was phenomenal (remember this was before every home had a colour printer attached to a computer). And who wouldn't like to make £100,000 from a single classified ad? Or have a constant supply of £10 cheques arriving by post?

Mail order bookselling was sold as the ultimate in kitchen table enterprises. Start up costs were minimal. All business was conducted by post. You could do this in your spare time. Your age, sex, colour, all became irrelevant because your customers never met you. Indeed, the fact that there was no face to face selling was another major attraction. You simply sent out your offers and waited for the cheques and postal orders to land on your doormat. According to the spiel, the mail wasn't just going to arrive, it was going to pour through your letterbox!

Judging by the number of ads that appeared in the *Exchange & Mart* every week, lots of people were apparently already cashing in on the money-making wonders of mail order bookselling. The reality was very different as I was to discover during the few years that I went on to spend as a mail order bookseller. The vast majority of those selling manuals and reports made very little money. Few could afford to cast their advertising net wide enough to land the "hot business opportunity seekers" needed to sell their wares to. Most existed in a clandestine little world populated by others hoping to make their fortune by peddling what was basically rubbish. A stagnant backwater in which suckers turned mail order dealers were unwitting participants in the modern day equivalent of a nineteenth century medicine show in which assorted quacks attempt to sell each other cures for each other's ailments. A pond that has since all but dried up now that we have the internet.

Today's equivalent of the mail order manual is the e-book or digital book. Don't confuse these e-books with the electronic version of novels that you can buy from Amazon and elsewhere for a few pounds to read on your Kindle or iPad. The e-books that I'm talking about carry on the great traditions of the mail order dealers of old by making wild promises of success. Get girls. Lose weight. Make millions. That sort of thing.

Interestingly, most e-books aimed at business opportunity and vanity markets are sold at fantastically high prices, despite the marginal cost of producing an e-book being close to zero, and despite the fact that delivery costs are equally low (a buyer simply downloads the .pdf file containing the e-book so there are no postage costs). Why the high prices? There are only ever so many suckers to go around, but a real sucker will pay virtually anything for "secrets" of success. £5 was a lot to pay for a manual back in the Seventies. Today you'll pay ten times that for the same information by e-book. Maybe 20 times. Indeed, there are no doubt those who would rather pay more, much more in fact, in the misguided belief that nobody would sell real secrets for the price of a normal book. Price and value are obviously not the same, but we happily confuse both on a daily basis.

There are also always those who will take advantage of this strange quirk of human nature. If you're going to sell 1,000 copies of an e-book irrespective of the asking price, much better to get £99 a sale than £9.99. It also means you can offer huge commissions of 50-70% to anyone else who can find you suckers via their own marketing. The emphasis e-book gurus put on building mailing lists reminds me of how so-called boiler rooms work lists of investors who have bought worthless shares in the past. Once bitten, twice shy, doesn't apply to those in search of golden eggs. You can sucker punch some people over and over again. If someone buys into one get rich quick scheme, chances are that their ignorance, desperation or greed will lead to them buying into another. And another. And another.

Back on the chain gang

Don't shoot the messenger though. There is nothing wrong with the e-book format. It's equally true that there are business opportunity e-books available that can show you how to make money. Most however offer little new and rarely justify their high cover price: not on the grounds that the information isn't worth that much – it sometimes is – but on the grounds that the same information is often available elsewhere minus the hype for much less.

This is of course a picture that's repeated over and over again in the grubbier corners of the business opportunity world. On paper, even the humble chain letter looks like a sure-fire winner. As do the money circulation schemes that flare up on a regular basis, particularly during times of economic hardship.

Chain letters and money circulation schemes basically work as follows. You pay a fee to join and then earn a percentage of the membership fees paid by anyone you recruit. And you also earn a percentage of membership fees paid by anyone they then recruit. The more people that join because of your initial efforts, the more money you stand to make.

It's the classic pyramid scheme where those at the zenith stand to make some serious money while those further down the pyramid will be lucky to make any money at all. For every winner there has to be a number of losers because any money paid out doesn't come from thin air, it comes out of someone else's pocket. And of course, unless those at the bottom manage to recruit a new bottom layer, they might as well be throwing their pound notes into a fire for all the good participating will do them.

For everyone to make money, you would need a never ending stream of new recruits. Yes, there are billions of people in this world and yes the better schemes may have a good deal of mileage in them, but it's equally true that the vast majority of people have neither the inclination or the money to participate, and at some point you must reach the end of the line. New recruits dry up and the last people in the door quickly discover that they've lost their money.

Take a sample money scheme that requires you to recruit six new members. The pyramid structure of such an organisation is illustrated by the numbers below and after just nine levels would involve over ten million people. There hasn't been a scheme or scam to date that hasn't collapsed or been closed down well before it reached anything like those numbers of participants. The nearer the top of the pyramid, the more likely it is that you will walk away with some money. The nearer the bottom, the less likely. As you can see, there are a lot more people nearer the bottom. This is true of all pyramid schemes whether they are called chain letters or given fancy names like "investment circles" or "gifting clubs".

Level 1: 6
Level 2: 36
Level 3: 216
Level 4: 1,296
Level 5: 7,776
Level 6: 46,656
Level 7: 279,936
Level 8: 1,679,616
Level 9: 10,077,696

What stands out is how six people each enticing six people to join, who then each entice another six people to join, quickly escalates into thousands and then millions of people all looking to entice six more people. By Level 10, every man, woman and child in the UK could be participating and you would still have places to fill. The entire population of the USA could fill Level 11 with plenty of room to spare. This is the magic of numbers again and it shows that it's magic that can work for you and against you.

The lazy man's way to riches

Mail order bookselling wasn't all bad though. Sure, the product sucked and its market was limited, but for me everything else made sense. Work from home. Work hours to suit. Low start up costs. Huge profit potential. No barriers with regards to age, sex, colour or disability. As a business model it is hard to beat. You just need to get the product and the marketing right. Wouldn't it be fantastic if you could do just that? That's where Plan B comes in.

That's not to say that there wasn't (or isn't) money to be made from mail order bookselling. Especially if you are actually selling books. Amazon may use the internet as a marketing tool, but it is essentially a bookseller that delivers books to its customers by mail (or courier).

A man who definitely got his product and marketing right was Joe Karbo. Joe was something of a legend in small entrepreneur circles, particularly in the United States. His book, *The Lazy Man's Ways To Riches*, has sold over three million copies since it was first published in 1973. Selling over three million copies of a book is a remarkable achievement, staggering in fact when you consider that it wasn't available through bookshops. It wasn't even listed in Books In Print, something that mainstream publishers both in the States and in the UK would consider commercial suicide. But year after year, the book kept on selling: 173,000 copies in its first year alone and nearly 50,000 copies as late as 1986, six years after Joe's untimely death.

A self-made millionaire, Joe Karbo acted as his own publisher and simply contracted out the printing of his book. Before *The Lazy Man's Way To Riches*, he had several other big sellers - one called *The Power Of Money Management* and the other about horse racing. Legend also has it that Joe didn't actually write *The Lazy Man's Way To Riches* until he had received US$50,000 worth of advance orders!

For those who haven't read it, *The Lazy Man's Way To Riches* is divided in two. The first part - or Book One to give it its official title - focuses on what the author calls Dyna/Psych, Joe Karbo's own take on the power of positive thinking. Basically, you set yourself personal and financial goals based on your needs and desires, and then by using the power of your subconscious mind, you turn them into reality. The theory goes that if you want something and can convince your sub-conscious that you are going to get it by constant positive reinforcement of that message, then the chances are you will get it. Psycho bullshit, some might say, but any system that focuses the mind on the positive can only do good. And there are plenty of Joe Karbo disciples out there who swear by Dyna/Psych.

The second part, or Book Two, is a detailed account of what Joe calls "the most exciting business in the world", the direct response business. By direct response, he simply means selling directly to the customer following a response to your marketing, be it a full page advertisement in a magazine or a thirty second commercial on local radio. In the UK we call it direct marketing. No wonder Joe's excited by it. He claims to have been living in abject poverty before discovering Dyna/Psych and the direct response, or mail order, business. Within a year of *The Lazy Man's Way To Riches* first rolling off the presses, Joe was driving the ultimate status symbol of the day, a Rolls Royce. Joe was a mail order bookseller made good. Maybe there was some truth in those manuals after all.

If you come across the book, by all means pick it up and read it. It's a classic of its kind, and although much of the information in the original edition is aimed at an American market and dated in terms of costings and so on, there is still much to be gained by reading it. In fact, as an entrepreneur, you should always be reading because knowledge really is power and the gateway to unlimited ideas. Joe actually had $1,000.00 printed on the cover of his book, followed by "Not the selling price but guaranteed to be what it's worth to you - at the very least!"

No ordinary Joe

So why did Joe make millions from mail order bookselling while I struggled to make a few pounds? One answer would be that Joe was selling a 160 page book which contained valuable information and not a few sheets of paper held together by a staple, but in truth that would only play a small part in Joe's success. Until they had parted with their money, customers were unlikely to have seen Joe's book or my duplicated manual and so would be buying either in good faith. And in any case, Joe wasn't selling a book and I wasn't selling a manual. We were both selling information, and there is no doubting that if the information is good, there will always be those who will pay good money for it, irrespective of whether it comes printed on gold leaf paper or written on the back of a beermat.

The real secret of Joe's success was marketing. He had the advertising muscle and experience from past publishing ventures to reach millions of potential customers via high quality full page ads in widely read magazines. I, on the other hand, was a school kid paying a few pounds a month to run classified ads in photocopied business opportunity magazines with a circulation of a few hundred each (and I use the word "magazines" very loosely indeed). What's more, virtually all of the recipients of said magazines were probably in the same boat as me anyway. Trying to work out how to make thousands of pounds by peddling rubbish to fellow pedlars. Out of Joe and me, there was only ever going to be one winner.

That said, we did have a few things in common. Even as a kid, I appreciated that running a successful mail order business from home would be a great way to earn a living, and in subsequent years I've done just that. Indeed, I followed in Joe's footsteps by publishing and selling books direct to the public (and later to bookshops), all from the comfort of my own home. I'm still doing so today, as the book you hold in your hand bears testament.

Even more importantly, like Joe, I immediately understood that people would pay money for information – and that was back in the industrial age. Today, "selling" information is so easy you can give the stuff away and still make money, as you will discover later in this book.

If Joe Karbo was alive today, he would be in his element. He would be lapping up the opportunities afforded him by the information age like there was no tomorrow. Of course, the success that he had in his lifetime meant that he was certainly no ordinary Joe, but then again you are no ordinary Joe (or Josephine) either, and the same opportunities that Joe would have cashed in on today are available to you. Right here, right now, to borrow a phrase from Fatboy Slim.

It is now over 30 years since I first stumbled across information and its potential to make me money. I don't think I have ever stopped looking for the perfect business opportunity, one that not only provides me with the money to do what I want each and every day of my life, but also affords me the time to do what I want to do.

The advent of the information age and the internet has delivered both to my door and for that I count my blessings. I am also driven by a burning desire to share what I have discovered with others. I am not going to make any wild promises and I am not looking for greater fools either. Just people genuinely interested in finding out more about a way of earning money that just might transform the way you live your life forever.

It's not who you know. It's what you know.

"Knowledge will forever govern ignorance; and a people who mean to be their own governors must arm themselves with the power which knowledge gives."
James Madison

Wage slavery is a classic example of the well proven theory that if you repeat a lie often enough, it becomes accepted as the truth. And that's why so few people do follow in the footsteps of the likes of Joe Karbo and seek alternatives to a life of "making a living".

Rather than question the system that sees the vast majority of people fall well short of their true potential, we blame ourselves. Maybe we're in the wrong job. Maybe we aren't working hard enough. Maybe we just don't know the right people.

Wait a minute. We don't know the right people? We live in a small world. A very small world. A world that is getting smaller by the hour. We know more people than we care to remember, and the people we know, in turn, know more people than we could possibly remember.

Pleased to meet you

Did you know that you are only six people away from anyone else in the world? That's right. We all live inside a giant pyramid scheme. You know someone who knows someone who knows someone who knows someone who knows someone who knows anybody you care to name. It's called "the six degrees of separation". You've probably heard of it.

In fact not only are you only six steps away from anybody you care to name, you are actually related to them too. And not only are you related to them, they owe you money. I'm pulling your leg. They don't really owe you money. You owe them money (just kidding again).

The point I'm trying to make is that we hear things repeated so often - get a job, get a pension, lemmings jump off cliffs, you're only six people away from anyone else in the world - that we just assume they must be true. And the better it sounds the more we want to believe it.

It would be nice if we were only six people away from anyone else in the world, but we're not. Or at least it's yet to be proven that we are. The six degrees of separation is nothing more than an urban myth based on an experiment conducted in the USA in the 1960s. Psychologist, Stanley Milgram, wanted to know how closely connected random individuals in the USA were and so he sent several hundred letters to randomly selected people in the Mid-West who were asked to forward them on to specific people in the North East Of America. No address was given for the final recipient, just a name, location and occupation.

So if you had received a letter from Stanley Miligram, he might have asked you to forward a letter on to John Shepherd, a chef from Manchester, New Hampshire, for example. If by chance you happened to know the intended recipient, you could forward the letter directly. Otherwise, you were asked to forward the letter to someone you knew on first name terms who might be able to get the letter closer to or directly to the intended recipient.

Milgram apparently discovered that the average number of steps between the original recipient of a letter and the final recipient was six. Hence the six degrees of separation that has passed into folklore. The problem was that Milgram wasn't telling the whole story. Most of the letters never even reached their intended recipient. For example, of the 50 people from Kansas who started a chain to deliver a letter to someone in Cambridge, Massachusetts, only three were successful. And of those, the average degree of separation was nine.

Indeed, no similar experiment since has been able to duplicate anything approaching six degrees of separation. There's no doubting that the internet, together with our new found ability to interact with the world at a click of a mouse, has brought this particular urban myth a big step closer to reality, but then again a fifth of the world's population doesn't even have access to clean drinking water let alone a computer screen.

Revolutionary times

If you live in the Western world, clean drinking water isn't usually something you have to worry about on a daily basis. Okay we might be up to ears in debt to pay for them, but things like cars, telephones and other goods once considered luxury items (including clean drinking water at the turn of a tap), are now commonplace in households throughout this great nation of ours.

Electricity wasn't widely available in domestic homes until the 1930s and yet, today, few of us could imagine life without it. My own children, who have been raised on the marvels of Sky

TV, think I'm joking when I tell them that when I was their age, there were only three television channels - and that one of them wasn't MTV. When a child myself, I couldn't imagine what my own parents did as children before the advent of television.

There's no doubting that the industrial revolution has delivered us a lifestyle that our ancestors of even a century ago couldn't have dreamed of. Our standard of living today - even as wage slaves - is higher than that of 99% of the people who went to war in 1914, but that doesn't necessarily make us wealthy. Indeed, most wage slaves are in debt their entire lives to pay for this increased standard of living.

What's really exciting is that we are once again living in revolutionary times, with the information age now beginning to eclipse the industrial age. Revolutionary times that will give you and me the opportunities to throw off the chains of wage slavery and to pursue our dreams – something that only the wealthiest and most single-minded have been able to do in years gone by. So profound are the changing times that we find ourselves living in, that I would go so far as to say that at no time in the history of mankind have those economic opportunities been so great.

At the dawning of history, mankind lived in small groups of hunter gatherers and there was little scope to be anything other than hunters or gatherers. Success was measured in terms of survival. Wealth was of little real interest or benefit. Then around 10,000 years ago, man planted crops for the very first time in what is now modern day Iraq, Syria and Turkey. As soon as we began to farm, the ball game changed forever. Increasing numbers of people no longer migrated to find food and instead remained in the one place. Land became valuable. Crops became valuable. Those who owned the land became wealthy, often literally living off the labour of those who didn't own the land, but who worked it in return for "a living". If you didn't own land - the means of production - the chances of you becoming wealthy were virtually non-existent unless you had the power to take what you didn't have by force.

The industrial revolution changed the rules once again. The means of production moved from the fields to factories, mills, steelworks, mines and shipyards. Landowners were no longer the only ones who could be wealthy. Industrialists - those who owned the factories, workshops and mines - could join them at life's top table. Those who worked in the Workshop Of The World, as Britain became known, discovered very quickly that little of that wealth was heading their way. Indeed, the lives of many who left the land to work in the industrial wastelands of 19th century Britain were truly wretched.

Conditions have dramatically changed since then of course, but despite the incredible advances we have made in the last 100 or so years, few of us are wealthy. Owning the means of production has always been the key to true wealth, but here's the incredible thing about the revolutionary times we find ourselves living in. Today, you don't need land to make money. You don't need to own factories to make money. You don't need money to make money. Who you know no longer matters. In the information age, the means of production is sitting on a desk in nearly every house in the Western World. We call it the computer, and, together with the internet, it offers you the opportunity of creating true wealth for yourself and your family.

What is even more incredible is that the vast majority of wage slaves just don't see what's right in front of their noses. It's the equivalent of a peasant being given his own fields. A production line worker being handed the keys to the factory. A South African miner being given all the gold and diamonds that he can carry home. Most of us are so blinded by the chains of wage slavery that, rather than seize the moment, we play computer games instead.

Zoom zoom

Don't believe the information age can transform fortunes beyond our wildest dreams? Ask people who the richest woman in the UK is and most will say the Queen. In 2010, *The Sunday*

Times Rich List said that Elizabeth II was worth £290 million, the culmination of centuries of wealth building, but she's not the richest woman in Britain. Not by a long chalk. Neither is Jo Murray, but in just 13 years, the former secretary and teacher has amassed a fortune of £519 million. Since the publication of her first novel in 1997, *Harry Potter And The Philosopher's Stone*, under her pen name, JK Rowling, in fact.

Jo Murray owns information and sells it via multiple revenue streams. It has taken her little more than a decade to go from living in a bedsit to being worth twice as much as the Queen of England. Incidentally, only 1,000 copies of *Harry Potter And The Philosopher's Stone* were printed initially, with her publisher advising Jo to get a day job because she would never make a living writing children's books. He may well have been related to the fifth Beatle. Or was at least six people away from being so anyway.

True, authors have been making money for decades, but never so much so quickly. It really is different this time. During our agricultural past, the humblest of peasant could have told you that owning land would make you rich. During the industrial age, workers on the shop floor knew only too well that owning the factory was where the money was, not pressing buttons on the production line. The reality was that the peasant didn't own land, the worker didn't have the keys to the factory.

We, however, live in truly remarkable times. And that's why producing information, selling what you know and what people want to know, is something that you should be seriously considering when you are developing multiple revenue streams of your own. Today, it's not who you know that matters. It's what you know. And what you know is the equivalent to owning land, factories, a gold mine.

Just ask Lauren Luke if you still don't believe me. Lauren left school with no qualifications after falling pregnant at the age of 15. Two years ago, the 27 year old single mum was working in a dead-end job as a taxi dispatcher and living in a tiny one bedroom flat in South Shields. In fact, if you have heard of Lauren, chances are that you've also seen inside her tiny pink and black bedroom courtesy of the internet video sharing website, YouTube (http://www.youtube.com), because that bedroom has been the backdrop to her success.

Today, Lauren is well on the way to making her first million thanks to what she knows – how to apply eye make-up. That's right. Something as simple as knowing how to apply make-up can make you a fortune today for no better reason than millions of girls and women don't know how to do it.

Go back two years, and in a bid to earn extra money, Lauren started selling make-up on eBay. Most sellers include an image of the product they are selling, but Lauren did something different. She used what she knew. She used the make-up herself and included a photo of her made up face in each listing. E-mails started to pour in, asking how she had achieved each look. There were far too many to reply to individually so Lauren started to post simple unedited video tutorials of herself applying make-up on YouTube for her customers to watch.

Those videos have now been watched more than 50 million times, making her the UK's most popular YouTube user, and paving the way to a book deal, her own make-up range, and even her own Nintendo DS game, *Supermodel Makeover*. Lauren has developed life-changing multiple revenue streams working from her own home with little more than a computer, a webcam and what she knows. Zoom zoom indeed.

It's a kinda magic

I love magic tricks, although if truth be told I'm no David Blaine. At the moment I'm trying to perfect a trick whereby I have a pound and a penny in my hand and I make the penny disappear. No magician worth his salt will ever tell you how a trick is done, so I won't mention the fact that this one is performed using two specially made coins, but what I will say is that my sleight of hand needs a great deal of improvement.

Supposing you also loved magic and wanted to share your love of all things magic by selling magic tricks. You could of course open a shop, but unless it was in a town or city large enough to support such a shop, you would be lucky to still be in business at the end of your first six month lease. You would also have to pay other fixed costs such as business rates and utility bills, make sure the shop was staffed during business hours, and that you had enough stock to fill the shelves. Quite an investment of time and money. The right magic shop in the right place though, and you'll make money. In Glasgow, Tam Shepherd's Trick Shop has traded from the same small premises in Queen Street since the late 1800s.

In the industrial age, you could have supplemented your shop's income by also selling magic tricks by mail order. The idea would be to develop this additional stream of income by supplying customers far and wide with magic tricks by post. This would have involved additional marketing expenses and you would also almost certainly want to produce regular catalogues that you would send to customers past and present to encourage repeat sales.

Alternatively, you could forget the shop and run your magic business exclusively by mail order from home without the expense of retail premises or warehouses or offices or staff. As long as you had access to a postal service, you could run your business from the corner of a spare room, wherever your home happened to be, with minimum overheads. You could be living on a remote Scottish island while you supplied Londoners with magic tricks by post – without having a retail presence in the Capital, without paying the high cost of living that London is well known for, and without the stresses and strains of big city life.

It also means that you could run it in your spare time if it didn't provide a full-time income because, with all of your business being conducted by post, you wouldn't have to be available during business hours (unless you encouraged telephone enquiries and accepted telephone orders too). The post would arrive in the morning, you would sort out orders and requests for catalogues, package orders that were ready to go, and then post them out to your customers in the afternoon. And of course the trip to the Post Office could coincide with a visit to the bank to deposit all of those lovely cheques. If you happened to have other things to do during the day – a job to go to, a round of golf to play – you could just as easily rifle through the mail in the evening and send any orders the following day.

Be gone dark Satanic mills

The industrial age with its dark Satanic mills is slowly but surely giving way to the green and pleasant land of the information age, and for once the grass is indeed truly greener on the other side. Today, thanks to the internet and what is commonly referred to as The Web, selling magic tricks has become a whole lot easier. In fact, selling virtually anything has become a whole lot easier.

True, you can still open a shop, place advertisements in newspapers, and you can still send out paper catalogues, but you can also have a website to display your wares. A website can be the virtual equivalent of retail premises, a shop with potentially unlimited shelf space to display every magic trick under the sun. A shop that is open 24 hours a day, seven days a week, 365 days a year – all without a member of staff in sight. At the same time, it can be a full colour catalogue that can be updated at the click of a mouse and need never go out of date.

So successful can a website be that you may find that you no longer need to place advertisements or send out catalogues (although it rarely hurts to include further offers when sending out orders to encourage repeat business). A website might be all that you need – and with that comes incredible benefits of running what is a virtual business.

Customers can choose and pay for their magic tricks online and the whole process can be automated. Orders are sent to your inbox for processing and payments are sent directly to your bank account. The whole business can be basically put on auto-pilot for hours or days at a time, with your only physical involvement being to update the website when necessary, fill the orders, answer enquiries, and spend the money earned.

Just like a High Street shop or a pre-internet mail order business, you still need customers to make money. Simply building a website and sticking it out there in cyberspace is of little use if nobody knows it is there. It's the equivalent of installing a telephone line, telling nobody your number, and then sitting there waiting for the phone to ring.

What's so incredible about the information age though is that you don't always need to go looking for customers. They will come looking for you. Nowadays, if anyone wants to find something, be it a product, a service or information, chances are they will head straight to a computer and "Google it". Google is just one of a number of search engines eager to direct users in the right direction, but with an estimated 90% share of the UK market, chances are you know Google well. You enter a search word or phrase and the search engine then returns a list of results in order of relevancy. You then click on your choice from that list and go on your merry way to wherever that link takes you.

Potential customers will come looking for what you offer via the search engines and, as long as you rank highly in the search results, chances are they will find you too. Even the smallest of sites can benefit from this to the tune of hundreds if not thousands of extra visitors every month. If you can turn those visitors into customers, then you're on your way to making money.

Although never good to have all your eggs in the one basket, I know from personal experience that a niche internet business can happily exist on revenue derived exclusively from customers who found their way to its website via the search engines. It's actually mind-blowing to think that some of the biggest internet companies on the planet - the likes of Google, Yahoo and

Microsoft - are out there 24 hours a day, doing all of your marketing for you, without charging you a penny.

So not only might your website reduce or eliminate your need to produce paper catalogues, visitors derived from search engines may mean you need no marketing budget whatsoever. We already know a mail order or web based business can be run from home, so overheads are lower still when compared to a traditional bricks and mortar enterprise. When you consider that a small website need cost you no more than £50 a year to run, and then factor in the above, you can see the attraction of developing websites instead of opening shops to produce multiple streams of income.

It just gets better and better

Good though the above sounds, it gets better still. We were talking about selling what you know. This can be done in many ways, including digitally. We've already mentioned e-books. You can deliver all sorts of information electronically, as an e-mail attachment for example or in various formats via a download link. If people are willing to pay for that information, then they can order, pay, and have their information delivered via the internet – with no involvement from you beyond answering any customer service issues and counting the money as it goes into your bank account.

It is not only possible to run a business like this from home, but because it literally runs itself, you can be anywhere in the world, doing anything you choose, and still be making money. As long as your website is live, as long as the search engines are directing visitors your way, as long as those visitors want to buy your information, you can be making money from what are basically fully automated cash machines.

Going back to our love of magic tricks. Instead of selling physical tricks, what about selling information about how to do magic tricks? What about doing for magic what Lauren Luke has done for make-up? What about selling video and written tutorials that demonstrate how to perform magic? And what about doing all this via an automated website that takes your customers' money and delivers the videos to them electronically while you work, rest or play?

Of course you may still want to sell actual magic tricks – and the good news is that you can do this too without carrying stock and without having to fill orders yourself. Plenty of companies will happily pay you a commission on sales generated when you send your website visitors in their direction. Known as affiliate marketing, this is something that we will cover in much greater detail soon, but again, any money earned is paid directly into your bank account.

You could even charge visitors to access "members only" magic pages on your website, whereby they pay for your premium information. Or you could sell advertising space on your web pages. Even Google – the friendly search engine who sent you visitors for free in the first place – will pay you to place its advertising on your web pages! Again this is something I will cover in detail later in this book.

The long and short of it is this. It no longer matters who you know. What counts in the information age is what you know (or indeed what you can find out). What you know doesn't need to be rocket science. It can be as simple as how to apply make-up or where to get 25% off pipes and slippers. You can then sell what you know over and over again to people all over the world thanks to the wonders of the internet. You can do it without the need for an expensive office or retail premises. You can do it from virtually anywhere in the world and you don't even need to be working to make money. Take the day off and you'll still make money. Go to sleep and you'll still make money. Give your information away and you'll still make money.

And best of all? You can start today.

Plan B

"Do what you love. Know your own bone; gnaw at it, bury it, unearth it, and gnaw it still."
Thoreau

Early February, 2009. As I munch away at my breakfast cereal while watching Sky News, I'm very pleased I don't have to face a long commute to work given that much of Britain is covered in snow. London's buses normally carry six million people every working day, but they aren't running at all today because of the dangerous road conditions. There are also severe problems on the London Underground too. Public transport has basically ground to a halt in the Capital and my television is showing pictures of people trudging through the snow to get to work on foot.

My daily commute consists of walking from said television and down a flight of stairs to my home office. Come rain or shine, I don't have to put a step outside my front door unless I want to. And while some people can spend an hour or more travelling to work in the morning and the same amount of time getting home again after work, it takes me less than a minute to reach my desk.

Even better, my desk can be wherever I want it to be. At the moment that's about 200 yards from the Mediterranean on the Spanish Costa Blanca, so even if I did venture outside, it would be sun not snow that greeted me. As long as I have access to the internet via a telephone landline, mobile broadband, or Wi-Fi, I can earn money pretty much anywhere in the world.

Better still, I don't have to even be at my desk to earn money. One of my first joys of the day is to check how much money I have made while I've been sleeping. A night doesn't go by without me making at least some money. I can be away from my desk for days, weeks or even months, and I still make money. I worked out that if I died suddenly, at least some of my multiple revenue streams would continue to function and bring in money for up to two years before finally grinding to a halt. I'm sure if I thought about it, I could plan things for them to continue even longer.

El Crisis

Spain might have better weather than the UK (although give me Scotland over Spain any day during the torturous heat of July and August), but it's a country not without its problems. The Spanish television news has been dominated by one story for months now – El Crisis.

If you think the UK has economic problems, spare a thought for Spain. Unemployment jumped by 199,000 in January, 2009, alone, taking the national unemployment rate to 14.4%, by far the highest in Europe (not that I believe the UK's official figure of 6.1% as I more than hinted at earlier).

And worse is still to come. The European Commission has forecast that the unemployment rate in Spain will increase to 16.1% in 2010 and 18.7% in 2011. It may even go higher. We've not seen unemployment levels that high in the UK since the early 1980s when reggae band, UB40, were riding high in the charts with their single, *One In Ten*, and millions of people were reduced to "A statistic, a reminder, of a world that doesn't care".

I know a lot of British ex-pats who live in Spain and who are struggling to make ends meet. Unless you speak Spanish (or indeed one of the regional languages, depending on where in Spain you live), finding a decent job has always been difficult. Today it is nigh on impossible.

Brits in Spain have traditionally made a living catering for other ex-pats – estate agents, restaurants, bars, building firms, satellite TV companies, what have you – but many have been badly affected by the downturn. Less Brits are coming out to Spain and more are going home, and so the potential pool of customers is shrinking. Those who remain are finding themselves having to watch the centimos as well as the euros and so are spending less, making it a double whammy for those trying to earn an honest crust.

Many of the 350,000 or so British pensioners who live in Spain are finding life especially difficult. Those who depend on pensions for their income saw their spending power fall by around 40% during the course of 2008, a combination of Sterling's dramatic fall against the euro and rising prices in Spanish shops. Many are having to eat into their savings to survive – and of course the fall in interest rates means those savings are making far less in interest than they were a year ago.

Many would love to go home – and I believe that up to half a million Brits who currently live in France, Spain and elsewhere will do exactly that during 2010, 2011 and 2012 as the economic problems continue and the strength of Sterling continues to wane. Many will have properties to sell, but that's easier said than done in a market dominated by falling prices and a huge surplus of new and resale properties. Sad though it is to say, for an unfortunate minority it's not even a case of being willing to accept less for your property. You couldn't even give away some of the properties that have been bought in haste by Brits in recent years.

Again though, just like the snow back home, Spain's economic woes do not affect me directly. Generally speaking, not a penny of what I earn comes from Spain and although the strength of the euro does mean I should earn less, the fact that I can earn money in dollars and euros, as well as pounds, insulates me from currency fluctuations to some extent. What's more, year after year, I find myself earning more money anyway for no more work.

I also benefit from the fact that Spain is a low wage country relative to the UK, so the cost of living is less than it is back in Blighty. Contrary to popular belief, Spain does have a winter and it can be cold (particularly at nights, and especially in the north and away from the coast), but our heating bills for example are a fraction of what they would be during a Scottish winter. Food and drink are also generally cheaper, as is petrol.

If I wanted to go home, I could pack up and leave tomorrow. Believing that Spain's housing boom couldn't last, I have never bought a property in Spain, preferring to rent for the part of the year that I spend here. The rent I pay has remained the same for the last three years (in euros that is), it's much less than I would have to pay for a mortgage on a similar property, and I've no maintenance bills to pay. I don't have any council tax to pay either (the Spanish equivalent is included in the rent), but if I did, it would be quite literally a tenth of what it would be back home anyway. My bins are also emptied every night, not once a fortnight.

Overall, I would guess the cost of living in Spain is about two thirds of what it would be in the UK and yet I'm earning exactly what I would do if my desk was in the UK. I could go and live somewhere where the cost of living was a tenth of what it is in the UK and still earn exactly the same, but I love living in Spain and so Spain it is for the time being.

I'm hoping that there will be people reading this who have always dreamed of living abroad because I'm living proof that it's a lot easier to do than you might think – especially if you have a Plan B that works just as well abroad as it does at home. What's also worth remembering is that the money you spend on flights, accommodation, and eating out during a two week holiday, is little different to what it would cost you to actually live in the same resort for two months, renting an apartment and eating in most nights. Something to think about if you have nothing to keep you in the UK during the cold winter months.

Plan B

For years now, when people ask me what I do "for a living", I've found it a very difficult question to answer. Usually, they are only asking out of politeness. They only want a one or two word answer. A sentence at most so that they can get on with the rest of their lives. I usual mumble something about the internet, hoping that will suffice. Usually it does, but it also runs the risk of me being asked to take a look at a faulty computer.

My problem is that I don't really have a job as such. I don't want one either. Instead I follow a plan. A plan I call Plan B. It's a plan that can be adapted no matter what your circumstances, and best of all it can be pursued in your spare time as well as on a part-time or full-time basis.

My Plan B encompasses much of what we have talked about so far in this book.

• It embraces the information age and takes full advantage of the opportunities afforded by the internet.

• It values time in a way that getting a traditional job rarely does.

• It allows you to work from home (or indeed from anywhere!), working whatever hours of the day or night suit you best.

• It enables you to develop multiple revenue streams that allow you to earn more money working less hours.

• It will allow you to sell each hour of your time over and over again.

• It will even make you money while you are walking the dog or asleep in your bed.

• It embraces the magic of numbers and sets compounding to work.

My Plan B is also very simple.

**My Plan B is to do enough work each day
to generate one pound.**

Yes, that's it.

Enough work to generate £1.

And when I've done that, the rest of the day is my own. The proverbial Gone Fishing sign goes up.

You're a hundred plus pages into a book about escaping the rat race and only now does the author mention that he only wants to earn a pound a day. The same author who told you that David Beckham was a decent bloke and that you had a genie at your disposal willing to grant you unlimited wishes every day of your life. As Clay Davis from *The Wire* would say, "Sheeeeeet!".

Fear not, dear reader. I'm not about to ask you to consider living on a pound a day. And I don't myself work all day for a pound coin. Instead, that pound's worth of work will earn me over £60,000 a year. That's because Plan B is an entirely different way of looking at work. It's not about devoting five or six days a week to work for 40 or 50 years of your life. It's about devoting the least time possible to work so that you can get on with living your life instead.

The key to Plan B's success is that I'm not selling my time. Instead, I'm using what I create with my time to make money. By following Plan B, I've discovered that by doing enough work every day to earn just one pound, not only is the rest of the day my own, but I end up earning far more than most people do working every hour God sends.

Sound too good to be true? At first glance maybe, but it's amazing what can be achieved when you employ the magic of numbers and compounding. Whatever work I do to earn me a pound will make me that pound not just once, but every day for a year with little or no additional effort from me. If my work for any given day continues to earn me money after a year, then that's a bonus (and it often does), but first things first: a pound a day for a year (or a total of £365 over the next 365 day period).

It could be that my day's work (which incidentally might take me ten minutes and not necessarily an entire day) earns me exactly a pound a day for the next year. Or it could be that the entire £365 is brought in on one of those 365 days in one fell swoop. Or it could be that one day's work only makes me £65 over a year and the next day's work makes £665. What matters is that it averages out at a pound a day over the next year. Give or take.

If I do this every day of the year, and assuming all goes to plan, the accumulated earnings over any 365 period would be £66,795. There's the magic of numbers for you. I arrive at the figure £66,795 by adding up all those pounds I hope to earn every day for a year. Obviously, I don't earn exactly that each and every year, but it's the ballpark figure I aim for when I pick up my bat in the morning and start swinging it in the hope of hitting home runs. No, it's not millions of pounds granted, and I'm not going to appear on the *Sunday Times Rich List* any time soon, but it's more than enough money for me, far more than the average wage, and best of all, it allows me to do whatever I want each and every day of my life.

Sometimes I have what I call a millionaire day. To earn a million pounds in a year, you would need to earn an average of £2,740 a day. Whenever I earn more than £2,740 in a day, I call it a millionaire day. It doesn't happen too often (yet), but it does happen. Just like Colonel John "Hannibal" Smith from the A-Team, I love it when my Plan B comes together and on millionaire days it really does come together.

That said, I am not in it for the money per se. I also have no interest in measuring my "success" by the number of fancy offices I have in capital cities around the world or the number of people I employ to fill them. I'm not that kind of entrepreneur. I'm more of a time entrepreneur, someone who values time more than money. I simply want to devote as much of my time to doing exactly what I want to do each and every day – and I want the money to be able to do it. My Plan B delivers exactly that.

So let's say that I start working to my plan on the 1st of January. On that first day, I plan on doing enough work to enable me to earn a pound.

On the 2nd of January I will aim to make another pound – and my work from the day before should contribute another pound to the coffers, making £2 in total for the day, £3 in total for the year to date.

On the 3rd of January, I will aim to make another pound, plus I hope to benefit from the previous two days' work by earning an additional £2, making £3 for the day and £6 for the year to date.

On the 4th of January I again do enough work to earn a pound plus I'll benefit from the previous three days' work, and earn £4 in total for the day, £10 in total for the year to date.

And so my year continues. By the 31st of December, I'm still aiming to make a pound, but I also get a pound for all the days that have come before, making £365 for the day – and a grand total of £66,795 for the year (for anyone interested in the maths behind my Plan B, it's basically the sum of all the numbers from 1 to 365 inclusive, and that equals £66,795).

I could of course set my sights higher or lower. Supposing I wanted to develop a Plan B that earned me £10,000 a year, my target would need to be set at 39p per day. If I wanted to earn a million pounds a year, my target would need to be set at £4 per day. That's right. With Plan B doing enough work to earn £4 a day will make you a millionaire within a year.

Here are a few more examples:

• 25p per day on Plan B would result in a total of £4,208 a year

• 40p per day on Plan B would result in a total of £10,731 a year

• 50p per day on Plan B would result in a total of £16,744 a year

• £1 per day on Plan B would result in a total of £66,795 a year

• £2 per day on Plan B would result in a total of £266,815 a year

• £3 per day on Plan B would result in a total of £600,060 a year

• £4 per day on Plan B would result in a total of £1,066,530 a year

So how exactly do I know if I've done enough work on any given day to earn a pound a day for a year? The simple answer is that I don't. Not exactly. No more than a car salesman knows how many cars he is going to sell today. But once you have been following Plan B for a while, you will develop a sense for the amount of work required to earn you your daily target, a sense that will be honed by the numbers that you produce as time goes by. And by numbers I am talking about the number of visitors that you attract to your site and how many of those you convert into customers. In other words, how many fish bite and how many you land. You soon know that for any given website, every 1,000 visitors to it will result in X number of click-throughs and Y number of sales.

Once you have a feel for the numbers, it is just a question of deciding what bait to use today. Visitors are the key to success for any website and it is down to you to see their numbers increase over time. It is obviously easier to sell Y number of things to 10,000 visitors than it is to 1,000 visitors. The surest way to do that is to add content to a website. By adding more hooks every day, while maintaining the bait on the hooks already in the water, your daily catch will continue to grow in size. In short, every page you add to a website compounds your ability to make money.

The trick is to aim to earn more than you actually need - and then if you do fall short it isn't the end of the world. I don't actually need to earn £66,795 a year. I don't need to earn anywhere near that amount. It just so happens that doing enough work to earn a pound a day ends up at that figure.

What's so beautiful about my Plan B is that the thought of earning a pound a day is not in the least bit daunting. Every day I believe that it's perfectly possible to do. It's no big deal. All I have to do is wake up, do enough work to earn one pound, and that's it. It's actually the equivalent of earning £183 per day every day of a calendar year which sounds like a much taller order – until you remember that with Plan B comes not only multiple revenue streams, but also the magic of numbers. To me it doesn't even feel like work. I only do what I enjoy doing anyway. To me it's one big game.

And here's why it's a lot easier to make money following Plan B than you might think. Suppose for a moment I'm an ordinary wage slave and I want to earn £66,795 a year. I need someone to pay me £5,556.25 a month or £1,284.52 a week. Jobs like that certainly do exist, but they come with strings attached – not least the number of hours your employer will expect you to be working each and every week in return for your wages.

Every hour that you work for a boss in return for an hourly rate of pay will earn you X number of pounds. That's the deal. You give your boss an hour of your time. Your boss pays you for it. As long as you keep your job, it's guaranteed money – but at a huge cost in terms of your time. The point is that you sell your time to your boss once and that's it. Once that hour has passed you can't go back and sell it to your boss again.

Plan B sees you approach things in a totally different way. Instead of earning X number of pounds for every hour you work, what you create with that hour becomes all important. The idea is that what you create in that hour will be able to make you money not just during that hour, but for hours to come. Days to come. Weeks to come. Months to come. Years to come even.

Each hour you invest in Plan B will do the same. If you can get excited by the fact that just one hour of your time spent working on Plan B can earn you money for hours, days, weeks, years to come, just think of the possibilities to earn money that unleashing ten hours of creativity can bring? Or 40 hours of creativity? Or the 2,000 hours you would normally devote to a nine to five existence during a typical year?

The information age makes all this possible. So much so that there's no need to spend five days a week for the best part of every year working. No need at all. Simply pick a daily target, do enough work to reach that target, and then go fishing.

Don't score own goals

Plan B is a little unusual with its "pound a day" target. I like it that way because it emphasises the awesome power of allowing time to compound the work that you do and the money that you earn. If you come from a sales background, you might be wondering why I don't just set myself a monthly earnings target, say £5,000, and aim for that instead? Isn't that the same sort of thing? In a word, no.

Most motivational gurus bang on about goal-setting and how you can do anything in life if you put your mind to it. I'm here to tell you that's simply not true. Each and every one of us is truly incredible, but that doesn't mean that anything is possible, that everything is within our grasp given the right amount of blood, sweat and tears. The reality is that we all too readily set ourselves goals and targets that doom us to failure.

That's not to say it's not important to have goals in life. It's extremely important. I see them as milestones on the way to your dreams. My goal is to do enough work to earn a pound a day and then walk away from my desk. If all goes to plan, I hope to make around £60,000 a year, but that's not the same as setting myself monthly targets of £5,000 or an annual goal of earning £60,000.

That is because there are two types of goals, internal goals and external goals, and they are very different animals. With internal goals, whether you achieve them or not is entirely dependent on you. A salesman might set himself an internal goal of knocking on 100 doors in a day. An athlete might set herself the target of running faster than she has ever run before. Beating your personal best is a good example of an internal goal.

External goals on the other hand depend on factors independent of you. Whether you achieve them or not is not down to you alone. Winning the lottery is an external goal because it is dependent on six randomly selected numbers matching your selection and you have no way of influencing the numbers that will be drawn. An external goal for our athlete would be to come first. For our salesman it might be to get five orders.

Imagine it's the final of the Olympics 1,500m track event for women. Eight of the world's best middle distance runners are on the starting line and all have set themselves the external goal of finishing first to claim gold. Unless there's a dead heat at the finishing line, seven of those athletes are going to go home disappointed having failed to achieve their goal of winning the gold medal. There was never going to be any other outcome. Each athlete's goal is dependent on the performance of the other competitors. An athlete could run the race of her life, breaking personal, national and even current world records, but if another athlete crosses the line in front of her she will have failed as far as achieving her goal is concerned.

Of those eight women in that Olympics final, all would have given every ounce of themselves to crossing that winning line first, but only one would ultimately succeed. Are the other seven failures? Of course not.

Similarly, if our salesman knocks on 100 doors he has achieved his goal. He has done what he set out to achieve and can go home a happy man. He can then knock on another 100 doors tomorrow. If he sets an external goal of getting five orders before he comes home, he can knock on all the doors in China, but his goal will only be achieved if he gets five sales. Four sales might be a fantastic achievement, but because it is one short of the external target set, he will have failed. That makes knocking on doors the following day that little bit harder.

The competitive nature of our wage slave society means that we are often conditioned to accept the challenges of achieving external goals - goals that we often have little or no chance of achieving. This leads to inevitable disappointment and the belief that we are somehow failures. If you have ever set yourself a goal or target and have failed to achieve it, chances are you now shun away from pursuing goals, believing that to do otherwise would just lead to further disappointment. The chances are you were chasing external goals.

Internal goals are totally different. Whether or not you achieve them is down to you. Nobody else. As an athlete on that starting line your goal might be to run faster than you have ever run before. To do so would be a fantastic achievement, a goal worthy of even the finest of athletes. If you ran the race of your life, running faster than you had ever done before, you would have achieved your goal whether you finished, first, last or somewhere in-between. And you would realise that the difference between success and failure is in the eye of the beholder.

It's the same with sales figures. Bosses love to set external goals for their sales reps, putting them into competition with one another. Whoever achieves the most sales this month gets a sticky bun. All of the sales reps go mad trying to outsell each other, working extra hours, never off the telephone, missing lunch, and yet at the end of the month there are only two winners. The wage slave eating the sticky bun and the boss counting his money.

It suits a wage slave society to have you chasing external goals. Most people will go through life thinking they are failures and will be grateful to eat from the crumbs that fall from the table of life if they chase external goals. Of course a few people will manage to achieve them - somebody wins the lottery every week - and so the pretence that external goals are somehow valid for us all to pursue is maintained.

As you begin to develop your multiple revenue streams make sure you are focusing on achieving internal goals and not external ones. By "doing enough work to earn a pound", I am setting myself an internal goal. It is up to me and me alone to do that work. If I knock off before doing so, I am only kidding myself. A monthly target of £5,000 would be an external target, totally dependent on others (visitors to my websites) to help me reach it.

One more important point. Setting and achieving internal goals is not the same as that well worn phrase of "try to do your best". Don't try to do your best. Do your best. If you are only trying to do something it suggests lack of preparation and lack of motivation and it usually results in limited success.

"As long as you try your best, that's all that matters," is a common enough phrase, but it's not the same as "As long as you do your best, that's all that matters." Not by a long chalk. Trying to do your best isn't good enough. Doing your best always is. Be a doer not a tryer. Set internal goals and then do everything necessary to achieve them (don't just try to do everything necessary). Success will follow.

A day in the life of Plan B

So let's see how I might make my pound today. Let's say that I'm going to add some content to one of my websites – a review of a gadget with ordering details for example. It might be a gadget that I've bought recently or it might be something that I don't own, but think will be of interest to others.

Supposing it is a gadget I've recently bought for my own use. What I will do is write a review of it, with the hope that people will read the review and go on to buy the gadget. I've no interest in stocking, selling and distributing the gadget myself however. That's too much like hard work. That consumes time. Instead, I will tell readers exactly where they can buy the gadget online. In fact, I'll include a link from my review directly to a web page where they can order the gadget from someone else. That someone else we will call the supplier, or the merchant, and that merchant will then pay me a commission for every sale I generate.

The gadget retails for £50 and, as an affiliate of the merchant, I'm paid a 10% commission (£5 in this case) for each one sold via my website's link to the merchant's website. How this is done will be explained in detail later in this book, but suffice to say at this point that there are hundreds of companies, big and small, from household names to small independent retailers, who will pay you a commission for sales that you generate for them. Finding these companies is as easy as visiting a handful of websites that act as middle men between what are called merchants (suppliers) and the likes of you and me (affiliates).

If the only work I did that day was that one review, I would need to sell one of those gadgets every five days on average over a 365 day period for it to earn me the equivalent of a pound a day and for Plan B to come to fruition (73 of those gadgets over the course of a year).

For an established website, with hundreds of visitors a day who would be interested in just such a gadget, it wouldn't be at all difficult to generate those 73 sales in a year. You might even sell thousands and earn thousands of five pound notes from that one review. Probably not all in one day, but over the days, weeks and months to come. It's equally true that for a new site with little traffic, 73 sales would be a very difficult total to achieve. Possible, but in truth unlikely. Given that, I like to hedge my bets.

It might take me an hour from starting to write the review to it appearing on my website. If I'm willing to work eight hours today, then I could write eight such reviews and place them on up to eight of my websites. Then I would have eight reviews working to earn me that pound a day. The odds of me achieving my target have just increased massively.

No page has to be a one trick pony either. As well as the gadget review, I could spend a few extra minutes integrating Google AdSense advertising into the page – and earn anything from a penny to a few pounds each time a visitor clicked on one of the ads placed on the page by Google (again, don't worry if it's news to you that Google will pay you to put ads on your website – all will be explained in detail later).

I can also add banner advertisements showing related products that might in turn result in sales. Or I could add links to similar pages I had created earlier - and maybe pick up some commission that way for gadgets I have already reviewed.

Or I could spend four hours writing gadget reviews and then spend four hours part developing a new directory style website whereby I earn money for each business that lists with me – say for example £9.99 a month or £119 a year or whatever is going to appeal to my target market given what I can offer in return for them listing.

Or I could spend an hour looking for domain names to register, either to develop myself at some point in the future or to sell on to someone else. I actually do spend 15-30 minutes almost every day looking at domain names that others have registered in the past, but have not renewed for whatever reason. I regularly find names that I can and then do sell further down the road for many times the cost of me registering them. Again, I'll tell you exactly how I do this later in this book.

Whatever I do, it's like pushing a snowball down a hill because every page that I add to a website adds value to that website by attracting new visitors - visitors who might visit other pages that I prepared on previous days and who might buy something that I wrote about a day ago, a week ago, a year ago.

Fishing is another good analogy. Everything you do to earn money is the equivalent of a hook baited to catch a fish or customer. The magic here is that each hook can catch an unlimited number of fish. It's like television. The fact that you are watching a programme doesn't mean that your neighbour can't watch the same programme. Millions of people can watch the same programme simultaneously. Indeed, the fact that millions can watch the same programme goes a long way to explain why footballers earn so much for just 90 minutes "work". The FA Cup Final, for example, has a worldwide TV audience of 400-500 million.

Not only that, the more hooks you create, the more fish you will attract to your stretch of the river bank. How cool is that? That's because, generally speaking, the more quality content you add to a website, the more visitors it will attract as time goes on.

And the beauty is that you don't have to be around to actually land those fish. That's all done for you. Going back to the gadget review, I write the review and that acts as a hook. I then go out to play. Any fish that it attracts (today, tomorrow, next month or even next year) are landed by the merchant supplying the gadget. It is their responsibility to land the fish – to process the order, take payment, deliver the gadget, and deal with any customer service related issues that may arise. My job's done when the review is finished and it appears on my website. I may have to check that I'm using the right bait from time to time (the price might change, the merchant might start selling an improved version of the gadget), but beyond that I don't have to spend my valuable time landing each fish, weighing it, gutting it, cooking it or even eating it. I just create the bait and drop the hooks into the water.

Once I think I've done enough work to make that £1, I can walk away from my computer screen a happy man. It may take me a full day, but the longer you've been building snowballs, the less time it takes. That's because those snowballs soon pick up a momentum of their own as they roll down the hill, and they quickly start to earn you money whether you're working, resting or playing. With a new website, you may be able to count visitors to a page you add with your fingers. 12 months down the road, a similar page added to the same website might be read by thousands of visitors. Millions even. Not surprisingly, that can do wonders for your earnings and it means you can work even less hours.

Sometimes I can be at my computer screen for an hour or less and the rest of the day is my own. Occasionally, it's just a case of turning on my computer, checking my e-mails, seeing that I've sold a domain name for hundreds of pounds (even thousands of pounds) and then taking the rest of the day off. A big domain name sale might give me the week off. Indeed, for the last few years, the accumulative effect of building snowballs has allowed me to take much of July and August off, with only the odd hour, here and there, spent making sure things are ticking over ready for my return in the Autumn.

Nothing that I do commits me to being at my computer screen during normal office hours. Not unless I want to be there. I don't deal with customers face to face. I don't have to be on the end of a phone. I can work whatever hours I choose. If I want to do something else during the day, there's nothing stopping me earning that pound in the evening or into the early hours of the morning. Who cares at what time I write a gadget review? Equally, I don't have to be at my desk to make that pound. Thanks to my laptop, I can be anywhere in the world as long as I have access to the internet. With mobile broadband and an ever increasing number of hotels, cafes and even entire towns offering free Wi-Fi access, working from anywhere you happen to be is getting easier by the day.

Parkinson's Law

As my good friend Ness from Barry would say, I won't lie to you. There are days when I spend every waking hour, feverishly working away. I can then spend ten, 12, 14 hours creating hooks, building snowballs. That's out of choice however, and when this happens, it rarely feels like work. It's usually when I have an Einstein moment, a brilliant idea for something, and desperately want to spend every hour that I can bringing that idea to life.

If you are used to following Plan A, you can probably relate to working long hours far better than you can to only working an hour a day, let alone ten minutes a day. So conditioned are we to doing a "full day's work" that you may even feel guilty the first few times you start work at say two in the afternoon and then knock off an hour later. A 40 hour week rolls off our collective tongues all too easily. The truth is that there's no reason at all why you should devote the vast majority of your waking hours to work - and if society tells you different, then society has got it badly wrong.

The biggest challenge that you will face is looking at work is an entirely different way. It is no longer what dominates each and every week of your life. It becomes something you do before getting on with the rest of your day. The rest of your life in fact. Or something you do when you come in from enjoying the best part of your day.

You have probably heard of Parkinson's Law. It states that work expands to fill the time available for its completion. That's as true today as it was over 50 years ago when it was first mentioned in *The Economist* way back in 1955 courtesy of Cyril Northcote Parkinson. Given that Parkinson's Law holds true in virtually every workplace you care to mention, and given that we want work to take up as little of our day as possible, it makes sense to devote as little time as possible to it. Earn that pound – or whatever target you set yourself – and be on your way.

It may still all sound too good to be true, but remember why it works. Just because you stop working, you don't stop earning. Your multiple revenue streams continue to work on your behalf, with the potential to make you money 24 hours a day, 365 days of the year. You can be watching TV, sat on a beach, climbing Mount Everest, and they will still be working away for you.

Remember when I said that for the first time in history, the means of production is sitting on a desk in nearly every house in the Western World? Well, you can think of your computer as an "information factory", a factory that produces information that makes money day and night, whether or not the owner of the factory puts in an appearance. Like a certain city in the USA, the internet never sleeps. Websites that you create will be hosted on servers that are hooked up to the internet around the clock. Whether your own computer or laptop is switched on or not makes no difference. You use your PC or Mac to create the information, but you then host that information elsewhere for others to access. People will therefore be able to visit your websites and make you money all day and all night long. That's the beauty of Plan B.

How big is yours?

I use what I know (or am willing to find out) to create informative websites that then give me opportunities to make money, but what if you know nothing that you think will be of interest to anyone else? Well, for starters, that's going to be extremely unlikely, but let's assume for one moment that you know absolutely nothing. That's when you sell what you don't know.

Let's imagine that you want to move to France, but apart from a smattering of schoolboy French, you know nothing. Rien. You don't know what type of properties are available in your price range, how the buying process works, how best to learn the language or how the education system differs from our own. There will be 1,001 questions that need to be answered for you to make your move a success. So you will surf the Net, go to property shows, maybe even go on viewing trips to France.

If you are serious about moving to France, and especially if do indeed take the plunge, you will soon know the answers to all of the above questions and more. Do you think others hoping to follow in your footsteps would be interested in knowing what you have discovered? Of course they would. And therein lies the makings of a website and other opportunities to develop multiple streams of income.

I am always making money from things that I didn't know. While most people will use the internet for research, very few realise that whatever they find out can be repackaged and "sold" on to others.

Let's take another example. Do you know how big the average human penis is? If you are a man reading this, it's a given that it's something that has certainly crossed your mind. That's true of all men going back centuries, millennia even.

According to Google, over 100,000 searches are made every month relating to penis size. Around 40,000 are made relating to AVERAGE PENIS SIZE (not the sort of thing you want to put in capital letters in a book, but there you go). In fact, around 10,000 searches are made every month in the UK alone for exactly those three words – average penis size. Which tells me that quite a lot of people are interested in knowing how big the average penis is and my guess would be that most of those searches are conducted by men who want to know how they themselves measure up.

I stumbled across this interest in average penis size by accident while checking the stats on one of my websites. I had written a short article on phalloplasty (the medical term for surgical penis enlargement) as part of a series of short articles on cosmetic surgery. I discovered that a significant number of people were finding their way to that article by searching for the phrase "average penis size".

A tiny discovery like this immediately gets me thinking about creating a niche website dedicated to answering just that one question - what is the average penis size? And so in March, 2009, I registered the domain name AveragePenisSize.co.uk with a view to building a niche website at some point in the future. That day came on the 30th of December, 2009, when I decided to quickly build a one page website to see how many visitors it would attract. If I remember correctly, I created that one page website, sorted out hosting and had it live online, all within a 30 minute break between TV programmes that I wanted to watch.

Then while surfing the net in early February, looking for Valentine's Day gifts to promote, I came across a site selling adult toys including penis pumps (yes, I know, it's amazing what I fill my days with). This prompted me to check how that one page website was fairing, and a quick look at the visitor numbers told me that during the month of January, 2010, 984 people had found their way to the AveragePenisSize.co.uk website.

So a thousand people, give or take, had visited my website after finding it via the search engines barely a month after it went live. In fact, most of those visitors had arrived in the final two weeks of January (as you might expect, very few people visited it immediately after its totally unheralded launch, with just 12 visitors in the first 17 days of the month). Given that, I reasonably expected more visitors during the month of February (actually, 1,221 unique visitors paid it a visit during February).

I don't know whether you'll find those figures impressive or not, but I was certainly impressed. By creating a very simple one page website to answer a very specific question, I am on target to attract 15-20,000 visitors during 2010. 15-20,000 visitors that won't cost me a penny to attract because they find my website via the search engines, and 15,000 plus opportunities for me to make money.

Obviously those visitor numbers are not guaranteed, but from experience I know that 15,000 will be the very least number of visitors I'll attract. For one, nearly all of my January visitors came from one search engine – Yahoo. Only eight came from Google. That's because my fledgling site was virtually nowhere to be found in the Google search results, but I know that if that changes at any time during 2010 I can expect ten times the traffic from Google than from any other search engine, simply because it is so widely used. If my Google rankings were the same as my Yahoo rankings, I could reasonably expect perhaps as many as 200,000 visitors during the year.

Now I'm thinking that this is a site with potential to earn me money. Supposing I did attract 20,000 visitors during 2010. I know exactly why they have come to my site. They want to know how big the average penis is. There's also a very good chance that some of those visitors are asking that question because they are concerned about the size of their own penis. And of those visitors, there's a pretty good chance that some of those would be interested in buying products that will increase the size of their penis.

Taking a stab in the dark, let's suppose that one out of every hundred visitors would be interested in buying just such a product. With 20,000 visitors that would equate to 200 sales a year. With 200,000 visitors, that equates to 2,000 sales a year.

One way to increase the number of visitors to a website is by adding pages, with each additional page complementing the other pages, and with each one reaching out to my target market in a slightly different way. Each page that you add has the potential to be ranked by the search engines for specific search phrases – and the more fishing rods you put in the water, the more fish you are likely to catch. Since every page is different, it has the opportunity to catch a different type of fish.

Going back to my Plan B, I decided to spend an entire day in February turning my one page website into a ten page website. This involved me trawling the internet to find relevant information relating to penis size and looking for products that I could sell. I then created the pages and uploading them.

As you will know my plan is to do enough work to make £1 a day for each day of the rest of the year. That means that I invested a whole day in the AveragePenisSize.co.uk website in the hope that it would earn me £365 over the next 12 months.

The site will make its money selling various products including penis enhancement pills, penis pumps and penis enlargers. Let's take VigRX for example, the world's best known penis enhancement herbal pill. A three month course of these pills will cost you £84.99 with free delivery at the time of writing if you buy them from Love Honey, an online retailer of adult products. Love Honey pay 16% commission for accumulative sales under £500, rising to 21% for sales over £500. So for every three month course that I sell, I stand to make at least £13.60.

If I was selling nothing but VigRX on the website, I would need to sell 27 courses over a 12 month period to make spending that day working on the website worthwhile in terms of my Plan B. That's two to three courses of VigRX a month.

Of course I'm also selling other products including a top of the range penis pump that sells at £179.99 via Shy To Buy, another internet retailer who will pay me 10% commission or £17.99 for each one sold. My trusty calculator tells me that I'd need to sell about two a month to make £365 over the next 12 months. Or one three month course of VigRX and a penis pump each month would do the trick too.

Or visitors may choose to buy a Jes Extender – as featured on *The Jonathan Ross Show* no less. It's £139.99 from Passion8, yet another online retailer who will pay me a commission for sales generated, in this case 15% or £20.99. Again 18 sales over the next 12 months would earn me my £365.

There's always the chance that a customer will add other items that I'm not advertising to their basket, boosting the commission that I earn even further. Or they may choose to click on a banner ad and buy something else entirely. Whatever it is they end up buying, I'll earn a commission on the total.

Basically, I'm only looking for two or three orders a month to make £365 over the next year. Even if I do only attract 2,000 visitors a month, I only need two or three of them to buy something for me to be quids in. That's a visitor to customer conversion rate of 0.1%. With 20 customers a month, a 1% visitor to customer conversion rate, I'd be looking at hitting my £365 target every month of the year.

A good day's work? I think so. I'll probably check the site every month, to make sure links are working and prices are correct, and if it does start earning money, I'll definitely spend time adding more pages. But basically, the work required for that small site was done in a day. Little will need changed for years to come unless I choose to further develop it (and I'll only do that if it is proving worth my while). That day's work could earn me £365 every year for the next ten years with next to no additional work. And who knows what it could earn over ten years if Google starts sending it traffic and I'm getting not 2,000 visitors a month, but 20,000 visitors a month.

Supposing that it doesn't make me a penny over the next 12 months though. Supposing that not a single visitor buys so much as a penis enhancement pill. It's quite possible that I'm not very good at convincing visitors to buy what some might view as torture implements from the Middle Ages. What then?

Well, I could always sell the domain name and the website. Do you think a company that does know how to sell such items would like to have a ready made website that attracts 20,000 or more targeted visitors a year? And if so, would £365 be too much to ask? Considering how much a marketing campaign to generate 20,000 plus visitors would cost, I think £365 would be a steal.

To me, whichever way I look at it, spending £5 to register the domain name and then devoting a day to developing it is a complete no brainer. Worst case scenario, I sell the site a year down the line with an asking price of £500. Not that I think it will come to that. It's more likely that my traffic will increase to something between 20,000 and 200,000 visitors a year for 2010 and that the site will make me my £365 and more. Not just this year, but for years to come.

Not bad for telling people what they want to know, even if that something is as banal as the size of your average penis.

Fluent in Geek

The AveragePenisSize.co.uk website is a good example of what I do to make money. I create a simple website that I hope visitors will find of interest, but I don't actually charge any money for accessing the information. I'm giving the stuff away. And being information, I can give the same stuff away to as many people who want it. Indeed, the more people who want it, the happier I am. Anyone can visit my website and leave it again without so much as a thank you. With a website like this, the information is the bait – any money is made by passing any fish caught on to other companies.

The missing link for a lot of readers of this book is that they don't know how to build a website and they don't know how to get it online once it's built. It's not difficult to do either. You certainly don't need a degree in Computer Science. If you can create a document using Microsoft Word and write and send e-mails, you're virtually there already. Before the end of this book, I will show you exactly how to build a simple website like the AveragePenisSize.co.uk one and I will show you how to get it online too (you will be pleased to hear that you get to choose your own subject matter).

I'm certainly no techie. The first time I ever used a computer was in a University. The only problem was that the computers were for the use of students – and I wasn't a student. Getting sat in front of a computer screen was easy because nobody ever asked what I was doing there. Getting the computer to do what I wanted it to do was another matter.

It may sound surprising today given the widespread use of computers, but at the time PCs were relatively new. Hardly anyone had one at home. I didn't even know how to use a mouse. In fact, I used to hold it in my hand upside down and carefully roll the little rubber ball with my finger to get the pointer exactly where I wanted it on the screen. Seriously. It took me ages to do the simplest of tasks, but my finger dexterity increased tenfold. This went on for days, until the student sitting next to me had obviously had enough of watching me make a complete fool of myself. Without saying a word, he took the mouse off me, placed it on the mousemat and moved it around so that I could see the cursor moving around on the screen. He then returned to his own work with a shake of his head.

That's how far down the learning curve I was. Even today if you ask me what size my hard drive is or what's the processing speed of my computer, I haven't got a clue. It simply doesn't interest me. I'm only interested in using a computer to make me money.

If I can do this, anyone can. And to prove it, I'm now going to ask for exactly one hour of your time. That's all we'll need to get your first website online.

How to start your first internet business in less than an hour

"A man who dares to waste one hour of life has not discovered the value of life."
Charles Darwin

I want to show you just how easy it is to start your first internet business. All you will need is a computer with access to the internet and some pocket money to register a domain name and to pay for your website to be hosted out there on the World Wide Web. All I will need is an hour of your time.

More good news. This is one of those "no previous experience required" job offers. It is going to be a stroll in the park. If you can do stuff like write and send an e-mail and fill in an online form, you are good to go.

I have also provided an online version of this chapter, complete with illustrations and hyperlinks, on the Get Out While You Can website (http://www.gowyc.co.uk) for those who need an excuse to go online, but I would recommend that you first read through this chapter in the book anyway just to familiarise yourself with what is required. Later in this book there will be a chapter showing you how to build a website using free website design software, but for now we are going to use blogging software called WordPress to get our first website up and running in less than 60 minutes.

First things first

Okay, the first thing to do is to register a domain name. A domain name is what most people think of as an internet website address. So, for example, the BBC's website can be found at http://www.bbc.co.uk, with the bbc.co.uk bit being the domain name. For demonstration purposes, I'm going to be using the domain name JokeBlog.co.uk which I actually registered in 2008, but for this exercise let's pretend I've just spent five minutes registering it for the first time via a domain registration company. A company like 123-Reg (http://www.123-reg.co.uk) for example, who I have used in the past for registering domain names and so can recommend. At the time of writing, the cost of registering a .co.uk for two years was £5.98 plus VAT (January, 2010).

Buying a domain name is no different to buying anything else online. You visit the website of your chosen domain registration company, use the search facilities to find a domain name that is available, add it to your basket or shopping cart, create an account so that you can manage the domain name after purchase, and pay for it at the online checkout. Simples, as a certain meerkat might say.

Name registered, it's time to buy a year's worth of web hosting. Again, this will take you five minutes tops. So that people will be able to access your websites 24 hours a day, it needs to be hosted on a web server, a computer that is always switched on and always connected to the internet. You could of course set up your own server, but most webmasters pay a webite hosting company to "host" their website for them. That's why you will need hosting.

Although most domain name registration companies also sell web hosting packages, I always think it is best not to buy hosting from the same company that you register a domain name with. Just in case of problems further down the line. Before becoming a Nominet Registrar myself, I used several domain registration companies and bought a hosting package from one of them. I subsequently cancelled it, but continued to be invoiced for the hosting – even although it was no longer being supplied and I couldn't possibly make use of it. I naturally disputed the invoices – only to find that my entire account was then frozen pending payment. This meant that I could not manage any of the domain names that I had registered through that company. When I eventually managed to talk to a human being, the issue was resolved very quickly, but this could have had dire consequences for my business.

Currently I'm using Total Choice Hosting or TCH (http://www.totalchoicehosting.com) for my own hosting needs and can therefore recommend them to you too. Their Starter Hosting Plan offers 40GB of monthly bandwidth transfer and 1,400MB of disc space for US$44 a year – more than enough for starting out and you can always upgraded at a later date if your website outgrows these confines. TCH also offer unlimited e-mail accounts and plenty of other bells and whistles that other hosting companies will charge you extra for.

Crucially, every Total Choice Hosting hosting package comes with cPanel, a control panel that allows you to manage every aspect of your website. Whichever company you choose to host your website with, ensure that they use cPanel for website management because it will make your life so much easier.

Once you have paid for your hosting, you will receive a welcome e-mail giving you information regarding the hosting package you have just paid for, including the username and password that you will need to manage your website.

It will also tell you what nameservers have been allocated to your hosting account. Nameservers – or to give them their full name Domain Name System (DNS) Servers - translate a hostname or a domain name (for example, JokeBlog.co.uk) to its corresponding binary identifier or IP address (in the case of JokeBlog.co.uk - 208.76.82.136). In layman's terms, nameservers ensure that visitors reach your site.

```
+===================================+
| New Account Info            |
+===================================+
| Domain: jokeblog.co.uk
| Ip: 208.76.82.136 (n)
| HasCgi: y
| UserName: jokeblog
| PassWord: **********
| CpanelMod: x3
| HomeRoot: /home
| Quota: 1400 Meg
| NameServer1: dns3.snhdns.com
| NameServer2: dns4.snhdns.com
| NameServer3:
| NameServer4:
| Contact Email: info@entrepreneur.co.uk
| Package: starter plan
```

Above: extract from my welcome e-mail from my hosting company, with nameserver details circled

In my case the two nameservers for JokeBlog.co.uk are dns3.snhdns.com and dns4.snhdns.com. You will need to know what your nameservers are so that you can go back to where you registered your domain name and update the nameserver records so that they point to your new hosting account. This will then link your domain name to your website hosting.

With most domain registrars this is very straight forward. With 123-Reg for example, you log into your 123-Reg control panel and under Manage Domain, select the domain name you want to manage and click Modify Domain.

Above: The 123-Reg Control Panel with link to changing Nameservers circled

You are then greeted by an option menu and the one you want to choose is Change Nameservers. Enter the nameservers detailed from your welcome e-mail and hit the Change Nameservers button. The two nameservers that were listed in my welcome e-mail were dns3.snhdns.com and dns4.snhdns.com so that's what I enter in the boxes marked Nameserver 1 and Nameserver 2 before pressing the Change Nameservers button.

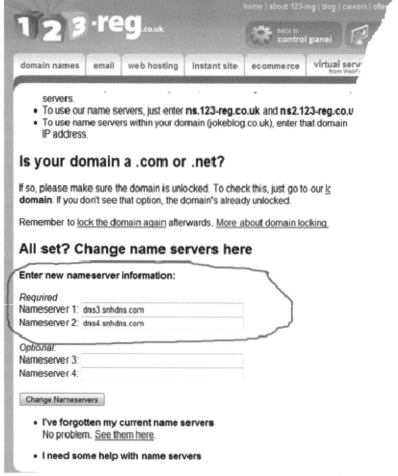

Above: I've entered the new nameserver information into the two boxes and now just need to press the button marked Change Nameservers

It can take anything from minutes to 48 hours for the nameserver changes to take effect and to propagate the internet, but once done your domain name and your hosting will be linked together. I've excluded this waiting time from the one hour it will take you to launch your first internet business. How To Start Your First Internet Business In However Long It Takes For Your Website To Go Live doesn't have quite the same ring to it. You can use this downtime to prepare content, walk the dog, wash the car, whatever tickles your fancy.

So we've registered a domain name and we've bought a year's worth of hosting for our new website. We've also changed the domain name's nameservers so that they point to where the website is being hosted and we've waited for the change to take effect.

Your first website

Once the nameserver change has propagated the internet, you can type your domain name into your browser (in my case www.JokeBlog.co.uk) and you will be greeted by a rather plain page with "Index of /" written on it. That's basically what your website looks like before any content has been added and before you have created a homepage. A naked homepage if you like.

Above: Screenshot of a typical cPanel

Now it's time to set up your first website – and you can do this in a matter of minutes without knowing anything about website design or construction thanks to cPanel which I mentioned previously.

Accessing your cPanel is very easy – details of how to will appear in your hosting e-mail. In the case of JokeBlog.co.uk, I simply enter http://www.jokeblog.co.uk/cpanel into my internet browser and then enter my hosting username and password (from your welcome e-mail) when prompted (a box asking for this information will appear on your screen). This allows me to gain entry to what is a password protected part of my hosting account.

Enter both your username and password correctly and you'll be greeted by the cPanel's homepage. This is the control panel for your website and a cursory glance at it will reveal the icons that you will click when you want to set up an e-mail account for your website, check your website statistics, create databases and so on. As with anything new, all those icons can seem overwhelming when you are starting out, but as time goes on you will find your way around. Poco a poco (little by little) as the Spanish say.

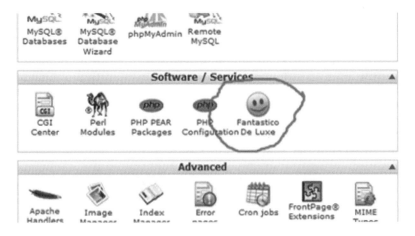

Above: cPanel screenshot with Fantastico Deluxe button circled

For now, I want you to scroll down the page until you come to Software / Services and an icon marked Fantastico Deluxe. Fantastico is an amazing piece of software that automatically installs a wide range of scripts that you can use to build a website or add functionality to a website. Click on the Fantastico icon and you'll be taken through to the Fantastico page that lists all of the scripts currently available.

One criticism sometimes levelled at Fantastico is that the scripts are not always the latest versions, but that needn't trouble us today. We're going to install WordPress, the free to use blogging software that will be the engine behind your first website. Whole books have been written about WordPress, but suffice to say it makes website creation so easy, your granny could use it. And probably does.

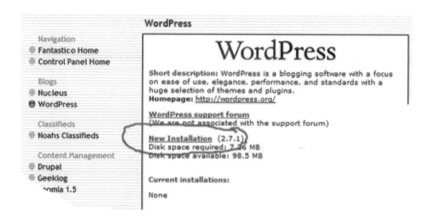

Above: Brief details of WordPress as provided by Fantastico - I have circled the New Installation link

Select WordPress from the list on Fantastico and brief details of WordPress will appear. You will also see a link allowing you to create a New Installation and you'll need to click that link to progress to the next stage.

The first WordPress installation window will appear and you need to fill in the details.

Install on domain - that should be filled in for you.

Install in directory - leave this blank because we do want to install WordPress in our root directory.

Admin username and password - you choose both (make a note of them for later use)

Base configuration - enter a nickname, a current e-mail address, the name of your site and a short description.

Then press the Install WordPress button.

WordPress

Install WordPress (1/3)

Installation location

Install on domain   jokeblog.co.uk ▼

Install in directory

Leave empty to install in the root directory of the domain (access example: http://domain/).
Enter only the directory name to install in a directory (for **http://domain/name/** enter **name** only). This directory SHOULD NOT exist, it will be automatically created!

Admin access data

Administrator-username (you need this to enter the protected admin area)   **********

Password (you need this to enter the protected admin area)   **********

Base configuration

Admin nickname   George

Admin e-mail (your email address)   info@ entrepreneur.co.uk

Site name   jokeblog.co.uk

Description   Joke Blog

[Install WordPress]

Above: Screenshot of the WordPress installation process

You are then taken to Step 2 of the installation process which confirms that a database will be created and where WordPress will be installed. All you have to do is press the Finish Installation button.

And that's it! WordPress has been installed on your website.

You can choose for details of the installation to be sent to you by e-mail (never a bad idea), but otherwise that's you completed your first WordPress installation.

Above: WordPress will replace the Index Of/ page with something not unlike the above

The proof of the pudding is when you enter your domain name in your web browser again (you may need to refresh your browser to see the changes). The previous "Index Of/" page will have been replaced by your new website's homepage - as powered by WordPress. Hello world indeed!

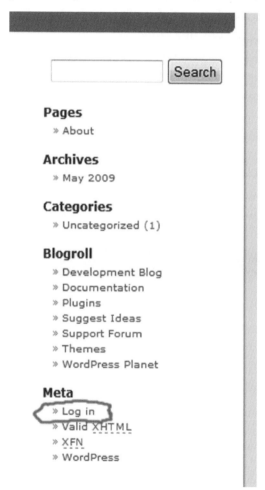

Above: **Screenshot of WordPress navigation links on the home page with Log In circled**

Hey presto!

You, my friend, are in business! Obviously, there is still work to be done, but less than an hour ago you didn't have the makings of an internet business and now you do!

That "Hello World" post that greets all those who have just installed WordPress is where your first content will go.

Visit your website - in my case www.JokeBlog.co.uk - and you will see that the right hand column of your brand new homepage features navigation links (see screenshot on previous page).

Under the heading Meta you'll find the Log In link. That takes you to the Log In page where you will enter the Username and Password that you chose during Step 1 of the WordPress installation. Fill in those details and you are taken behind the scenes of your website and WordPress installation, to what is called the Dashboard Page.

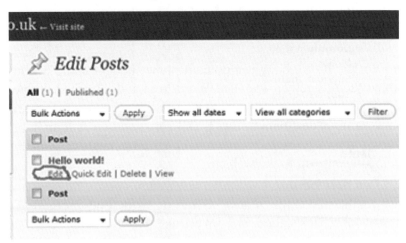

Above: Under Edit Posts, you will be able to Edit or even Delete posts that you make to your website

The first thing you will want to do is replace the "Hello World!" post with your own first post. This is easily done by clicking the Edit button under Posts in the left hand column.

That will take you through to a page listing your Posts to date - and there will be just the one "Hello World!" post. Click on it and a sub-menu will appear, the first option of which is Edit.

Click the Edit link and then you will be taken to the "Hello World!" post, ready for you to edit it. Now, it's just a case of overwriting it.

If you visit Joke Blog (http://www.jokeblog.co.uk) you'll see that I decided to replace it with a joke about B&Q's decking and I then pressed the Update Post button on the far right of the screen. WordPress then worked its magic and updated my website. That's why the homepage at Joke Blog no longer displays the "Hello World!" post and in its place is my "What's Going On At B&Q?" post.

With jokes like that I'm hardly going to make a living as a comic, but with what's left of our hour together, let's see if we can't at least make a start at making some money out of JokeBlog.co.uk.

So far, we've bought a domain name, bought some hosting, linked them together, installed WordPress and launched the new JokeBlog.co.uk website with a joke about everyone's favourite Bank Holiday destination, B&Q. All very good for half an hour's work, but now we need to spend the next 20 minutes or so adding an income stream to the website.

I've decided that I will alternate funny posts with ones that just might make me money - starting with one promoting a classic joke pack called The Joke Box. It's currently on sale at Stocking Fillers (http://www.stockingfillers.co.uk) for £6.99 and it just so happens that Stocking Fillers are one of hundreds of companies who will pay you a commission on any sales you generate for them.

Stocking Fillers, run by the better known Hawkin's Bazaar, pay 8% commission on sales, so for every Joke Box I sell I stand to make 56p. Not a fortune, but remember all I have to do is introduce the customer. Hawkin's Bazaar carry all the stock, fill the order and deal with any customer service issues. If the customer that I introduce decides to buy other items while shopping at Stocking Fillers, I'll be paid a commission on those purchases too.

So I need to create a new post about The Joke Box and I do this by visiting the JokeBlog.co.uk WordPress dashboard page again via the Login link on my homepage.

In the right hand column under Posts, I simply choose Add New and start writing (or blogging as it's called). Once finished, I press the Publish button on the right of the screen and my new post gets automatically added to the JokeBlog.co.uk website.

The link through to Stocking Fillers contains a tracking code so that any resulting sales will be tracked to me and I will be paid any commission due. I got the tracking link from Affiliate Window (http://www.affiliatewindow.com), an affiliate network that is home to hundreds of merchants including Stocking Fillers. It's actually Affiliate Window that collect commissions due from all the merchants on their network that I sign up to and promote, and it's Affiliate Window that pay me any commissions due every fortnight. Not just from Stocking Fillers, but one payment from all merchants that I have generated sales for on the Affiliate Window network.

I talk about affiliate marketing in detail later in this book, but the above is an example of just how easy it is to integrate it into even the most basic of websites.

Bells and whistles

Talking of the most basic of websites, JokeBlog.co.uk isn't going to win any website beauty pageants. It's bland, colourless, boring. The good news is that it doesn't have to be this way because WordPress offers you endless opportunities to change the look and feel of your website as well as its functionality.

Think of WordPress as the engine that powers your website. It has been developed in such a way that you can change its outward appearance without affecting the engine's performance. In fact you can change the look simply by installing a new Theme. A Theme changes the look of your website without modifying the underlying WordPress software. What's so amazing is that there are hundreds of Themes to choose from.

You'll find over a thousand different ones at WordPress.org and they are all free to use. Hundreds more are available to buy from websites like ThemeForest (http://www.themeforest.net), Premium WordPress (http://www.premiumwp.com) and Gorilla Themes (http://gorillathemes.com) where you will find some truly awesome designs for your website for an equally amazing small amount of money. You can even go down the custom route and pay someone to design a WordPress Theme (or customise one) especially for you. My own blog at Entrepreneur.co.uk is just a simple WordPress website with a premium Theme installed. I just add the text. WordPress does everything else in terms of layout and design.

Themes are only the beginning of the limitless things you can do with WordPress. There are thousands of Plugins available too that allow you to do almost anything you can imagine with a website. Whatever your heart desires you can guarantee that someone somewhere has made a WordPress Plugin to do exactly that. There are Plugins for image galleries, advertising, contact forms, video, audio, social networking, everything. The holiday company Sunshine.co.uk even has a Plugin called Sunpress that allows you to quickly create and manage a holiday website using their affiliate programme (you'll find it on the Paid On Results network). Again, you'll find a directory of nearly 10,000 Plugins (maybe more by the time you read this) over at WordPress.org.

The real beauty of a WordPress powered website is that it can be updated from anywhere in the world and from any computer with internet access because it is entirely web-based. That means you can be on a year long round the world trip for all it matters and still be able to update your website whenever you have internet access.

Show me the money!

You might be wondering if a website like this could make any real money. I guess the same thought might have crossed the mind of Eric Nakagawa when he started the strangely named I Can Has Cheezburger? website in January, 2007.

After complaining to his friend, Kari Unebasami, about having a bad day at the office, she sent Eric a funny picture of a cat, Happy Cat, and a few others from her collection. The sort of funny animal photos that people with nothing better to do with their time forward on to each other via e-mail on a daily basis.

The pictures literally made Eric laugh out loud and so he registered the domain name icanhascheezburger.com (http://www.icanhascheezburger.com) and posted the picture of Happy Cat on it. Several more pictures followed and the two friends then decided to turn it into a blog so that visitors could leave comments and maybe even send in their own funny images for inclusion.

It was supposed to be a joke, but the almost instant incredible popularity of the site meant that by May, 2007, Eric had quit his job as a computer programmer to work on the site full-time. Seriously. I first came across the site in July, 2007, when it was one of a dozen or so money-making blogs featured in one of my favourite magazines, *Business Week*. The article said that I Can Has Cheezburger was making an estimated US$5,600 a month in advertising revenue alone. "If you hit a niche and you can build a community, you might not have a $1 million idea, but you might have a $10,000 or a $100,000 idea," Eric was quoted as saying.

US$5,600 a month equates to US$67,200 a year – or a little under £1,000 a week for simply posting funny pictures of cats on the internet. Funny pictures that were for the most part already available on the internet anyway, but not under the one roof offered by I Can Has Cheezburger. As the site's popularity grew, visitors started submitting images and videos – and by January, 2008, the site was receiving a mind-blowing 8,000 submissions a day!

Multiple revenue streams anyone? Eric and Kari started with so-called lolcat merchandise (t-shirts, fridge magnets and the like) and lucrative book deals have followed. The I Can Has Cheezburger website was actually sold in September, 2007, for two million dollars, allowing its two founders to start work on a new project, a website dedicated to – wait for it - funny pictures of dogs . . .

No job. Just eBay. Ask me how.

"When you feel that you have reached the end and that you cannot go one step further, when life seems drained of all purpose: what a wonderful opportunity to start all over again, to turn over a new page."
Eileen Caddy

Car boot sales, where you literally sell stuff out of the boot of your car at venues around the country, are a great way to clear unwanted household clutter and earn some money doing so. It's estimated that over a million people buy and sell at them every weekend during the Summer months.

If you have ever loaded up your car early on a Sunday morning to do a car boot sale, chances are you'll know how demoralising it can be to bring home a lot of the things you spent hours ironing, cleaning and sorting. It goes with the territory and the trick seems to be to simply box them up and take them with you the next time you do one. Of course, you'll bring most of it back home yet again but . . .

The last time we did a car boot sale as a family was way back in 2001 (another downside of car boot sales - most of what you earn is spent on keeping the kids amused with ice creams, bouncy castles and buying other people's unwanted toys). One of the things we brought back with us was a couple of pub bar towels. We had only wanted 10p each for them, but there were no takers.

It was about this time that I discovered the online auction site, eBay. Bar towels are very easy items to send through the post and I noticed that eBay had a section devoted to collecting breweriana. So I thought I'd list my two bar towels. I started the bidding at £1 each and waited for the auctions to close ten days later. If I had sold both for 20p at the boot sale a couple of weeks earlier I would have been happy enough. On eBay one sold for £3.20 and the other one, a Babysham one, sold for £10.01.

If you have yet to discover the marvels of online auctions, I recommend you do so straight away. And they don't come any bigger than eBay which now has over 90 million registered users worldwide (including 14 million in the UK) who buy and sell everything from the junk they've found in their attic to helicopters and woolly mammoths.

eBay is like the biggest antiques fair, flea market, boot fair and auction house you could ever imagine. Entry for buyers is free and as they walk in they can be directed instantly to a list of everyone selling anything that they are interested in buying. At any one time, you will find up to ten million items for sale and everything is categorised and fully searchable across every category. In fact, eBay will even e-mail you if something you're looking for - a type of model train for example - gets listed!

Items that you can't give away at car boot sales can fetch surprising sums on eBay as I discovered with my two bar towels and have witnessed with many items since.

Roll up! Roll up!

Every Saturday at Penrith in Cumbria there is an open air market and we often used to drive down to it from Scotland once every few months as part of a day out in the Lake District. Not long after selling my two beer towels, it just so happened that one of the stalls at Penrith was selling promotional items for famous name drink brands like Heineken, Red Rock, Boddington's and Coca Cola. I've no idea if the stall is still there, but at the time, you could find the same stallholder at Morecambe's market every Sunday and no doubt elsewhere in the North West of England on various other days. As well as drinking glasses, the stall sold everything from umbrellas to juggling balls, bar towels to fridge magnets, t-shirts to beer taps. And of course, a nice selection of brand new bar towels for 50p each.

With eBay in mind, I decided to take a closer look at what was on offer. I know nothing about breweriana so decided to play it safe by buying three bar towels that featured well known brands and looked good from a design point of view. Total cost £1.50.

When I got home I listed one of them on eBay with a starting price of £2 plus postage (I was hoping to recoup my modest outlay in one fell swoop). Ten days later and it had sold to a lady collector of breweriana from the USA for £5.50. I told her about the other two great bar towels that I had and she ended up buying those two for a grand total of £17.50 including postage. Not bad for my initial outlay of £1.50 and the cost of sending them to California - £2.20 by air mail including a padded envelope so that they arrived in pristine condition.

It got better. Encouraged by my initial success as a trader in fine breweriana, I returned to the stall the following Saturday and came away with a carrier bag full of goodies. I have to point out that the breweriana for sale at the Penrith market stall was very cheap. No matter how hard you tried, it was actually very difficult to spend a great deal of money. My bag full of breweriana cost me £5.00. In fact if you manage to spend a fiver, the stall holder rewarded you with a free promotional CD (you had a choice of a Rolling Rock CD or a Boddington's CD - look like you couldn't decide and he gave you them both).

One of the many items I brought home with me that day was a packet of six Rolling Rock dice. The dice cost 50p for the packet, but I decided I would sell two at a time - with a starting price of £1. When the auction closed, the highest bidder, an American, paid US$17.50 for my two Rolling Rock dice that had cost me less than 17p (30c) to buy. Within hours of the auction closing, other bidders were e-mailing me to ask if I had any more and offering to pay the same US$17.50 for them. I sold my other two pairs and kicked myself for only buying one packet (I also couldn't wait for the following Saturday so that I could buy up every Rolling Rock dice I could see).

It gets even better. A man who ran an unofficial Rolling Rock Museum in Latrobe, Pennsylvania (where the beer was first made and still brewed until 2006), contacted me asking if I had any more dice or anything else Rolling Rock related. Apparently, Rolling Rock related memorabilia was very collectable in the USA and promotional material produced in the UK was often unique to the UK (in fact even the bottles the beer comes in is slightly different - I know this because a dozen or more people subsequently asked me to sell them empty bottles for their collection!).

I told the museum man that I was hoping to get some more dice and asked how many they might want. As many as I could get them came the reply. I also said I had a Rolling Rock shaped promotional CD if they were interested. They wanted that too and multiples if I had them.

All but three of the items that I had got from Penrith that Saturday sold on eBay for the princely total of £87 just ten days after I had paid £5 for the lot. Needless to say I went straight back to Penrith at the earliest opportunity and came away with as much as I could carry. The stallholder actually asked if I owned a chain of pubs, but again - despite being laden - I found it incredibly difficult to spend much money. My total for the day came to £12, with my most expensive item being a £3 Rolling Rock ice bucket.

When it came to choosing the free CDs, I asked for Rolling Rock ones and asked if he had any more that I could buy. He had boxes of them. In fact for £3 I could have a box of 50.

I wanted to offer the Rolling Rock museum some dice and CDs at a reasonable price because they were buying multiples, but at the same time I didn't want to see them flooding eBay in the USA with the items I'd got for them and spoil my little party. So I decided to sell them 12 pairs of dice (total cost to me just £1) and 25 CDs (total cost to me £1.50) for US$100 plus postage. This was a great price for me and for them - and to sweeten the deal I said I would include a Rolling Rock ice bucket. I received full payment the same day through Paypal.

That still left me with all the other breweriana I had bought to list on eBay which I did over the coming few weeks. I sold more dice, I was getting more for each CD than I'd paid for a boxful, beer towels were still very popular, and so it went on.

Another popular brand name turned out to be Murphy's, partly because of the Irish connection (Americans with Irish roots love anything to do with Ireland) and partly because people with the surname Murphy bought items. A Sisters Of Murphy's plastic bar mat (which could double as a giant mouse mat as I pointed out in my listing) sold for £18 - I had paid 50p for it. The buyer admitted that it was more than he wanted to pay, but he loved it nonetheless.

Within six weeks I had turned my initial investment in breweriana of £1.50 into just over £500. By the end of that time, prices were tailing off, but there was still easy money to be made and no doubt still is in breweriana or a thousand and one other areas. £500 isn't a fortune, but it's still a considerable sum of money - particularly when I must have spent no more than five hours spread over those six weeks to get it from an initial investment of just £1.50.

Often people say to me that they would love to start their own business, but just don't have the seed money to get things started. Either that or they just don't have the time. I would imagine that dozens of people who would love to escape the rat race walk past that market stall in Penrith every Saturday. The same opportunity that I saw is right before their eyes. And yet they keep on walking. As I've said before, opportunity is always knocking, but you have to be in to open the door.

One of the best ways to make money is to concentrate on what you enjoy doing. That's a very important part of discovering success, not just financially but on a personal level too. I had no great love of breweriana, but I do love markets and get great pleasure out of buying low and selling for a profit. Irrespective of what I'm buying or selling, I love a deal.

The key to my success however was simply this. Virtually on my doorstep was an abundance of something that just wasn't available everywhere. And more importantly, it wasn't available where it was most wanted. By using eBay, I was able to offer that something to people who were willing to pay a premium for it - simply because they couldn't get it where they lived. All over eBay are examples of people doing exactly the same thing and making a good living doing so.

For example, one guy on eBay deals exclusive in shaped metal Disney pin badges. In fact there are a few of them that do it. Most are Powersellers, a sure sign that they are selling plenty of badges week in week out. Most of these sellers, not surprisingly, also live in Orlando where Disney memorabilia is harder to miss than find. Most of their buyers won't live in Orlando or anywhere near it.

Sometimes, the best opportunities are right in front of our noses, but we are so conditioned to only making money while at work that we walk straight past them. In fact there are people who spend hours surfing around eBay looking for things to buy when they could be spending some of those hours looking for and listing things to sell.

Take a closer look at what's on your doorstep. Is it something that is selling on eBay? And is it something that you can buy and sell for a profit? If so you too might be able to turn

£1.50 into £500.   And who knows what you'll be able to turn that £500 into by investing it in other multiple revenue streams.

No job. Just eBay. Ask me how.

Back in 2004, The University Of Essex was given a grant of £120,000 to carry out research into eBay to find out why the auction site was so successful and what effect it has had on business and the way people shop. One of the aims of the two year long study, according to Dr Rebecca Ellis who lead the research team, was to evaluate whether eBay could be a viable form of self-employment for people. We didn't need to wait two years or spend a penny on research to discover the answer to that one. eBay was already a viable form of self-employment for thousands of people in the USA, the UK and elsewhere.

I tell everyone who will listen to start trading on eBay if they want a taste of working from home and want to earn some money to boot. Initially, the most I usually get is a smile. A smile that says, "You're pulling my leg". People don't want to believe that "playing on the computer" can earn them more than doing a day's work. When in fact it can. Next time I see them that smile is ear to ear and they can't wait to tell me what they got for something that had been gathering dust in the darkest corner of their attic.

If you haven't already considered eBay as part of your escape from the rat race strategy, do so today. I say this for one simple reason. It is a fun way to make real money. Chances are you may already have sold a handful of item on eBay and thought no more of it. Think back to what was achieved in that magical month of February featured earlier in the book. Ask yourself what just might happen if you go the full 28 days with eBay and don't walk away on day one or day two.

The first UK eBay millionaires

When Jamie Murray decided to sell his Playstation 2 games console on eBay in the Summer of 2005, he would never have guessed what it would lead to. After getting £100 for it, he realised that there was a demand for PS2s on eBay and thought that there would be even more interest as Christmas approached. So he started buying up secondhand consoles that were being sold in the local newspaper and ones that had been poorly listed on eBay and hadn't attracted much interest. He ended up with around 30 consoles and sold them all, pocketing £1,500 in the process. Not bad for someone who left school at 16 to work as a £60 a week porter.

Jamie realised that there was money to be made online, but wanted to sell something that was less bulky and easier to send than gaming consoles. He plumped for the memory cards that gamers used and that were starting to be used with mobile phones too. Orders poured in and three years later he had a business with a turnover of more than £3.5 million and was employing eight people.

Mark Radcliffe was a 21 year old trainee manager at Tesco earning £7 an hour when he decided to invest £200 of his savings to start an internet business selling mobile phone accessories via eBay. He ran the business from a spare bedroom at his parents' house in Southport, with the garden shed acting as stockroom.

Ten years on, Mark was supplying 36,000 customers a month with electronic consumables and had a business turning over more than £3 million a year. He was living in a £700,000 home with a Ferrari and an Aston Martin in the driveway.

Jamie and Mark have both obviously worked incredibly hard to achieve millionaire status via eBay. But you're not stupid. I don't really need to tell you that. One very important point I do want to ram home though, no matter how bright you are. Don't just read the above stories and then do nothing about it. Here's two guys making tens of thousands of pounds a month on eBay for Pete's sake. Your first thought should be how can I do the same?

Could you start a business selling items - old or new - on eBay? Is there a category on eBay that will allow you to combine one of your passions with making money? Can you think of a business in your home town that would benefit from using eBay as an alternative shop window? Could you earn money helping them do just that?

Give it some serious thought because making money doesn't have to be hard labour. Escaping the rat race can be as easy as trading on eBay for a couple of hours every night until you earn more from sitting at home than you do going out to work.

Imagine it. No work. Just eBay.

I'm not pretending that selling thousands of items every month on eBay isn't work. If you want to make a million pounds selling small ticket items anywhere, prepare to work. As far as Plan B goes, that sounds a little too much like a full-time job and then some. That said, many of the processes normally associated with selling are fully automated with eBay. Billing and the collection of payment can be automated by Paypal (you can even pay and print off postage labels with Paypal). Once you've created an auction listing for a product, it can be used over and over again just by pressing the re-list button. You don't need to go looking for customers. The millions of eBay users will come looking for you (think of eBay as a search engine for products).

With Plan B you don't need to make millions with eBay. Not unless that's what you want to spend your time doing. I use the examples of Jamie and Mark to show you the incredible potential. The point is you could use eBay to make an extra £50 a month, £500 a month or £5,000 a month. It could simply be one of your multiple revenue streams that you spend a few hours a week developing. It could even be a case of selling a few unwanted items to get the seed money together to launch the business of your dreams. Oh, and unlike car boot sales, it never rains on eBay!

The more items you list on eBay, the better you get at doing it and the quicker you are at listing items too. Use your first few dozen auctions as your learning curve. There is real money to be made on online auctions and you can make that money working from home during hours that suit you.

I won't waste your time or mine telling you how to use eBay. It actually makes it very easy to buy and sell items (hence its runaway success) and its website provides page after page of help to get you started should you need it. What follows instead is some advice based on my own eBay buying and selling experiences, advice that will hopefully fast forward your own success.

Will it sell?

Before you even list something you have to ask yourself is it worth listing? Better still, ask eBay if it is worth listing.

Perform a search for the item you are thinking of listing and see how many other people are selling something similar and whether or not they have received any bids.

Even better, perform that same search and on the results page look down the lefthand column for a link named **Refine Search**. Scroll down until you come to the subheading **Show Only** and select **Completed Listings**. Now you will be shown how much money items have actually sold for. This is important because many auctions experience bidding frenzies just as they are about to close and it will give you a good idea of what you might get for your own similar item.

Also study the auction listings that appear to have attracted higher bids. What differences could have accounted for this success?

And remember, just because a category is hot, don't assume your product will do well in it. I have done very well selling rare vinyl records on eBay. Whenever I tell people about my latest success they immediately say, "Wow! I've got some records. Maybe I should put them on?"

Sadly, *Des O'Connor's Greatest Hits* is not going to make you a fortune. Sorry, Des.

It takes as much time to list something that'll make you money as it does something that won't get any bids. The trick is to spend more time listing the former and less time listing the latter ;-).

But never just assume something won't sell just because you don't think it will. Do your research. You might be pleasantly surprised.

Specialise

The best way to get started on eBay is to sell items that won't cost you a penny to find. And the best place to find such items is your own home. It is both amazing and frightening how much clutter we collect over our lifetimes. eBay and other online auction sites give you the perfect opportunity to get rid of a lot of it and to make some money doing so. As you do this you will quickly discover what sells well and what doesn't.

Chances are you will discover little niche markets totally by accident - simply by listing that horrid vase that Aunty Mabel gave you or that dusty old Chopper bike that you found buried in the garden shed.

The most successful eBayers are the ones that specialise. That's because they build a reputation in a particular field and attract the attention of people interested in those items. People who will always check their auction listings and who will help push the price upwards by bidding. They will also bid on multiple related items. Repeat customers are the cornerstone of virtually all successful businesses from corner shops to drug pushers.

If you have a love for something, that's where your eBay success will be found. If you can bring passion to your listings, you will attract more bids. And if you have the background knowledge to fully detail your listings, the price will climb even higher.

A quick aside. Don't fall into the trap of being a buyer of things you have a passion for. If you want to make money, you need to be a seller! Sounds obvious, but I know plenty of eBay "sellers" who buy more than they ever sell. Great fun, but not very profitable.

Feedback

At the end of each auction, you have the opportunity to leave feedback to tell others whether the buyer or seller (depending on what side of the bargain you are on) was a good person to trade with. Every time you get a positive feedback from someone, your feedback increases by one. The higher your feedback rating climbs, the more confidence bidders will have in purchasing from you.

In fact I have often bought items from people with low feedback ratings with the sole purpose of re-listing them myself, knowing that my much higher feedback rating will attract more bids and allow me to turn a profit.

When you start out on eBay your feedback is not surprisingly zero. You can increase it quickly by bidding on small ticket items and paying promptly for them. Buy ten items at a pound each from ten different sellers, pay immediately (preferably by Paypal - see below) and you will quickly get your feedback up to ten and gain your first all important feedback star.

Now you can start selling. But don't sell your best items first. Save them until your feedback rating has grown even more (100 plus) because that is when you will get better money for them (I learned this lesson the hard way – ouch!).

When you leave feedback for a buyer, make sure it is positive. Sellers can no longer leave negative feedback for buyers, but buyers can still leave negative comments about sellers. By awarding positive feedback quickly to a buyer, you reduce the chances of getting negative feedback in return if something small goes wrong.

I would rather leave no feedback than negative feedback, except in extreme circumstances. If a seller reneges on a deal, complain to eBay. If a buyer never pays use eBay to get your selling fee back and eBay will automatically put a black mark against the buyer (as part of its three strokes and you're suspended policy).

And be warned. No matter how good you are at providing the best service possible, the day will come when you get negative feedback from someone. It's a certainty. Some clowns take great pleasure in spoiling perfect feedback records. I had completed over 1,000 deals before I got my first negative feedback. It was from someone who had only seven feedbacks themselves, three of which were negative. He said the record I sent him had arrived broken due to poor packaging. He never e-mailed to tell me this, he just left me bad feedback. I contacted him to apologise (even though I knew I had sent the record in packaging specifically designed for mailing vinyl). I asked him to return the broken record so that I could refund him and claim against Royal Mail for damage in transit. Apparently, he hadn't kept the record - he had binned it in disgust. He had however kept the packaging and could return that so that I could see how damaged it was . . .

I have also received a negative from someone who complained about non-delivery of an item - and then apologised because they realised the fact that they hadn't sent payment might have had something to do with the tardy arrival of their book.

Life happens.

Paypal

If you are serious about making even a spare time living via eBay it is essential that you have a Paypal account (http://www.paypal.co.uk). Paypal basically lets you instantly send and receive money from your Paypal account to anyone with an e-mail address (as long as they have or open a Paypal account).

eBay now owns Paypal and so it is fully integrated with its auctions. Payment buttons can be automatically inserted into all of your auctions (if you choose that payment option) and the beauty is that you receive payment far quicker - often before you have had time to see how your finished auctions have done.

One massive advantage is that it offers multiple currency accounts, allowing you to accept American Dollars, Pounds Sterling, Euros, Yen, even Polish Zlotych or Israeli New Shekels, if you choose too. All can quickly and easily be exchanged into your main currency and then deposited into your bank account.

The majority of auction winners use Paypal to pay for what they have bought. It has its critics, but for my money Paypal has revolutionised online credit card processing and is up there with the likes of Google, Amazon and of course eBay itself in defining the web. And a lot of criticism seems to be based on misunderstandings of how Paypal works anyway.

It is free to withdraw money from your Paypal account - you simply transfer the money to any bank account in your name. I do this on a regular basis, preferring the money in my bank account.

You can also use Paypal to accept credit cards on websites as your portfolio of revenue streams develops. What I have discovered is that if you give customers the opportunity to pay for goods and services via Paypal, and they have money in their Paypal account from selling a few items on eBay, they aren't slow at spending it.

Turbo Lister

Creating each auction listing from scratch can take up a lot of time and the more auctions you can get started each week, the more money you will make. If your profit on each auction averages £5, then you need to list 100 successful auctions a week to make £500. If you can make £50 profit an auction, just ten successful auction listings a week are necessary.

Assuming you'll fall somewhere between the two, you will need software that will help you list new items quickly. That's where eBay's own free auction listing tool, Turbo Lister, comes into play. It is easy to use and will allow you to list hundreds or even thousands of items efficiently. You can save the listings you create and use them again and again and even schedule listings to start automatically at a future time.

Other auction manager software exists, most of it available for a fee, but Turbo Lister will certainly get you off to a good start. You'll find more information at:

http://pages.eBay.co.uk/turbo_lister/

Making the most of each listing

Each component of a listing can be used to increase the chances of attracting bids. The better your auction listing, the bigger your profits.

1. Category

When you list your item, the first thing you will be asked to choose is the category you want it to be listed in. eBay has a fantastic category suggestion tool that you can use to see where similar items are listed. It not only tells you how similar items are categorised, but throws up suggestions that you might not have considered.

A book biography of a rock band might attract more bids if listed with that band's vinyl records (a magnet for the band's fans) than under music books for example.

http://pages.eBay.co.uk/tools/

Using a Hornby train set as an example I searched for TOY TRAIN.

26% of all toy train auctions are listed under Toys, Bean Bag Plush:Television Toys:Thomas Tank Engine.

26% are listed under Toys, Bean Bag Plush:Wooden.

7% are listed under Collectables:Trains, Railwayana:Other Trains, Railwayana.

This tells me two things. My Hornby railway set is most suited to the Collectables:Trains, Railwayana:Other Trains, Railwayana category. Out of the above three anyway. And that TOY TRAIN probably isn't the best description for it. So I try again with HORNBY TRAIN SET.

45% of matches are found in Collectables:Trains, RR Models:Model Railway: Hornby:Other Hornby Models

22% in Collectables:Trains, RR Models:Model Railway: Hornby:Locomotives

I know Hornby collectors will scour both of these, but my train set fits best in the first of the two. I can now search in that category to see what techniques the most successful auctions employ to attract bidders.

What if my Hornby railway set just happened to be based on Thomas The Tank Engine? I would keep to the Hornby category, but include Thomas The Tank Engine in the title if at all possible. This then attracts two niche markets - Hornby collectors and people searching for Thomas The Tank Engine products.

2. Auction title

For my money, an auction's title is the most important part of any auction listing. When people are browsing page after page of auction listings, the title is what stands between them clicking through to your auction or somebody else's. Equally, if a potential bidder is using the search facilities to locate items of interest, it is your title that will lead him or her to you more often than not.

I always try to put as many keywords as possible in any title. For example, returning to my model train set. I won't just put TRAIN SET FOR SALE. I will think about how people might search for a model train set. What other words might they use instead of train set? Is the type of train set important? What other train sets are listed and what auctions (and keywords) are attracting most views and bids? So I might come up with something like:

HORNBY MODEL RAILWAY TOY TRAIN SET BOXED

I have used capitals in the above, but in listings I rarely do for the simple reason that the human eye responds better to lower case letters than upper case (we recognise words by their shape, but that shape is lost when we use capitals). So I would have:

Hornby model railway toy train set boxed

"Hornby" is the brand name - collectors will be looking for this. "Model railway" and "train set" are both perfect search phrases - and you will also get people searching for "toy train" or "toy railway set". I cover as many bases as possible in the words allowed.

If I can distinguish my listing from others I will always do so - and that is where the word "boxed" comes in. Collectors love boxed items. It also says to potential bidders, "It is still boxed - I have looked after this train set".

This can make a real difference. My Mum once listed an AA car badge on eBay. It was one of the vintage ones that was given to AA members back in the 1960s. At the time they sold on eBay for about £10, but because of a low feedback rating (my Mum was relatively new to eBay) and other listing factors her badge sold for just £8. She was really surprised when the buyer knocked on her door and said they had come to collect the AA badge in person. That's because the buyer was me.

I immediately listed the AA badge again, adding just one word to the description. The word "MINT" (in capital letters too). What my Mum hadn't realised was that all of the AA badges selling for about £10, no matter their condition, had been used. My Mum's badge had never been on a car. It was in mint condition. I improved the listing using the techniques that will follow and both my Mum and me watched the auction with interest. Ten days later it sold for £41. That word "mint" in the title made my auction irresistible to anyone looking for an AA badge in pristine condition.

3. Description

The devil is always in the detail. And when it comes to describing your item, the more detail you give the higher the price it will sell for. There obviously is a balancing act to perform here. If your item is never going to sell for more than a small amount, you are wasting your time providing more detail than is necessary, but for items that could or should attract high bids, then the more detail the better. For example, the condition of your item is often of crucial importance, but is often glossed over in auction listings. People often say no more than "good condition" or "excellent condition" when such phrases are largely meaningless unless qualified. After all, there is no benchmark to say what "good condition" actually means. We all have our own pre-conceived ideas.

Better to say "in excellent condition with some wear to edges of box" or "in very good but played with condition" or "in good condition but with small mark in top corner". People will appreciate your honesty.

Always include brand name, catalogue numbers, reference numbers or anything similar where appropriate. If it has a box say so. If it comes with instructions say so. If it's a limited edition say so. Every bit of additional information might just be what a potential bidder needs to press the bid button. If there is any sign of wear and tear, say so too. As well as demonstrating honesty, it will decrease the possibility of a disappointed bidder.

If you can add any personal touches do so too. People like to do business with people they can relate to. "Originally bought as a Christmas present two years ago, it has spent much of its life in its box in the loft. It deserves a better home!"

Also when creating your description listing, keep it simple and clear. Don't use wacky fonts. Don't use weird colours that induce headaches. Don't use special effects or sound or anything else unless it adds to your auction listing.

4. Pricing

eBay charges both a listing fee and a fee based on final selling price. The higher your start price, the bigger the listing fee.

If you have an item that your research on eBay shows attracts few bids, you have little choice but to start the auction at more or less the price you want for the item and you have to accept the corresponding listing fee.

But if you are listing an item that you know will generate bidding interest, you can afford to start the auction at a lower price - thereby saving on listing fees and also encouraging bids because everyone likes a bargain. The lower the start price, the more bids you are likely to attract until the item reaches the price most people expect it to sell for. But by this point, you will already have attracted a number of bidders - and those bidders are most likely to drive the price upwards as they are now emotionally involved with the item. As soon as someone places a bid, they start to believe that the item can be theirs. And that's what drives them on to bid again and again to ensure that what they think of as theirs stays theirs. That's why items often attract far more money on eBay than they would elsewhere.

Most of my auctions I start at under £5 - even if I expect to get far more for my item. By encouraging bidders to enter the bidding process at lower levels, I know that those who develop an emotional bond with my item are likely to be there at the end if a last minute bidding frenzy takes place. As a seller, I love a bidding frenzy!

5. Pictures

Pictures help sell items so wherever possible include at least one good image of the item you are selling. If you have a digital camera use that. Get in close for better results. If you have a scanner, you can use that too - even for three dimensional items that aren't too big. Place the item carefully on the glass and instead of putting the cover down, cover the item with a plain (preferably white) material such as a tea towel. Press the scan button and you will be surprised by the quality of pictures you can achieve using this method.

6. Delivery

Again, make it crystal clear how much you are charging for postage. If you are serious about making money from eBay, get yourself some postage scales and a postal rates booklet from your local Post Office. Then weigh your item, add the cost of packaging and give potential bidders the price they will pay. If you are willing to send your item overseas, give a price for both international and domestic bidders.

Incidentally if you are willing to sell internationally, your listing automatically appears on the relevant eBay websites around the world - there is no need to list the same item on eBay.com and eBay.co.uk for example.

7. Finish time

When an auction is due to finish can have a marked effect on the final price. For example, people who work are usually busier at the start of a week than the end of a week. So on Monday they are less likely to have time to look at eBay. Come Friday afternoon, as things wind down for the week and thoughts turn to the weekend, they might have more time.

There is also little point in having business items close outside of business hours. An auction for machinery that closes at 4pm Thursday will usually do better than one that closes at 4am Thursday.

For personal items, I have found more success when my auctions close during the late evening, when bidders are home from work and are more likely to be looking at eBay. And personal items also do well when they close on Saturday or Sunday too. If possible I list personal items on Wednesdays and Thursdays for ten days. This means they will close on a Saturday or Sunday and it also gives me two weekends' worth of exposure.

If you are willing to ship internationally, bear in mind time differences between different countries. If you are in the UK and hoping for American bidders, make sure the item closes when it will suit them. I used to sell a lot of collectables to Japan. Tokyo is eight hours ahead of London so I took this into consideration when setting closing times for my auctions.

For time zones for different countries see here:

http://www.timeanddate.com/worldclock/

For a small fee, you can actually choose the exact time you want an auction to close - irrespective of the time you list it. Often worth considering if selling abroad to countries with big time differences to you.

Cashing in on other people's eBay mistakes

Many items on eBay go for much less than they are worth because:

1. The seller has no feedback or a very low feedback score and so fewer people will bid

2. Many items are so poorly listed that few people will find them let alone bid on them

3. Many items are often listed in either the wrong category or at least not in the category where they would get most attention

Spot these bargains and you can make money by doing things properly and by cashing in on a high feedback rating (which you need to build for eBay success generally). Buy these items for low prices from less experienced eBay sellers and then re-list them and sell them for a profit. That's what Jamie Murray did with gaming consoles on his way to eBay millionaire status.

Buy a collection, sell individual items

Often a collection will sell for far less on eBay than what the items in it would have sold for individually. An example of this was an autograph collection with over 100 signed photos, letters and other items, including some very rare and sought after ones. I bought the lot for just over £300 - about £3 an autograph.

The reason for the low price is that most people don't want 100 signed photos. They might already have some of them or only collect certain ones. What's more, fewer people have £300 to bid, but might still be willing to pay £50 for one of them.

Similarly, I bought the copyright, negatives and prints to about 220 related photos for £2,000 on eBay. It worked out at less than £10 a photo - when to buy just a print of a similar photo will cost you up to £14.99 elsewhere on the web. The photos I'm keeping and will develop into an internet based business, but the likes of the autograph collection are crying out to be sold individually - both on eBay AND as the starting stock for an online autograph business.

Another example. Guinness merchandise is very collectable and a man listed four identical bar towels in one auction. Who wants four identical ones? Most people just want one so won't bid. I bought them for little more than what collectors would have paid for one and resold them individually.

International rescue, eBay style

Anyone who trawls eBay regularly will know the feeling when they find just what they want, but the seller won't ship outside the USA and you're in the UK or vice versa. A lot of sellers simply can't be bothered sending anything abroad. Many don't even know how to.

So why not start a business offering your services as a middleman? For example, a seller in the UK will ship only to the UK and you live in the UK. An American buyer wants the item, but cannot bid without having a UK shipping address. And that's where you come in. For a fee and onward shipping costs you will take delivery of the item in the UK and forward it on to the USA, allowing the American buyer to bid. This is a gap in the market just waiting to be filled. Maybe you can see yourself filling it.

A man with a plan – an eBay case study

A few years ago, I came across someone who had got selling on eBay down to a fine art. He doesn't seem to be active on eBay anymore, but his business model is one that could be adapted to a wide variety of eBay-based businesses, something that should interest anyone wanting to make money from online auctions.

The seller had found himself a very lucrative niche on eBay, selling plans for making battery powered children's cars. So if you wanted a scaled down model of a Jeep, he was selling the plans you'd need to build one. And if you wanted a Ford Model T that your kid could ride around the garden in, again here was your man.

Buyers paid between £15.00 and £35.00 plus postage for a set of plans. Presumably, the seller had to do nothing more than put a set of plans in an envelope and put them in the post (as an aside, you might be able to streamline a similar operation further by offering plans as downloads, but perhaps plans - given the exact nature of them - are usually best supplied in hard copy format. You can often charge more for physical products too. You did get full size pattern sheets as well as an instruction manual and working drawings with the car plans so a downloadable version might not have been ideal).

Each auction was a Buy It Now fixed price auction, with a number of sets available during any one auction. Looking at his feedback, he sold the same plans over and over again, meaning that he spent very little time creating new auction listings. He simply re-listed auctions as they ended, and as he only sold four different sets of plans, it must have taken him all of ten minutes a week to keep the listings live.

Although no longer active on eBay, when I last looked he had sold 600 plans over a 12 month period at an average of £20.00 a set. That's £12,000 - a thousand pounds a month for re-listing the same plans on eBay and then sending them out to buyers. Add an hour or two for putting the plans in an envelope, keeping accounts, and walking down to the Post Office, and you're probably talking no more than a few hours of "work" a week.

That was just for starters though. Although the auctions were only for the plans, the listings made it very clear that once you had the plans, you could also buy all the parts you needed from a comprehensive price list that the seller included when sending the plans. So as well as making money from selling plans, he could make money (without any eBay listing or selling fees) by selling parts to his customers too. He might not have supplied these parts himself - I have a feeling he simply included the parts list of the company that does supply the parts. A shrewd move that would attract more customers, but keep his involvement to a minimum.

The seller also knew exactly how to target niche markets. Engineering-minded customers might just want the plans and would source parts themselves, but others with little or no experience in building anything like this would no doubt buy everything from that list. He catered for both niches, and all the niches that lie in-between.

Another example of niche marketing was the fact that the seller specifically targeted not only people who would be making a car for their own children's use, but also those with an eye for a business opportunity. Several listings mentioned the fact that, once built, the cars can be worth five to ten times the build cost. Others mentioned the idea of charging for rides in the cars at fêtes and car boot sales.

In the auction titles, the seller also targeted people looking for the full size version of the cars. For example, anyone searching eBay for a Jeep would have come across his listings. And if Daddy is going to get a new Jeep, what better than to get Junior a scaled down version?

He also listed the plans in various categories, thereby reaching different niches with each auction listing. The auction listings themselves were well written, built enthusiasm for the plans, and were always accompanied by multiple photos of finished cars and happy smiling children.

I don't think the seller was even the prime source for these plans, although I could be wrong. He was based in Sheffield, but the plans were produced by Real Life Toys Ltd of Biggleswade. Indeed, they still produce the plans and sell them online at http://www.realifetoys.com.

Plans for children's battery powered aren't the only plans you could sell on eBay. Here's some ideas based around house plans.

What about plans to build treehouses for example?

What about plans to build dolls' houses?

What about plans to build real houses?

What about finding a book of plans that was published in Victorian times? What about making them available again for today's market? Plans of genuine Victorian dolls' houses for example?

What about finding another company that produces plans and ask to sell them for them? Perhaps there's a company in Germany that produces fantastic plans in German that you could buy the rights to for the English language market?

If you could produce your own plans for something that would find a market on eBay and beyond, but didn't know exactly what was required to deliver a complete set of plans, here's a solution. Why not buy a set from Real Life Toys Ltd? See what they offer and write the cost off as market research.

Selling plans on eBay is one of the best examples of how to make money from selling information (what you know!) with minimum effort that I've seen. And if you can come up with an idea along similar lines, you too could be in the money.

Food for thought – another eBay case study

I just want to share one more case study with you. Not only does it show the incredible impact that eBay can have on a business, but it throws up all sorts of possibilities that might interest you.

Restaurant.com was a dotcom failure on the brink of collapse in 2001. When it first opened it doors for business on the 1st of May, 2000, Restaurant.com looked the very picture of success. A year and a half in the making, and with US$7.5 million invested in it, it claimed to be the most comprehensive database of restaurants in the USA with 350,000 entries.

It's business model was simple. Become the number one portal for eating out in the USA and then make money by selling "mini-websites" (basically pages within Restaurant.com) to restaurants. The complete package being offered to restaurants included everything from dining reviews, online reservation facilities, wine lists, menus, even a 360 degree tour of the establishment - all for an annual subscription fee of US$895. With 350,000 potential clients, the future looked very bright indeed.

The problem was restaurants weren't buying it. Within a year, Restaurant.com had got through all of its start-up capital and was on the brink of bankruptcy. Founder, Scott Lutwak, was on the verge of throwing in the towel when he came across an idea that transformed the fortunes of Restaurant.com.

The interesting thing for you and me is that the same idea could be successfully applied to different markets or indeed restaurants in another country by a small entrepreneur working from home. Think about how you could create a similar venture where you live when you discover what Restaurant.com has become.

Today, Restaurant.com is no longer a restaurant portal. Today, Restaurant.com sells discount coupons or gift certificates redeemable at over 15,000 restaurants nationwide. Fixed value coupons worth US$25, US$50, US$75 and US$100 can be bought from the website for less than half of their face value and then used to pay part or all of the bill at the restaurant of their choosing from Restaurant.com's massive database.

If you visit www.Restaurant.com you'll see how easy it is to use. Simply select a state then a city, choose the type of food you want to eat, select from the list of restaurants that appear, add the relevant discount voucher to your shopping cart and proceed to checkout.

Restaurant.com sells thousands of discount coupons. In fact hundreds of thousands of coupons. The reason it sells so many coupons is because everybody is happy. Restaurants are happy because they get people through their doors when tables might otherwise be empty. It costs them nothing to work with Restaurant.com - their only commitment is to honour the discount coupons. If nobody turns up, it hasn't cost them a penny. Each restaurant still gets what is now called a "micro-site", a simple one page website with all the information you need plus a picture or two. It also gets to choose what vouchers it will accept.

Restaurant.com is happy because it gets to keep all of the money it gets for selling the discount coupons. And of course diners are happy because they can eat out for less whether they fancy a pizza or a slap up meal.

The beauty of selling discount coupons over the internet is that there is no physical product. No discount coupons to produce. No delivery costs! After making their purchase, customers simply download the coupon and print it out using their own computer and printer. This business model is crying out to be duplicated in other markets and other locations by entrepreneurs working from home.

Could it work in London or Glasgow or Paris or Sydney? Why not? Or why not target the holiday market and produce discount coupons for Benidorm's restaurants or the sidewalks of St Tropez? And forgetting restaurants for the moment, can you think of other markets that this idea could be adapted and applied to? Why not discount coupons for tourist attractions in Florida or the UK? In fact the hospitality industry has many opportunities for a business selling discount coupons.

Imagine a website that offered a guide to and discount accommodation vouchers for use at hotels in the UK? Or bed and breakfasts in France? Or shops in one city? Could you run a business like this from home and make a good living? It's certainly worth considering.

One more thing. What's the best way to sell your discount vouchers? Well, apart from a great domain name and the free media publicity such a venture would attract, would you believe the answer is online auctions? Restaurant.com's main marketing tool for years was eBay. I'm not sure why (I have asked, but got no reply), but Restaurant.com stopped selling its certificates on eBay in May, 2008, having completed an incredible 1,429,853 sales!

No job. Just eBay. Think of the possibilities.

You don't need no Rich Dad

"Only those who are asleep make no mistakes."
Ingvar Kamprad, founder of Ikea.

A while ago now, I came across an article about a story told by Robert Kiyosaki in his book, *The Cashflow Quadrant*. Kiyosaki is one of the most successful motivational authors of all time, with book sales approaching the 30 million mark. He is best known for his best selling book, *Rich Dad Poor Dad*, and *The Cashflow Quadrant* was the sequel to it.

In *The Cashflow Quadrant*, Kiyosaki develops a lot of the themes introduced in *Rich Dad Poor Dad*. Its focus is mainly on generating passive income by means of investing in the likes of property and businesses, with financial independence being achieved when your monthly passive income exceeds your monthly expenses.

The specific tale I came across revolves around a village and its need for water. Local businessmen were asked to establish a service that would bring water from a nearby lake, and two of them, Ed and Bill, took up the challenge. Ed rushed out, bought some buckets, and started running back and forth to the lake. While Ed was earning money, Bill went away and for the next six months worked on creating a pipeline. He then returned with a construction crew, built the pipeline, and was soon the village's main water supplier. Work done, it allowed Bill to build pipelines to other villages and so his business grew. Meanwhile, Ed was still running back and forth with his buckets in an attempt to compete with the pipeline.

Obviously Bill is the hero of this story in *The Cashflow Quadrant*, but it got me thinking. If I had been one of the village's entrepreneurs, what would I have done? Would I have been a Bill or an Ed? And I decided I would have been neither. I would have politely declined the invitation to supply the village with water.

Running up and down a hill with buckets of water all day long isn't my idea of fun. I'm not interested in investing bucketloads of time and (borrowed) money in projects either. Not when there's no real need to.

There are plenty of excellent money making opportunities that require hard labour and there are plenty that need massive commitment on your part in terms of both time and money. There's nothing intrinsically wrong with either, but there are also just as many opportunities out there today that don't require hard labour or huge investments and it's these opportunities that provide the foundations for a successful Plan B.

As I've said before, we were all born to be entrepreneurs, and thanks to the age we live in, we don't have to carry proverbial buckets of water or build the proverbial pipeline to prove it. Richard Branson is probably Britain's best known and loved entrepreneur. His Virgin empire apparently knows no bounds. The wage slave society loves holding the likes of Richard Branson aloft as an archetypal entrepreneur because, although many will admire him, few will feel truly able to emulate him. Bottom line, we simply don't have the cash to launch an airline or to buy a train franchise. That leaves us thinking our lot in life is to hump buckets.

I love Bob Dylan's definition of success. Getting up in the morning and going to bed at night and doing whatever it is you want to do in-between. Carrying buckets? Building expensive pipelines? Maybe once upon a time, during the industrial age, but we now live in the information age. It's the computer in the corner of your room that holds the key to your future success because the internet has revolutionised the way we can live and how we can make money. And anyway, a pipeline by definition restricts flow – that's why I would rather stick to snowballs.

Plan B in a nutshell

Here's my ten second elevator pitch for Plan B. Starting today, you can work less hours, work the hours you choose, and earn more money, doing whatever it is you want to do with your time, all from the comfort of your home. And your home can be wherever you want it to be!

Let's break it down. **Work less hours, work the hours you choose.** To me this is more important than money because time is something that I value above all else. Time with my family. Time doing what I enjoy doing. Time doing whatever it is I want to do. Each day, every day. In fact forget money. Time is the most precious resource you will ever have.

You should seek out opportunities and ideas that allow you to plan your day around yourself and your loved ones. You need to be developing multiple revenue streams that allow you to work the hours of your choosing. The internet allows you to do this. Websites are available 24 hours a day, seven days a week, 365 (sometimes 366) days a year, give or take a few hours of inevitable downtime. You can be open for business even when you're not even working. What's more you can tend to your business at times that suit you. Mornings, afternoons, evenings, weekends. You choose.

Even better, you no longer have to work as many hours (you can if you want to of course!) because so much of the day to day grind of business can be automated online. The very fact that your websites will be working for you around the clock means you can put your feet up. Contrast that with a traditional retail outlet. If it opens from 9am to 5.30pm, six days a week, the shopkeeper has to be there in person to serve customers or he has to employ someone to do it in his place. On a wet Monday there might be only a handful of customers all day, but someone still has to be there between 9am and 5.30pm just in case.

If that handful of customers did their shopping between 9am and 10am, and the shopkeeper knew nobody else would be coming, he could spend the rest of the day fishing. Unfortunately, he has no idea when a customer might come in, so he is stuck in his shop, twiddling his thumbs, until closing time. That same wet Monday, a coachload of customers might drop by at 6pm, only to find the shop shut. By then the shopkeeper might well be fishing, but he's also losing business.

Via the internet, the customer can order online any time of the day or night. A great deal is made about how you can shop online in your pyjamas. The other side of that coin is that you can take orders in your pyjamas too – even if you happen to be tucked up in bed asleep in those pyjamas. The customer can pay you by credit card and everything is processed automatically without you lifting a finger. You can make far better use of your time because if a handful of customers place orders, you can process those orders when it suits you. Process them first thing in the morning and the rest of the day is yours. If you are selling digital products, your customer can even get instant delivery. Or if you are simply sending customers to other websites in return for a commission, someone else will be filling the orders.

Earn more money. A money-making internet business can be started for the price of a meal out, but don't make the mistake of thinking low upfront investment means low returns. The fact is that the cost of launching an online business has tumbled over the past ten years to the point where it is almost negligible – and at the same time the amount of money being spent online has rocketed. Annual UK online sales are expected to exceed £40 billion for the first time in 2010 and that figure is going to keep heading north for a long time to come. That's quite a pie to shove a finger or two in.

Throughout this book I bang on about you being able to start an internet business for less than £50. The interesting thing is, you can start ten internet businesses for not much more. Hosting costs can be shared between websites. For around £400, you can host as many as 100 or more small websites for a year on what is called a reseller hosting account. Including domain name registration, that works out at not much more than a fiver a year per website, per internet business. That's 100 internet based businesses, each with the potential to earn at least a spare time income. Over a period of time, you could be earning more money than you ever did as a wage slave thanks to their combined earning power - all without leaving your own home.

100 websites is a lot of websites to juggle, but it underlines just how easily and cheaply you can get an idea to market these days. You might make the same money concentrating on just one website. Or ten websites. The secret of course is choosing the one or ten websites that are right for you and that have the potential to make money. The first one or ten website ideas you come across probably won't be the right one or ten, but that's the beauty of being able to risk so little to find out what works for you and what doesn't.

Doing whatever it is you want to do with your time. This is where a lot of people miss out. You only live once so why waste your valuable time doing a job or work that you don't want to do? Choose only those opportunities and ideas that make work feel like play. Not only will you enjoy what you're doing, but the other upside is that you'll earn more money too because your passion and love for what you do will be infectious.

Working from the comfort of your own home. I've been a home based entrepreneur since before leaving school. I once rented an industrial unit complete with office, warehousing, toilet and kitchen, but still preferred to work from home. I like the idea of being a one minute commuter. Thanks to the internet it has never been easier to work from home. All you need is a computer, a phone line and an internet connection, and away you go.

And your home can be wherever you want it to be! Your computer, phone line and internet connection can be in Bristol, Belfast or Bermuda. It can be in Sheffield, the Shetlands or Sydney. It really doesn't matter anymore. Town, city, village, back of a VW Camper Van. You can now live and work wherever you choose. With that comes many lifestyle advantages, not least the ability to move away from congested city centres with high property prices - if of course that's what you want to do!

Since the day wage slavery began, people have been looking for escape routes. Carrying buckets and building pipelines were and still are viable options, but for possibly the first time in history, and certainly for the first time in our lifetimes, there is another way forward. And that way forward is to develop low cost multiple revenue streams, primarily via the internet, that allow you to work less hours, work the hours you choose, and earn more money doing whatever it is you want to do with your time - all from the comfort of your home and from wherever you want that home to be.

Break that last paragraph down for yourself and seriously consider the implications for you.

How many hours do you want to work?

How much do you want to make?

What would you like to do with your time today, tomorrow, for the rest of your life?

And where would you like to do it from?

They can be difficult questions to answer, particularly if you are conditioned to accepting a life of wage slavery. That's why so many people find it difficult to know where to start when planning a new life for themselves and their family. You need to be answering these fundamental questions before you start to plan your escape from the rat race because your answers will lead the way to the multiple revenue streams that are right for you. Then it is downhill all the way.

Chickens and eggs

Which came first, the chicken or the egg? Scientists at Sheffield University working with even more scientists from Warwick University think they know the answer. The chicken. Apparently, the formation of eggs is only possible thanks to a protein found in the chicken's ovaries.

We have our own chicken and egg puzzle to solve before starting work on a Plan B. Which comes first, the product or the market? The answer is the market. Identifying a need or want should always come first. Without a market, a product will flounder. Without a product, the market still exists, albeit with one or more of its needs and wants unsatisfied by that particular product.

So the first thing you need to do to get this party started is to identify markets and their wants and needs. Even better, identify niche markets (markets within markets) and their wants and needs. Better still, identify WITH niche markets and WITH their wants and needs. And the best way to do the latter is to look for opportunities to satisfy the wants and needs of niche markets that you are part of. In other words, scratch your own itch.

There is nothing stopping you looking beyond your own world for money-making ideas and opportunities, particularly if you can identify a need or a want that you know you can help satisfy. If you find yourself short of ideas though, there is probably no better place to find opportunties than with markets you are familiar with.

If you are a parent to a five year old, think about the wants and needs of other parents of five year olds. If you collect stamps, think about the wants and needs of other stamp collectors. If you are losing weight, think about the wants and needs of others who are fighting the flab. As well as the knowledge and passion you bring to the table, doing what you enjoy will turn work into play.

One man who oozes passion about what he does is Martin Lewis of Moneysavingexpert.com. If you have seen him during his now regular TV appearances, talking about how to save money or unfair bank charges, you'll know what I mean. Martin has been working as a money saving expert since the year 2000 when he wrote a newspaper column and appeared on various TV and radio shows as a consumer champion. About this time, he started sending e-mails to friends, offering money saving advice. Before long he had a list of 1,000 friends, and friends of friends, who he sent his tips to and who visited the simple one page website he had created to showcase his latest tips.

Sensing that there was potential in developing the website further, he paid a website designer in Uzbekistan £100 to create a more professional version. The site was launched in February, 2003, and "the Dumbledore Of Debt", as he has been called, has never looked back. The more media work Martin got, the bigger the site grew. The bigger the site grew, the more media work Martin got.

Today the Moneysavingexpert.com website welcomes more than eight million visitors a month, with nearly four million people subscribing to his Money Tips e-mail. What's more, the website has made him a very rich man. A multi-millionaire in fact. All thanks to his passion for collating and sharing information about saving money, whether its a two for one meal deal at a restaurant chain or the credit card charging the least interest on purchases.

How has he made those millions when the site is free to use and displays no advertising? Look closely at many of the recommendations made on the site and you will see an asterisk next to them. Martin earns a commission from each sale generated by such recommendations via affiliate marketing. Eight million visitors every month generate a helluva lot of sales. With the same amount of passion and dedication, there is absolutely nothing stopping you from doing exactly the same in your chosen field. Incidentally, if you need a web designer in Uzbekistan (or anywhere else for that matter), try the likes of eLance (http://www.elance.com), Guru (http://www.guru.com) or Odesk (http://www.odesk.com).

Ideally, you want to do what Martin does. Fill your days with joy and passion. Take your time choosing ideas and developing opportunities that genuinely have the potential to earn you the money you want to have in your pocket every day and that will get you out of bed in the morning, raring to go. The temptation might be to try to run with every opportunity that knocks, every idea you come across - whether or not they will make you money and whether or not you will enjoy pursuing them. Without the joy and passion, what's the point? Your time is priceless, never forget that.

To me, fixing a car is hard work. I couldn't spend all day doing that. But some people love nothing better than to spend their day tinkering with cars. If that's you, fantastic. What is work for me is play for you, but don't stick your head under the bonnet unless that's what really sets your world on fire. Similarly, if you ever find yourself half-heartedly working on something that doesn't really interest you at this moment in time, start working on something that does. The key is to keep to the

Plan. To keep moving forward. As long as you are doing enough work every day to hit your Plan B target, you can't go far wrong.

Eggs and baskets

Your Plan B will develop into a portfolio of revenue streams that make it increasingly easier to earn your pound (or 50p or £2) a day as time goes by thanks to the snowball effect. Add only those ideas with true potential and that you will thoroughly enjoy pursuing. You don't have to choose ten or six or two or any number of opportunities and ideas on day one. Let your multiple revenue stream portfolio grow as time goes by. You also don't have to start pursuing each and every one of your income streams from day one. Develop one until you are at a point where you don't need to devote so much time to it and then pick another string from your portfolio to add to your bow.

Many of today's internet based opportunities can be put on autopilot very early on and will contribute to your bottom line for years to come. Take a downloadable product like a digital report or a piece of software for example. Build an attractive website that is optimised for the search engines and that sells a product that will appeal to your target market. Make the purchasing and delivery of the product fully automated. Then leave it on autopilot while you develop your next idea. Or a fully automated auction website where customers provide the website content and payments are processed automatically. Or an automated classified website. Or an automated dating website.

Yes, all will need updating at least periodically, and all will demand a certain amount of your time, but there will also be days when you do nothing more than count the payments coming in. Days you can spend developing other revenue streams.

Conventional wisdom says you can only make money while you are working. While you are putting the hours in. The internet says you can make money while you're sleeping, while you're in the bath, while you're on holiday. That's why Plan B works. Selling things on online auction sites for example can easily net £500 a week working evenings only. You don't have to physically tend to each auction for its duration. eBay does that for you.

Nothing like this was possible a generation ago. Whole industries are being turned upside down by the information revolution. When the CD format first began to replace vinyl, many people inside and outside the industry said that nobody would want to buy CDs. I was working in the music industry at the time and have to admit that I couldn't see CDs ever replacing vinyl. One reason was that the album cover artwork was such an intrinsic part of the product that reducing it to CD booklet size seemed to devalue it and therefore the product. And yet CDs have all but replaced vinyl in our shops and we now pay more for CDs than we ever did for LPs.

When the internet came along and people could download music, the same argument was raised. It was thought by many that CDs would remain unchallenged because music fans wanted something physical to collect. Napster and its millions of users begged to differ. Then we were told that the popularity of the likes of Napster was largely due to the fact that music could be downloaded free of charge and that a business model where people had to pay for music downloads was doomed to failure. In April, 2003, Apple Computers launched iTunes where you could download over 400,000 songs for 99c each. That same year, on the 12th of December, the 25th million song was downloaded from this automated website. That was 2003. At the time of writing (February, 2010), iTunes was fast approaching ten billion downloads.

But what about the gift market? What about all those CDs bought as Christmas presents? What about the millions of pounds worth of iTunes gift certificates that are now found in stockings come Christmas Day? Welcome to the digital music revolution as the iTunes website says.

I'm not suggesting that a one man band could run iTunes or that it is purely on autopilot, but you get the idea. You must see the potential. Canadian, Markus Frind, certainly understands the potential. He started his hugely successful free dating website, PlentyOfFish.com, in his spare time and only gave up his job to work on it full-time when it brought in US$4,000 in a single month. He then taught himself everything he needed to know about affiliate marketing, Search Engine Optimisation and making money online, and now earns millions of dollars a year from it. That's right, millions of dollars a year from a free dating website.

A dating website simply collates and shares information about people looking for dates. Virtually all of the content is provided by the users themselves. Markus found huge success largely because his site is completely free to use. That too flies in the face of conventional wisdom. How on Earth does he make any money from a free dating website? The answer is Google AdSense. Those little ads that appear on PlentyOfFish.com have made Markus a fortune. I can remember, back in 2006, when those little ads earned Markus one million dollars in just three months and he posted about it on a forum for webmasters. You'll be pleased to hear that there is a whole chapter devoted to how you can make money from Google AdSense later in this book.

A dog that chases two rabbits catches neither

Markus has done very well thank you very much by devoting his time, energy and passion to building the world's biggest free dating website. He is making millions from that one revenue stream so has no need to pursue other opportunities. You might strike gold too with the one big idea or you might end up making your money from a cluster of smaller ideas. Both make sense for Plan B. As the Louisville Lip, Muhammad Ali, would have it, it is perfectly okay to fly like a butterfly from revenue stream to revenue stream, as long as you sting like a bee when you do get down to work.

Plenty of well meaning people will tell you to focus on just one idea. One website at a time. Always finish what you start. That sort of thing. Such talk is more conventional wisdom from a bygone age. An age when how much you made was largely determined by how many hours you worked. An age when you had to be physically doing something to make money. An age when a trade implied physical labour and when specialisation was the key to success. That's why conventional wisdom teaches us to focus on one idea at a time.

Nobody's suggesting that you set up simultaneously as a plumber, a mechanic, a florist, a stuntman, a dentist, a hairdresser, a market trader, a gardener, a baker and a candlestick maker. Trying to run ten traditional small businesses on your own is little different to trying to hold down ten different jobs. For me, that's not only madness. It's suicidal.

However, there is no reason why you shouldn't have ten websites in various states of development, all contributing to your income. No reason at all. That's if you want to work on more than one website at a time. It's your time. You decide what you do with it. Just focus on making money, not working hours.

In a portfolio of revenue streams, there will be times when one project will consume all of your time. It may be that you have one all-consuming big idea that will be all you ever work on. At other times, you may find yourself working on four or five smaller projects at the same time. It's all good as long as what you do is making a positive contribution to your future. If you are creating website content for example, whether you create ten new pages for one website in a day or two pages each for five websites, the result is still ten more pages that can make you money.

Conventional wisdom is exactly what it says on the tin. It's what you are expected to follow for no better reason than that's how people have done it before you came along. A dog that chases two rabbits catches neither - that in a nutshell is the argument against having more than one website. Just remember this. You are not a dog.

We live in changing times. Conventional wisdom still applies to both wage slaves and a lot of traditional small businesses, but not necessarily to you any longer. Today, the potential for you to make more money working less hours is greater than it has ever been in all of history. That being the case, why would you want to live your life as if none of that incredible potential existed? Why would you want to be confined by the chains of conventional wisdom that are of such dubious value in times of immense change?

You can still make your fortune pouring all of your time and energy into just one idea as Jeff Bezos over at Amazon or eBay's founder, Pierre Omidyar, will happily testify. For something to succeed on this scale demands 110% commitment. Common sense, let alone conventional wisdom, says that if you want to create another Amazon you simply don't have the time to sleep, let alone pursue other business ideas. Equally if your one idea demands every minute of your working day, there is little scope for starting new ventures. That is one side of the Plan B coin.

Flip it over and, by harnessing the awesome power of today's (and tomorrow's) technology, we can develop a portfolio of smaller business ideas into multiple revenue streams that combine to deliver financial independence - without filling each and every day with work. There are countless opportunities that just simply don't require your complete attention. I'll probably check sites like the Average Penis Size website once a month, just to make sure prices are correct and links work. I don't have to devote my life to it. There's absolutely no need to. So there's really nothing to stop me starting another website. I actually juggle 50 or so niche websites, 50 or so multiple revenue streams, not because each of them is perfect, but because I want to. It makes me happy. Simple as.

Don't worry. Be happy.

Where you will come off the rails is if you have a website that requires your complete attention every day to succeed – and then you start another website that also needs your complete attention every day to succeed. You will end up tearing your hair out trying to keep up with two underperforming websites. That's not what I am advocating. What I want to see is you making the best use of your time in a bid to make your Plan B come true. To do that you will need to select, develop and prioritise revenue streams that help you succeed in the minimum amount of time. The key to successfully developing your Plan B isn't the number of revenue streams in your portfolio, but that you make best use of your time each day.

The beauty is you aren't committed to pursuing any of your ideas forever more. Your portfolio can be added to at any time and ideas that don't work can be shelved. Even success stories can be sold on to make way for new challenges. The secret of success - and we're not just talking monetary success here - is deciding what you want to do with your time each and every day of your life. Work only really becomes work when you would rather be doing something else. And when that happens you should have the freedom to go and do that something else. That's what escaping wage slavery is all about. That's what financial independence is all about. That's what your Plan B should be all about.

I'm fortunate enough to be in a position to only have to follow Plan B, but what if you work six days a week and can't spend each and every day following Plan B? Taking my AveragePenisSize.co.uk as an example, two or three hours each weekend for a month would be enough to create just such a website. If you did that every month for a year, you would have a dozen websites with the potential to earn you money. 12 sites with the potential to earn you £365 over a 12 month period, or a total of £4,380. Not a fortune granted, but enough to fund a couple of memorable family holidays or to buy a decent secondhand car. In short, enough to make a difference. Enough to see that there is light at the end of the tunnel. Enough to encourage you to devote even more time to your Plan B in the months ahead. And who is to say that one of those 12 sites isn't going to make you much much more than £365 in a year? One might be the next Facebook.

As far as making money goes, the old rule book has been thrown out of the window and a new one is being written by today's internet based entrepreneurs. Investing fortunes in pipelines is one way to make money. Working all hours carrying buckets is another. Then there's Plan B. Invest in yourself and develop low risk multiple revenue streams that make you money whether you're working or not. Sounds like a plan to me.

How does your garden grow?

"Forget what we're told,
Before we get too old,
Show me a garden that's bursting into life."
Chasing Cars, Snow Patrol

I'm always having ideas for potential websites and obviously some of my ideas are better than others. To sort the good from the bad, traditional business theory would have me embark on weeks or maybe months of market research to see whether my latest idea has the makings of a viable business proposition. Before you know it, you are up to your eyes in business plans, feasibility studies, financial forecasting . . .

That's all fine and dandy if you need to invest large sums of money in your idea. It's even more important if you need to borrow those large sums of money. Bankers and their kin aren't big fans of great ideas delivered on the back of an envelope. What real value these neatly presented documents actually deliver though is dubious to say the least. Humans are pretty bad at predicting the future. We're not even very good at understanding the present. Given the complicated world we live in, that's hardly surprising, but being humans, we like to pretend we can do both. Has anyone ever created a business plan that didn't show a profit in years two and three? Not that made its way to a prospective lender anyway.

My favourite ideas are the ones that I can get up and running in a matter of days for less than £50. In less than a week you can have had an idea, have created an online business, and have started the marketing ball rolling. All for less than the price of a meal out.

If you do invest £50 in a business venture, the most you can lose is the same. Fifty quid. Why would you waste hours on market research, let alone days, weeks and months, if the most you could lose was £50?

When was the last time you spent £50? When was the last time you bought a pair of shoes or enjoyed a good meal out? Did either involve weeks and weeks of due diligence and market research? I doubt it.

Things move so quickly on the Net that if you do spend months researching an idea, chances are someone else is going to beat you to market anyway. So every time you have an idea that just might have legs - BANG! - do something outrageous and run with it. And that's especially true if you only need to spend a few pounds to get things moving.

There are people out there who will tell you that you can't possibly start a business for £50. The fact is you can. Okay, you'll need a computer and an internet connection too, but chances are you have both of them already. Most households now have both as standard. As we've already seen, £50 will buy you a domain name, hosting for your website and the caffeine needed to fuel those adrenaline-soaked first few days. That's all you need in this day and age to start your own business. You don't even need to give up your day job. Give the TV a miss for a few evenings a week and put your spare time to better use by getting a new business off the ground.

The man who wanted to be eBay

Back in 2002, I met a man who wanted to start his own online auction site. To me that would be a great idea if he could have got it started in a matter of days for very little money and had a niche market in mind to target his website at. But he had other ideas. Much bigger ideas. He wanted to be eBay.

He had found a company who were going to build him an auction website that would incorporate all of the features that anyone who uses online auction sites takes for granted: from automated listings to feedback facilities. And all for the princely sum of £10,000. This was to be his platform to rival eBay.

To me that was £10,000 down the drain. To go head to head with a giant of the internet like eBay is going to cost you a lot more than £10,000. Even back then, eBay's UK site was attracting around a billion page views a month. What was it going to cost to get anywhere near that many page views in terms of marketing a brand new auction site?

This man was so certain that he was on to a winner though that there was no cautioning him otherwise. I know that incredible things can be achieved by human endeavour, but this had non-starter written all over it. Here was someone who did need to do some market research before parting with such a large sum of money. Market research that would inevitably have told him his idea was not a good one.

So I made a suggestion. Rather than commit yourself to a £10,000 custom made auction site, why not test the water with my approach. Invest £50, get a website up and running, and see what response you get. Within a few minutes of searching online, I had found software to create an auction website for just five dollars. Ironically enough, I found it for sale on eBay.

The software might not have been quite as good as his £10,000 bespoke solution, but it did have all the main features an auction site required. For all we knew, it might have been better than the ten grand solution. For five dollars it was certainly worth buying, tinkering with, and putting it up there on the worldwide web to see what interest there was in his alternative to eBay.

At first he didn't believe that off the shelf auction packages were even available. After all, he had been quoted £10,000 for development. The truth is that clones of successful website models are generally easy to make and can be done at a fraction of the cost borne by those who are first to market. Incidentally, that's as true today as it was back in 2002. Probably more so.

Anyway, he reluctantly agreed to take a look. After doing so, he did admit that it looked interesting, but he was still not convinced. Did I know where he could see a demo or example of the software working? Doh. Here was a man who was quite happy to spend £10,000 on an idea that wasn't going to happen in a month of Sundays, but wanted to see a demo of an alternative that he could buy for just five dollars. Why not just throw caution to the wind, pay those five dollars, and try it yourself? What have you got to lose? A little time and five dollars by my reckoning.

The man just couldn't see the wood for the trees. He simply wasn't willing to believe that he could launch a serious alternative to eBay for just five dollars. Of course he was right. The problem was that he wasn't willing to entertain the idea that his £10,000 website wasn't going to mount a serious challenge to eBay's market share either.

He did in fact spend that £10,000 on his own auction site, an auction site that sadly no longer exists today. I did take a look at it a year after launch and he had managed to attract just 325 registered users. There were barely 500 auctions in progress despite his selling fees being less than eBay's. Who knows what the man spent in total on an auction site that had as much chance of challenging eBay as I do of meeting Elvis.

All the market research in the world is no substitute for getting your product out there and seeing what actually happens, but it needs to be done with as little risk as possible. Thanks to the internet it has never ever been easier to do just that: in days rather than months and for the price of a night out at the theatre.

Ask Google

My market research before deciding to spend £50 lasts about five minutes and it revolves around just two questions. Does my idea satisfy a genuine want or need of a niche market? And are there already people searching the worldwide web for what I want to offer them? If the answer's yes to both, you are in with half a chance. If the answer's no, forget it.

So how do you find out what people are actually looking for online? The quick answer lies with Google and its Keyword Tool. Completely free to use, it was designed to allow users to get new keyword ideas for Google Adword advertising campaigns, but we're going to make use of it to see what keywords and phrases people enter into Google when searching for information.

You'll find it at:

https://AdWords.google.com/select/KeywordToolExternal

Here's how it works. You choose a keyword or keywords that are related to your idea, enter them into the box provided (if you want your search to include adult keywords you can use the filter option to do so), and Google will produce a list of related searches that include your keywords. It will also tell you how many times each one was searched for during the previous month.

The default results show broad matches, but by ticking a box in the right hand column, you can fine tune those results to show exact matches. For example, according to the Keyword Tool broad match, approximately 5,400 people search for the words DOG BOWLS and 5,400 people search for DOG BOWL every month using Google.co.uk (The Keyword Tool used to draw data from across the Google search network, but recently changed to using data from just Google.com and for local searches the likes of Google.co.uk). That will include PINK DOG BOWL for example as well as BOWL DOG and any other searches including those two words in any order. 1,300 people searched specifically for just the two words DOG BOWLS and in that order according to the exact results. There is a third option – phrase match. This simply shows any phrases searched for that include the words DOG BOWL and can include other words before or after the phrase.

The Keyword Tool results shouldn't be taken too literally. Sometimes it throws up data that just doesn't look right and it would be completely wrong to plan your life around them. It was never meant as a tool to determine the viability of a website. By using this Keyword Tool though, you can quickly discover whether or not people are actually searching for whatever it is that you think will fill a particular need.

Just as importantly, it tells you the keywords and phrases that those people are using as they search the internet for your proposed product or service. Something that will be of big time importance when it comes to designing your new website. We've talked before about pages being bait in the search engines to attract visitors to your website. What better way then than to make sure each page is created in a way to target exactly what you know people are actually searching for?

Here's an example. Approximately 170 searches are made in the UK every month for the search phrase PERSONALISED DOG BOWLS. It's fair to assume that most of those searches are made by people who would like to buy a personalised dog bowl for their pampered pooch. If I sold dog bowls, it would make sense to actively target those searches in a bid to capture some of those sales. I would therefore create a web page or pages about nothing but personalised dog bowls in the hope that the search engines would rank the page or pages highly in search results for personalised dog bowls.

I might even go so far as to launch a mini website dedicated to nothing but personalised dog bowls. Or I might create a website that specialises in personalised pet accessories and sell not only dog bowls, but also collars and dog clothes too. Not the biggest of markets granted, but done properly, a very simple website targeting this niche could generate hundreds of sales a year.

I know the marketing gurus will be screaming at me to research how many personalised dog bowls are produced and sold every year and to hold focus groups with dog owners, but I already know everything I need to know about the potential for a small website dedicated to selling just personalised dog bowls or just personalised pet accessories. All I need to know to risk less than £50 anyway. In fact, I'd be risking less than £10 if I started such a site because I would use hosting I'd already paid for as part of a multi-website hosting package (usually known as a reseller hosting package where you get to host a number of sites on the one account).

Let's try another example. Black socks. Are there people on the internet searching for black socks? Would a website dedicated to just black socks be successful? Let's ask Google. Tap the words BLACK SOCKS into the Keyword Tool and you'll see that 260 people in the UK and 1,900 people worldwide used Google to search for the exact phrase BLACK SOCKS during the previous month (the actual number of searches across all search engines will undoubtedly be greater).

Does that tell you anything worth knowing? If you had a website offering just black socks do you think you could make any money selling them to those 260 people in the UK or indeed the 1,900 worldwide? Samy Liechti and Marcel Roth, co-founders of Blacksocks.com (http://www.blacksocks.com), discovered that you could. Launched in Switzerland in June, 1999, to offer the world's first "personal sock management system", customers around the world have since bought hundreds of thousands of pairs of socks via "sockscriptions". And all from a very basic website (obviously the main theme is the colour black). Indeed, in September, 2008, Blacksocks.com celebrated the sale of its one millionth pair of calf socks.

Does Google's Keyword Tool tell you that you're about to make your fortune online? Of course not. Does it guarantee success? No. But in less than five minutes you have enough market research under your belt to know whether your idea is worth the few quid it will cost you to put it in front of the only "focus group" that actually matters. The general public.

A million dollars in four months

You can spend hour upon hour trying to come up with the next big thing, but it's often the case that the simplest of ideas are also the best. Alex Tew, a then 21 year old Nottingham University business management student, wanted to make enough money to pay his way through university and came up with the blindingly simple idea of The Million Dollar Homepage (see it for yourself at http://www.milliondollarhomepage.com). The website offered a total of one million pixels for sale at US$1 each. Anyone could advertise on Alex Tew's homepage by buying at least one 10×10 pixel block for US$100, which they could then use to display an ad or logo, together with a link to their own site.

It's an idea that could so easily have bombed and fizzled out without a trace. If the idea had popped into my head instead of his, I would have given it little further thought to be honest. To me it was a stupid idea. If he had asked me for advice before launching it, I'd have said that the chances of him making a million were slim to say the least. Shows how much I know. That said, I would have added that it was only going to cost him less than £50 to give it a go and find out for himself, and if he had the money to spare, to go for it.

Thanks to a lot of offline publicity and the power of the internet, Tew struck gold. He launched The Million Dollar Homepage on the 26th of August, 2005, and by the end of the year he had banked US$999,000! The last 1,000 pixels were auctioned on eBay, adding a further US$38,100 to the kitty.

Not surprisingly, The Million Dollar Homepage spawned countless immitations, none of which succeeded. The success of the original site was based purely on the publicity generated, which in turn meant increasing numbers of advertisers wanted to be associated with it. Without the same oxygen of publicity, the copycat sites were mostly stillborn.

Alex himself went on to launch PixelLotto. The idea was to sell a million pixels at US$2 a piece, with US$1 going to himself and US$1 going into a prize fund, with the eventual winner receiving a one million dollar prize. His idea was to do this over and over again, starting afresh every time the million dollar prize was awarded. Things didn't quite work out as planned and PixelLotto only generated US$153,000 for Alex (with 10% going to charity) and the same amount for the one and only winner, a man from Kenya. Not as successful as The Million Dollar Homepage granted, but a nice little earner nonetheless for an idea that again could have been launched for less than fifty quid.

How does your garden grow?

So you too have had an idea. Google's Keyword Tool tells you it's probably got potential. Time to plug it into the mains and add it to your Plan B.

Surely there is more to it than that? Not really. Here are a few simple truths.

- You don't need to invest huge sums of money to start a business.

- A website that has no advertising budget can attract both customers and orders.

- A simple website can make money.

- A business that you can run from home working the hours that suit you can make a substantial contribution to your income.

The key is to zoom in on a niche market and serve its wants and needs better than anyone else does. Build websites that people will want to visit. And visit again. And again. Amazing things start to happen when you build sites like that. Search engines will not only list you, they will rank you. And if you are ranked highly enough, they will send you traffic. Tons of traffic. Turn visitors into customers and you make money.

Also in amongst that traffic will be journalists and others looking for information to write articles. If you are lucky, they will mention your website in their articles and that will lead to more traffic. For example, earlier this month one of my websites was mentioned in *The Times* newspaper and the article appeared on their website too. The result? A spike in traffic.

If you have an established website and think that visitors will like a new site that you are launching, tell them about it. Other webmasters who come across your site might also tell their visitors by linking to your site (and of course, there's nothing stopping you approaching other webmasters and asking for a link). If you are really lucky, your visitors will tell others about your site, perhaps via a forum post, Facebook or a blog, and you will get even more visitors. Word of mouth can be truly explosive as far as traffic on the web is concerned.

And so it goes on. For me, a website is like a flower. Plant it in good soil (memorable domain name, clean design), give it plenty of nutrients (quality content that's regularly updated), make sure it gets plenty of sun (search engine rankings, press coverage, links, etc.,) and before long you will have people peering over your garden wall to look at it (visitors).

This approach won't work for every website, but it does work - particularly for sites that target niche markets. Although sites can take off literally overnight, it usually takes a year or two for one of my sites to really establish itself. Meantime, I keep feeding it with new content to help it grow.

Finding your niche

I talk a lot about niche markets in this book. Niche marketing is where you target a product or a service at a particular segment of a larger market. What I do for the most part, and what I hope you will soon be doing, is provide the information that members of a niche market need to be able to satisfy their wants and needs for products and services.

How small can you go when defining a niche market? That depends very much on the product or service and the customers' spending power. If you were selling islands for example, the number of potential buyers will be small, but the commission earned on each sale might mean you only have to sell one island every two or three years to make serious money.

Equally, who would think your local graveyard would be a "niche market"? The fact is that those gravestones and the information they contain are of real interest to people tracing their family ancestry in your area, people who may not be able to visit the graveyard themselves because they live too far away. You could take photos of all the gravestones in local cemeteries and sell them on a CD via a website or eBay. Take the photos once and sell them over and over again.

When deciding what niche market to target, it's also important to remember that not every member of that niche market will be in buying mode. When people use the internet to find information, a proportion are simply gathering general information and have no intention of buying immediately. We will call them window shoppers, the "just looking" brigade.

Then there are those who have a good idea what they want and may want to consider their options – models, price, colours, alternatives - before making a purchase. We will call them contenders.

The third group are ready to buy. They know exactly what they want, probably right down to the model number, and want to know where they can buy it. We will call them dead certs.

So, for example, a website that provided information for people looking to buy a 3D TV might have reviews of the best ones available, together with maybe a price comparison between three major online retailers (all three of which will pay you a commission per 3D TV sold). Visitors in buyer mode would love this sort of information. For those who haven't quite made up their minds, the contenders, those reviews will prove interesting – maybe even interesting enough to convert them into buyers. You might like to add a page or two especially for them to let them know what 3D TVs are available with a quick feature comparison. Window shoppers might become contenders or even buyers after reading the above information, but they may simply be wondering what all the fuss about 3D television is anyway? That's when general information about why they should buy a 3D TV would be useful.

In an ideal world, our chosen niche market would contain just dead certs – and it is possible to target your website at dead certs by your choice of content. Unfortunately, we don't live in an ideal world and so contenders and window shoppers are also going to find their way to your website. That's not such a bad thing, especially if you cater for both in the hope of moving them further along the buying decision process, but it does mean that you will never be able to convert every visitor to a customer. Nowhere near it in fact. Not that it matters. Often a conversion rate that you can count on the fingers of one hand will be all that you need to make money.

Right in front of your nose

If you yourself are part of that niche market, so much the better. You will be instinctively in tune with its needs and wants.

Although we may not realise it, we all know things that others would pay us to know themselves. Whatever fills your heart with passion, whatever sets your mind on fire, whatever you would spend your time doing if you could do anything you wanted to do, day in day out, that's where to look for business ideas that will allow you to make money from what you know.

And what you know doesn't need to be rocket science to make you money. Life becomes more complicated by the day and more and more of us are looking for answers to questions like:

How do I lose weight?

How can I pass my exams?

How do I know this car I'm buying is not a ringer?

How can I improve my golf game?

What is the best 3D TV?

What should I know about buying property at auction?

How can I learn to cook?

How do I cook the perfect turkey for Christmas dinner?

How can I make more money than I currently do?

Where can I take the kids on a wet weekend?

Where can I find a red raincoat?

Where can I find a pink dog bowl?

These are the sort of questions I try to answer day in day out as part of my Plan B. People don't just want answers, they want them fast. If you can provide those answers when people want them, then there is a great deal of money to be made.

I build cheap, simple websites around the answers and then seek to turn visitors to those websites into money. You could quite easily do the same. If you think about it, every aspect of your life relies on information, much of which you take for granted. Your home town for example. You probably know it like the back of your hand. Where to eat, places to visit, times of buses, fantastic little shops tucked away in back streets. Visitors to your town would love to have access to that knowledge – and there's nothing to stop you sharing it with them.

Empire building

We have already seen how easily you can get a website up and running using WordPress. Once you familiarise yourself with WordPress and begin to customise it with a Theme and Plugins, you can create very professional looking websites. You may even find yourself moving on to one of the other free to use content management systems such as Joomla! (http://www.joomla.org), Drupal (http://www.drupal.org) or Mambo (http://mambo-foundation.org). As with WordPress, any of the above can be installed easily and quickly by using Fantastico on your website's cPanel, and although all involve learning curves, it's incredible the help and support you will receive from other users via their respective community forums.

If you are serious about empire building on the internet, I would seriously recommend that you take a website design course. Chances are there will be such a course on offer locally – ask at your library. HTML (HyperText Markup Language) is the most commonly used markup language for web pages. I know a lot of readers will be zoning out after reading that last sentence (I was too), but HTML is actually very easy to learn.

With What You See Is What You Get (WYSIWYG) design programs, your HTML knowledge can be virtually non-existent and you can still build HTML websites, as you will soon discover in the walkthrough chapter that will show you how to build a simple site using free WYSIWYG software.

W3schools (http://www.w3schools.com) offer free and easy to understand online tutorials covering all aspects of website development including HTML. It is a site well worth spending a few hours at, working through the tutorials to get an insight into how easy it is to write HTML code for web pages.

LearnDirect (http://www.learndirect.co.uk) also offer a 15 hour course entitled Web Publishing And Design With HTML

4.01 And XHTML that you complete online (XHTML is simply a stricter and cleaner version of HTML). At the time of writing, the course costs £50 and will teach you the basics of web design using HTML, XHTML and Cascading Style Sheets (CSS).

Although I do use WordPress on a number of my websites, most are built using basic HTML (I haven't even really graduated to Cascading Style Sheets – I use tables to layout pages). The software I use to build websites is Adobe Dreamweaver. It's not cheap to buy, but it is the industry standard software and it is a lot easier to use than you might think thanks to its WYSIWYG option alongside the code based design options. I barely scratch the surface of Dreamweaver's full capabilities when building my very basic websites, but again if you want to dig deeper there are courses and books aplenty to help you do so.

For a free alternative to Dreamweaver, consider either SeaMonkey, the software I'll be introducing you to shortly, or KompoZer (http://www.kompozer.net), another free web authoring system that combines web file management and WYSIWYG web page editing. Like SeaMonkey, KompoZer is designed to be extremely easy to use, making it ideal for those wanting to create websites with little or no knowledge of HTML or coding. SeaMonkey and KompoZer are actually very similar – I mention this just in case you already use KompoZer and were feeling obliged to switch to SeaMonkey. If you have a Mac, you might want to take a look at Rapidweaver (http://www.realmacsoftware.com), which is a lot cheaper than Dreamweaver, although not free.

Keeping it simple

Just as I've no idea how a car works and am just happy that it gets me from A to B, so it is with websites. My lack of web building expertise is not the drawback you might think. It means I can only build simple websites. And the good news is this. Simple websites make money.

Indeed, one common theme running through some of the most successful websites is this. Simplicity. Take Google for example. Go to www.google.co.uk. Does life get any easier? You'll find little more than a search box. Now take Yahoo. Go to www.yahoo.co.uk. Mmmmm. More clutter than your average loft space. It's no coincidence that the lean mean Google machine is the number one search engine in the UK by a long long way. As Google proves, less can be more.

Similarly go to the BBC's website - www.bbc.co.uk. Busy yes, but ordered, simple and clear. No sound effects, no Flash presentations, nothing but the facts m'am. And that's also true of eBay, Amazon and other hugely successful websites like Craigslist. Take a peek at www.craigslist.com. Does it look to you like:

a) a website designed by someone using free software?

b) an image free website circa 1997?

c) a website generating millions of dollars a year?

Take your pick because all three ring true. Craig Newmark started Craigslist in 1995 as a virtual noticeboard for San Francisco. Since then, it has grown into a true community, one that is now very much part of San Franciscan life and one that is now spreading its charms to other cities, both in the USA and abroad. London even has its very own Craigslist (http://www.craigslist.co.uk).

Craigslist is basically a classified ads site. The interesting thing is that it is free to post messages to every single category except for jobs. That's right, job ads are Craigslist.com's only source of income (unless of course you want to buy a t-shirt). There are no banner ads, no annoying pop ups, nothing. Just good old fashioned plain text and hyperlinks to even more good old fashioned plain text. But click on a few of those job text links and you start to see how Craigslist is pulling in the dollars. Each one is worth $75 to Craigslist and every day hundreds of job ads are posted. So many in fact that Craigslist earns hundreds of millions of dollars a year. The beauty is that all of the content on Craigslist is produced by the community. The posting of ads is fully automated, and thanks to the "flag for review" feature, the Craigslist staff don't even have to police every posting - the community does most of that work for them.

So why is it so successful? A number of reasons. First, making something look this simple is a real art. Start using Craigslist and you'll see that behind the basic look are some nifty features such as being able to use an anonymous Craigslist e-mail address that forwards messages on to you. Craigslist works incredibly hard at keeping it this simple.

Secondly, Craigslist has stayed the course. It's been online since 1995. I hear from people who have been online for only a matter of months and are throwing in the towel because they aren't making any money. These things can take time. This is something we talked about earlier in The Magic Of Numbers. Do you think Craigslist was making millions in 1996 or 1997? By keeping going, Craigslist has built a true community, one that allows it to not only charge $75 for job ads (far less than the likes of Monster by the way), but one that provides those advertising the jobs with some of the best job-seekers around.

For me that's the key to Craigslist's success. Another "me too" job website would have been trampled over years ago by the Monsters of this world. Who would bother visiting a website called Craigslist if it just listed a few jobs? But by building a community of users who can list pretty much anything they like (from a car for sale to a "casual encounter"), it is loved by hundreds of thousands of San Franciscans and millions of people worldwide.

Thirdly, Craigslist is a classic example of a niche website. It didn't need to serve the world. Since 1995 it has served just one city. San Francisco. True, there are now Craiglists for other cities both in the USA and elsewhere, but it serves them one at a time. The San Francisco site just serves San Francisco, New York's Craigslist just serves New York and so on.

Craigslist has simply evolved into something fantastic. There was no master plan to build a massive community and then use it to attract job advertisers. If there had been it probably would have failed. It's a blueprint for successful classified ad sites the world over. Including perhaps your own town or city where a similar site might make money for you. Maybe as part of a town or city guide website. Incidentally, even if there are already websites devoted to your town, that doesn't mean that there isn't room for another one. Go niche. Focus just on shopping, eating out, family days out, family history, even graveyards.

What makes a good website?

There are countless examples of websites that look like the finest of dining experiences and others that look worse than a dog's dinner. Good websites. Bad websites. But which are which? What exactly makes a good website?

If you agree that a website should serve a purpose, a good website would be one that delivers on that aim. If that purpose is to deliver X amount of leads a month or Y number of sales, then a website's ability to do just that should determine whether it's good or bad. If its sole purpose is to look pretty or make use of every bell and whistle available, then let it be judged on those grounds.

Problems arise when you go down the beauty pageant route in terms of design, and then lose sight of the real purpose of having a website in the first place. Naturally, you would want a website to portray a positive image of your business (it is after all the internet equivalent of a shop window), but unless the purpose of a website (delivering leads, sales, whatever) is stitched into the very fabric of the site's design, it's unlikely to serve its purpose fully. The Web is awash with beautiful looking websites that simply don't deliver what they might, simply because they've been built for all the wrong reasons.

When it comes to Plan B, I only build websites and add content to them for one reason. To make money. So for me, a website that does that is good. A website that doesn't is bad. And although I do my best to avoid dog's dinners, for me what a site looks like and how many fancy features it has comes a distant second to how much money it makes.

Take two

When you start looking at websites in terms of the bottom line (as in how much it makes you), you can tell how good or bad a website is by looking at just two figures. The number of unique visitors the website attracts every month and how many of those visitors convert. By convert I mean how many of those visitors buy something, book an appointment, sign up for a newsletter – whatever you require them to do to fulfil the purpose of your website. If you are selling books, you will want sales. If you are selling conservatories, you might want appointments instead. If you are selling financial services, you might want newsletter sign ups.

Supposing for a moment that you sell conservatories and the main purpose of your website is to get visitors to it to book appointments. The more appointments, the more chances for you to sell a conservatory. A good website would be getting you those appointments. A bad website wouldn't.

To increase the number of appointments booked via your website there are two things you can do: Increase the number of visitors to your website (and by visitors I mean targeted visitors, as in people genuinely looking to buy a conservatory) or increase the conversion rate so that more of those visitors book an appointment. Best of all, do both. Do both by making sure that every aspect of your website is working to achieve those two aims, rather than showing off the talents of a web designer.

Let's go gardening

Grab your gardening gloves because we're going to do a bit of gardening. Earlier, I said that a website is like a flower and I just want to expand on that thought because it encompasses everything you need to know about building simple but effective websites.

Your first task is to plant your website in good soil. Your choice of domain name is part of that, but there's a whole chapter regarding domain names coming up so I won't repeat myself here. Arguably more important is the website's actual design. If you are using WordPress or a similar content management system, much of the design will be taken care of by your choice of Theme or skin. If you are creating your own websites from scratch, remember the old adage to keep it simple:

● Do not fill your pages with unwanted garbage like counters, tacky animated gifs and unnecessary javascripts

● Make sure your site is primarily text and image based

● Use video and sound only when it is absolutely necessary

● The background should be white, text should be black, links should be blue (don't underline any other text)

● Use colour wisely and sparingly: the idea is to generate money, not give visitors sore eyes and headaches

● Use plain simple readable fonts that are on virtually every computer: Arial, Times New Roman, Courier New, Helvetica

● Check that your website looks like you want it to in the most commonly used browsers: Internet Explorer, Firefox, Safari,

Chrome and Opera

A professional looking logo can add a great deal to the appearance of a website. There are a number of logo companies offering to design a logo for you for a few pounds upwards, but when you run a number of websites, logo and indeed banner design can become very expensive - unless you can do it yourself. The good news is that you can easily do it yourself.

The first thing you will need to get is Selteco Bannershop™ GIF Animator V5.0 for Windows which is available via download for £30 (or thereabouts – it is actually priced in dollars) from Selteco's website at www.selteco.com. This is a superb piece of software that quickly and easily allows you to create logos, buttons and banners, that include both text and graphics. It is so easy to use, you'll be producing logos and banners in minutes. Any shape. Any size.

Animating banners is just as easy. Bannershop creates an animated effect by assigning each image a frame that is timed to be replaced by the next frame at set intervals in a continuous loop (you can change the duration that each frame appears for and can stop the loop whenever you want). The fonts you can use are only limited by the ones you have installed on your computer (as part of an image they will appear as intended). I tend to stick to bold plain typefaces that can easily be read.

As for images, Bannershop allows you to import images from your own files or collections. If you're wondering where you'll get exactly the right image you require, time after time, look no further than Clipart.com (http://www.clipart.com). Here you'll find over ten million pieces of clip art, web art, photos, fonts and even sounds - all royalty free and fully searchable. Within minutes you'll be able to find exactly what you are looking for - plus plenty of other options you might not have even considered without such a vast selection at your disposal.

There are no download limits (use as many images as you want) and no per use fee either. You can buy unlimited access to

Clipart.com for anything from a week to a year (a week will cost you US$14.95, a year US$159.95). The beauty is that you can look through the entire collection before paying a cent. This allows you to prepare the groundwork for several projects, join for a week, and get everything you need for US$14.95.

With Bannershop and Clipart.com, you'll be producing quality logos, banners and buttons in no time. You can either use them for your own websites or set up a small business offering your new found skills to other webmasters.

To start your own logo and banner design business simply buy a domain name and a basic hosting package, and set up stall. You will only need a home page, an about page, pricing page and a sample page to get things going. At the very least you will have acquired software and developed a new skill to apply to your own web based ventures, but with some web based design companies charging hundreds of dollars for logos that you could very easily do in minutes, the potential is definitely there to develop an extra stream of income, perhaps even a full-time one if you find you have a flair for this sort of thing. Just another idea.

Read all about it

After planting it in good soil, you must also ensure that your website has all the right nutrients. For nutrients read quality unique content that is updated regularly. For a niche website with few competitors you will not need to update it as much as you will a website fighting for its life in a very competitive market. For the latter, you will need to provide fresh content every few days, maybe daily, definitely weekly. For the former, weekly, maybe monthly updates will suffice. Make sure all of your websites remain fresh and relevant whatever the level of competition.

Use the Google Keyword Tool for guidance with regards initial content if you are stuck for ideas. Plan your content around what people are already searching the internet for. Once your site is established you can also plunder your own visitor statistics to see what brings visitors to your site and you can then tailor more content for them.

When preparing content for a website it's really important to bear in mind that people don't read web pages in the same way that they read printed pages. People don't actually read web content. They scan it quickly, stopping only when something grabs their interest. Then - click – and they are somewhere else entirely. That's why brochure style websites are nowhere near as effective as their offline counterparts. So you've got to draw them in with web specific techniques. Grab their attention by using:

- Lots of white space

- Headings and sub-headings

- Bullet points

- Short sentences

- Short paragraphs

- Bold text to highlight keywords

- Spell-checked plain English

Information at the top of each page – heading, first paragraph – should make it very clear what the page is about. If it is of interest, the reader is then more likely to read what follows. The further down a page, the more in-depth the information can become. Really detailed information can be on supplementary pages if need be. The idea is to provide content that quickly and effortlessly delivers your visitor to where you want them to be. Clicking on the Buy It Now button. Signing up for your newsletter. Whatever you want them to do, make it fantastically easy for them to do it.

Web users spend about 80% of their time looking at content above the fold. It's not that they won't scroll down, but if and when they do, eye tracking research has shown that they pay far less attention to the content below the fold.

The advice that usually accompanies the above is to keep your pages short too. That's nonsense. There is nothing wrong with long pages, nothing at all, providing that the content is web friendly. If you want proof that long pages work, simply visit Amazon.co.uk. Amazon have spent millions on understanding what works and what doesn't when it comes to selling online and most of their pages go on and on and on.

That's how Amazon customers like it. The thing to remember here is that there are an awful lot of Amazon customers out there and you could do a lot worse than follow Amazon's example, not least because it will make an awful lot of people comfortable on your website too. Notice too that despite the very long pages, the navigation and search box at the top remains constant, the positioning of the Add To Basket button remains constant. All are above the fold in terms of visibility – there is no scrolling required to find them.

Page consistency across a website rocks online. Remember, visitors won't necessarily arrive at one of your pages from your homepage. The search engines might bring them directly to it. That's why it's important to let them know where they are. Don't worry about repeating information about your site on every page. As long as it is done sensibly (header with logo, constant and clear navigation to key areas of your website, side bars with links to other relevant content), it will be appreciated by visitors.

It could be that you want to create something with more functionality than a basic website, but don't have the skills to do it. Those skills may come in time, but until then there are always options. If you are using WordPress or another content management system (CMS) to build your website, chances are that what you are looking for is already available, whether free of charge or for a small fee. In fact, however you are building your websites, there are scripts and programs available to do almost anything you can think of. You can either search online for what you want or check out sites like Hot Scripts (http//hotscripts.com) and JavaScript (http://www.javascript.com).

For a custom solution, you will find freelance developers galore at websites like Guru Employer (http://www.guru.com), Elance (http://www.elance.com) and vWorker (formerly known as Rentacoder and now at http://www.vworker.com). Through sites like these, it is possible to hire excellent freelancers at surprisingly low prices, largely because you have developers from around the world looking for business, including those from countries where the cost of living is much lower than it is in the UK. The key to success on sites like this is to know exactly what you want and to communicate it clearly to those you want to work with. Vague briefs will almost certainly result in disappointment.

Let the sun shine

Now you need to make sure your content gets plenty of sun. Your content will play a big part when it comes to search engine traffic so it's important to optimise it to get the best results. Again, there's an entire chapter on its way dedicated to Search Engine Optimisation (SEO), but a few things are worth mentioning here.

You should make sure that the content of each page includes the keywords and keyword phrases that you want the search engines to use to rank each page, but – and it's a big but – do not overdo it, especially if it's at the expense of the quality of the content and the human visitors who will have to read it. Search engines don't like keyword stuffing and neither do humans. In fact, here's a tip you would do well to remember. Write for humans first, humans second and search engines third.

If your content is good enough, press coverage and links from other websites will naturally follow. Press releases might help move things along, but only if you genuinely have something of interest to send out. If what you have to say is not genuinely newsworthy, forget it.

You can further promote your site by becoming active in related forums (don't spam them; participate in them, become a respected member and only ever soft sell your site when truly appropriate or via signatures). As you'll discover in the chapter on Search Engine Optimisation, I'm no fan of sending begging e-mails to other webmasters asking to swap links. It's so badly used and abused that you might as well be sending out e-mails selling Viagra (I get literally hundreds of link exchange e-mails every week and so do most webmasters with established sites).

Don't forget about internal links either. Make sure that your content is well organised and use categories to divide content on larger sites. Content Management Systems like WordPress take care of most of this for you, but if you are building websites yourself, it is down to you to make sure your website is easily navigated. Make sure that each page has an internal link to at least one other on the site and that it is never more than three links away from your home page. If your homepage is the top level, make key pages and category pages level two and less important pages level three. Use keywords in links too where practical rather than using phrases like "click here" or "more". Keywords in external and internal links help the search engines identify and rank the pages that they link to.

Before long you will have people peering over your garden wall and this is where it gets really interesting. Turning those visitors into money.

Show me the money

"There are more opportunities today than there have ever been, but - and this is the biggest bit - if people don't recognise them, can't exploit them, don't have the capacity, the education, the confidence and the self belief then it doesn't matter how many opportunities there are."
Tom Hunter

Hopefully by now you are sold on the idea of Plan B. You like the idea of the low start up costs of making money online. You like the idea of working less hours and of course you love the idea of making money not only while you're working, but for hours, days, months, even years, after you've done that work.

But where exactly is this money going to come from? You will be pleased to hear that there are lots of ways to monetise information, even if you are giving the stuff away, and the remainder of this book is going to be largely dedicated to showing you exactly how.

If this is a completely new world to you, it may all seem overwhelming at first glance. A lot like learning to drive or using a computer for the first time. You will soon get into the swing of things though. Making money from information can be as easy as adding a snippet of code to a web page.

Here's how people like you are making money from small niche information websites:

Pay at the door

If you think of niche websites as the online equivalent of specialist magazines or local newspapers, you could go down the route of charging visitors to view the information on your website or at least parts of it. *The Times* and *Sunday Times* will be charging visitors to read their online content by the time you read this. It will inevitably mean far fewer online readers, but not necessarily less revenue than the sites are currently making. One report I read suggested that even if only 10% of those who visited the website while it was free are willing to pay for that same content, News Corp will be quids in. Other websites, such as *The Economist*, have successfully charged for premium online content for years now.

It would be a mistake to think that you have to be Rupert Murdoch to charge people to view pages on a website. Premium content comes in many shapes and forms. John Clare for example runs a niche property website that specialises in the unique and unusual (http://www.property.org.uk/unique). Some of the properties are available for all to see, but there are also member only pages that feature even more properties for sale. Access to the restricted pages costs £35 a year. I've no idea how many people have joined, but John only needs 1,000 to do so to earn £35,000 a year.

Creating a members only area of a standard website is as easy as password-protecting the directory that contains the pages you want visitors to pay to see. This can be done simply and easily by using the Password Protect Directories facility that you will find under Security on your website's cPanel (part of your website's hosting package). You could then provide the password to those who pay you. Similarly, if you are using WordPress, there are Plugins available that will password-protect certain pages or categories.

For a more professional solution and to automate the entire process you could use off the shelf software such as MCP4 (formerly Membership Client Pro) which costs US$120 a year including installation or a US$200 one-off fee if you don't require much hand-holding (http://www.mcp4.com). Subhub is another option (http://www.subhub.com). It provides managed membership software that allows you to build and manage your own membership site and then charge for access to your own premium content including articles, a forum, digital downloads, video and audio. It costs from £49.97 per month.

Sell Ad Space

Of course there are also magazines and newspapers that have no cover price – the freebies that get shoved through your letterbox or are piled up high at train stations and airports. Advertising revenue is what keeps the printing presses rolling. You can go down this road too by selling advertising space on your website.

Again, don't think you have to have millions of visitors coming to a website every month for advertisers to be interested. Many would rather talk directly to much smaller niche markets: specialist websites with a very focused audience give them the opportunity to do just that.

At the very least you will need a rate card page on your website, giving advertising rates. Potential advertisers want to know that they will earn more in revenue than it will cost them to advertise so give them the relevant facts and figures regarding your website that will help convince them.

There are three basic online advertising models:

● **Per impression** This is where you charge advertisers every time their advertisement is displayed (I nearly wrote viewed, but just because it appears on a page doesn't mean it's been seen). Advertisers are normally charged per thousand impressions – something that is known as Cost Per Thousand or CPM in the trade (slightly confusingly, but the M refers to the Roman numeral for thousand). This is an increasingly hard sell in my opinion, especially for smaller websites. I've seen it described as the online equivalent of junk mail and I like that analogy.

- **Per click** This is where you charge advertisers every time their advertisement is clicked. Again, this is a hard sell, not least because advertisers are more likely to put their trust in something like a Google AdWords campaign than you (no offence meant). That's also why it's a lot easier to let the likes of Google handle your Cost Per Click (CPC) and Pay Per Click (PPC) advertising and we'll talk about Google AdSense in depth shortly.

- **Per time period** This is where you charge advertisers to display their advertisement for a specific time period, usually a month or a year. If you are going to make money selling advertising directly, this is how you are most likely going to be able to do it. Advertisers will want to know the number of unique visitors that the site attracts, together with any other relevant information relating to your audience, and your advertising rates.

Advertisers will expect to pay more for premium positions (home page, above the fold, within rather than around content) and will expect to be able to choose from one or more industry standard banner sizes.

Advertising banners today come in all shapes and sizes, but the majority conform to industry standards and you would do well to design your pages with these sizes in mind. It means that advertisers do not need to go to the expense of creating custom size banners when they probably have standard sizes ones already available. The most popular ones (measured in pixels) are 468x60 and 120x600 in size. Other common sizes are shown opposite, although different size banners are increasingly being used where possible to help advertisers stand out from the crowd.

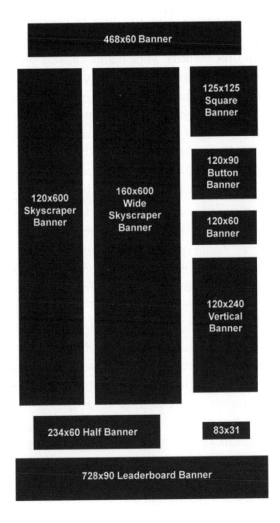

Above: the most commonly used banner sizes

Sites that can attract a number of advertisers can sell the same ad space several times over by using what is known as a rotating banner. This is also known as Share Of Voice, where a number of ads are shown in rotation, most commonly in premium positions. At the time of writing, you could buy leaderboard banner advertising on the homepage of *The Independent* newspaper's website for 28 days for the rate card price of £395, but you would share the space with up to 14 other advertisers on strict rotation. In other words, your banner advertisement would appear once every 14 times the homepage was viewed over those 28 days (*The Independent* hopes to sell as many of those 14 slots as possible). You can get ad rotator scripts for free that can be used on websites (Google it) and there are also free Plugins available for WordPress and other free content management software.

You can also sell text advertising alongside banner advertising. This is often very attractive to advertisers because there is no text equivalent of "banner blindness" (a lot of surfers intuitively ignore banners because they dismiss them as advertising and therefore not genuine content). Text ads are more flexible too, being able to appear virtually anywhere on a page.

A word of warning when selling ad space, particularly text ads. What you are effectively doing is selling links, something that Google and other search engines frown upon because links are used as part of the formula to rank search results. By buying links, some webmasters have sought to artificially boost their rankings and this has resulted in Google penalising both those selling and buying links. That's not to say that selling advertising or even links is unethical. Just make sure you do it by not offending the search engine gods. This is easily done by using the nofollow attribute in your page's code:

```
<a href="www.bbc.co.uk" rel="nofollow"> click here</a>
```

That code would link to www.bbc.co.uk, allowing visitors to click on it and visit the BBC website. At the same time, search engine robots would not follow the link and so no unfair advantage would be gained in terms of that link helping to boost the BBC's search engine rankings.

Depending on how much of your time you want to devote to raising money via advertising revenue, you have a number of options open to you:

● Actively sell advertising space by approaching businesses and others that you think would be interested in advertising on your website. You can do this in person, by phone or by e-mail.

● Get someone else to sell advertising for you. There are a number of companies that specialise in selling ad space on websites and blogs in return for a commission, companies like Blogvertise (http://www.blogvertise.com), Smorty (http://www.smorty.com), Blogads (http://www.blogads.com) and the very innovative Project Wonderful (http://www.projectwonderful.com).

● Let visitors to your website know that you accept advertising by including a rate card and other relevant information regarding traffic on a dedicated page on your website (see how other webmasters do this when surfing the Web yourself).

● Employ any combination of the above.

Google AdSense

You can also allow Google to sell your advertising space for you via its Google AdSense program. Google sells advertising on your behalf mostly on a Cost Per Click basis. You simply add a few lines of code where you want text and image ads to appear and leave the rest to the Big G. So successful can this be that it deserves a chapter to itself and you'll find one later in this book. There are alternatives to Google AdSense that might be worth considering, particularly if your website is aimed at a US audience, including Chitika (http://www.chitika.com) and Adbrite (http://www.adbrite.com). Yahoo's Publisher Network which you may still see mentioned on the Web was closed in April, 2010.

Affiliate Marketing

Instead of being paid a flat rate per advertisement that you display on your website, you could charge advertisers only when a sale or similar action resulted from an ad appearing on your site. Businesses then only pay you when their advertising is successful. Not surprisingly they love the idea. So much so that a whole industry has grown up around it called affiliate marketing. Books have been written on affiliate marketing, but to whet your appetite I have devoted a chapter to it that you will come to in due course.

Digital Products

As well as selling other companies' products and services, you can also sell digital products such as how to e-books. The big advantage of selling digital products is the generally very high commission rates paid on sales: the number one source of digital products, Clickbank (http://www.clickbank.com), offers commissions of up to 75% on sales. To give you some idea of the size of the market for digital products, Clickbank has sold an incredible one and a half billion dollars worth and counting. There is also nothing stopping you creating your own niche digital products to sell on your own website and via Clickbank's army of affiliates.

What makes digital products so attractive is that the cost of producing and distributing each additional unit is virtually zero. You are effectively selling the same product – a digital file – over and over again without any additional production costs. Similarly, distribution via a download button is also virtually zero. Once you have recouped the initial investment of producing the digital product in the first place, every sale thereafter is virtually pure profit. Hence the ability to pay commission rates of up to 75% via Clickbank. You can also sell digital e-books via Amazon's Kindle Program where you will keep 70% of the cover price or through other self-publishing websites like Lulu (http://www.lulu.com).

Listings

If you run a property for sale website, you can charge individuals and indeed estate agents to list their property with you. Similarly, if you create a jobs related website you could charge employees and recruitment agencies to advertise jobs on your website. A puppy website could charge breeders a listing fee to list puppies for sale. A classified ad website could charge per ad. A specialist auction site per listing. If you have ideas along these lines, there are website templates and scripts aplenty, including WordPress Themes and Plugins, that will help you automate much or all of the listing and payment process for listing style websites. Some you will have to pay for, others are free to use. As always, use Google to find them.

A quick word about property websites in particular. Bear in mind that certain professions are bound by laws. For example, there are few restrictions to you opening a gift shop in the UK, but you wouldn't expect to be able to open a doctor's surgery or a solicitor's office without having the appropriate qualifications for doing so and without having to work within a legal framework. So it is with certain types of websites too. If you are starting a property website, make sure you understand your obligations under the relevant legislation, especially the Estate Agents Act.

Directory

In a similar vein to listings, you could create a directory, either as a website in its own right or as part of a website. A good idea is to offer a free basic directory entry, at least initially, so as to help populate the directory and make it useful. That will in turn attract traffic and those listed in the directory will increasingly benefit. Once established, you could introduce a paid premium directory entry that might give better positioning on a page or the ability to add extra information to their entry to make it stand out.

Alternatively, you could create a directory where all entries earned you a commission per booking via affiliate marketing. This would be easy to do for hotels for example given the large number of travel companies, including hotel chains, who will pay you a commission per booking.

Newsletters

You are not limited to selling advertising space on web pages. If you offer visitors the opportunity to sign up to a regular newsletter or for e-mail updates, you may well be able to develop a very lucrative income stream by selling advertising space or including affiliate offers. Voucher code websites will inundate you with e-mails giving you discount codes to use at online retailers simply because they earn a commission for every sale made.

Sponsorship

As well as selling advertising space, you can offer advertisers the opportunity to sponsor a website or sections of it. A website dedicated to training puppies for example may find a dog food company that would be interested in being associated with it by way of sponsorship. Alternatively you may find a company that is willing to provide prizes for a competition, or freebies for your visitors, in return for publicity.

Not all websites are equally suited to selling advertising space and sponsorship may well be the answer in such cases. Forums are a notoriously difficult sell to advertisers, but sponsorship opportunities might be of greater interest. For example, if you had an overseas property forum, there is every chance that a company that runs overseas property fairs would be willing to "sponsor" the forum (or sections of it) to promote their fairs. Work hard to give potential sponsors value for money without adversely affecting your forum users' experience and you can create a win-win situation for all concerned.

Donations

If you are providing valuable information free of charge to your visitors, you can always ask them to donate to the running costs of the website. One advantage of the donation route over selling advertising is that your content can be seen not to be influenced by advertisers, something that would be very important for certain types of sites: those offering impartial stock market advice for example.

If you have a Paypal account (sign up for one at http://www.paypal.co.uk), not only will you have the ability to accept payment for goods and services (including advertising), but you will be given access to Donate buttons that you can place on your website.

For those using WordPress as a platform for websites, there is a great Buy Me A Beer Plugin that works with Paypal (for non-drinkers, there is a Buy Me A Coffee alternative). For WordPress and any other website, you might also want to take a look at the free to use Chipin widget (http://www.chipin.com).

Consultancy

Your website may well be the perfect springboard for you to get consultancy or similar work in your chosen niche. A successful website can help underline your expertise in a particular field and from that you may be able to offer consultancy services. Similarly, you may be asked to speak at seminars or conferences, or you could even arrange your own, with your website being your primary marketing tool.

Write A Book

If your website proves successful and you become something of an authority figure in your niche, there may be an opportunity to write a book or produce a DVD for the same market. With digital printing allowing you to print one copy of a book at a time if need be, the financial outlay is tiny compared to the days of the traditional printing press (that said, for larger print runs of a thousand or more copies, it is well worth getting a quote from a printer). Websites like Lulu (http://www.lulu.com), Wordclay (http://www.wordclay.com) and Blurb (http://www.blurb.com) can help realise your publishing dreams. The book you hold in your hand was initially produced using Lulu.

Merchandise

If one or more of your websites lends itself to selling merchandise, you could make money from selling t-shirts, caps, badges and other related products with your website branding on them. Great for building visitor loyalty and for promoting the site too.

If you are selling merchandise, or anything else for that matter that requires you to receive money directly from a customer, there are various readily available options open to you. It was once the case that the only way to accept credit card and debit payments was with what is called a merchant account. Traditionally, merchant accounts were only available to established businesses through banks, and small start-up enterprises found it hard to get one. What's more, the costs involved in having a merchant account and the length of contract required were often prohibitive to small start-ups.

The internet has totally changed the ball game though. Banks and other merchant account providers have had to move with the times, providing accounts for brand new start-up internet companies that simply couldn't begin trading without them. Internet payment systems were also quickly developed to help oil the wheels of e-commerce, in competition with traditional providers, and suddenly the ability to accept credit card payments was thrown open to even the smallest of enterprises.

The most successful of the new breed of internet payment systems is Paypal, its number one position fuelled by online auctions (Paypal is owned by eBay and millions of eBay users have Paypal accounts).

When it comes to accepting credit card payments online, Paypal is often seen as a poor man's choice - a perception that is often based on a misunderstanding of what Paypal actually offers. One falsehood that is repeated time after time is that if you use Paypal to process your credit card payments, you can only accept payments from people who already have a Paypal account. This simply isn't the case. If you have either a business account or a premier account with Paypal (both are free to set up at www.paypal.co.uk), you can accept payment from anyone with a valid credit or debit card. And the good news is that includes American Express as well as Visa, MasterCard, Visa Delta, Visa Electron, Maestro and Switch. If you have a number of small websites, you can also use one Paypal account to process payments for up to eight of them.

For a small entrepreneur looking to start accepting payments online immediately, Paypal takes some beating. I also use Google Checkout (https://checkout.google.com/seller/) which allows me to process card payments from Visa (including Visa Electron), MasterCard and Maestro (including Switch/Solo). Like Paypal, there are no monthly charges and it is free to join. If you do want a full blown merchant account, and the monthly fee that goes with it, RBS Worldplay is the number one choice in the UK for online sales (http://www.rbsworldpay.com). For instantly delivered digital products, definitely consider Clickbank for both payment processing and marketing (http://www.clickbank.com).

Sell The Website

There is a thriving market for websites and you could always cash in by selling one or more of yours. An established website can be a very valuable piece of real estate. Some people buy a domain name, add a website to it, get it going, and then sell it within weeks or months of launch. Others sell established websites after years of development. The price you get will depend on a number of factors including visitors numbers and earnings. There are also those who buy abandoned or underperforming websites, give them a lick of paint, and then flip them. Domain name forums are a good place to sell them as are sites like Sitepoint (http://www.sitepoint.com).

Mix And Match

The beauty of virtually all websites is that you won't be limited to using just one of the above income streams. Any website might lend itself to developing any number of income streams. A travel website for example might sell advertising directly, incorporate Google AdSense and affiliate marketing, have a directory with paid entries, offer visitors a weekly newsletter, and produce its own range of digital travel e-books. Mix and match until your heart's content.

The information that you create and then offer in the form of web pages acts as the hook that will attract the fish to your website. Once there, any of the above will act as bait and if any of those fish bite, you will make money. The better the information, the more fish you will attract, and the more chances you will have to make money.

What's in a name?

"A good name is better than precious ointment."
Ecclesiastes 7:1

For me, the inspiration for a new website usually comes in one of two ways. Either I have an idea and then I look for a domain name to bring it to life. Or I come across a domain name that is either available to register or is for sale and it gives me the idea. Whichever happens, a domain name will always be central to my plans. Every website needs a domain name, and whereas I spend next to nothing on marketing my websites, I am willing to pay thousands of pounds for the right domain name - and do exactly that two or three times a year.

According to DNJournal (http://www.dnjournal.com), the online journal for the domain name industry, there were no less than eight reported seven figure sales for 2009 - Toys.com (US$5,1Million), Candy.com (US$3 million), Fly.com (US$1.76 million), Auction.com (US$1.7 million), Ticket.com (US$1.525 million), Russia.com (US$1.5 million), Call.com (US$1.1

million) and Webcam.com (US$1.02 million). No doubt there were others. Many big money domain name sales go unreported due to non-disclosure agreements between buyer and seller. And all this at a time when the world was in the grip of a global recession.

Although not quite in the dotcom league, there have been some big money .co.uk sales during the last couple of years too. Take a look at Domain Prices (http://www.domainprices.co.uk) and you'll find page after page of reported UK domain name sales (again the vast majority go unreported). Cruises.co.uk sold for an eye-watering £560,000 in February, 2008, making it the most expensive UK domain name on record to date. In July of the same year, Phones.co.uk changed hands for £175,000. Both trumped the previous biggest sale, Recycle.co.uk, which sold for £150,000 in September, 2007. Other six figure sales of late include Software.co.uk (£150,000), Sport.co.uk (£135,000), OnlineCasino.co.uk (£100,000), HorseRacing.co.uk (£100,000), Ink.co.uk (£111,000) and Mobile.co.uk (£120,000).

Why would anyone in their right mind pay such huge sums for domain names that once upon a time were registered for just a few dollars or pounds? Why would someone like me, who regularly launches websites for just a few pounds, spend more on a domain name than I have ever spent on a car for example? The likes of eBay, Google, Facebook, YouTube and MySpace seem to have done very well thank you very much without the need to splash out fortunes, large and small, on domain names, so why do names regularly change hands for such large sums?

All aboard Cruises.co.uk

Let's take a closer look at Cruises.co.uk. It was actually bought by Cruise.co.uk, an internet based company that specialises in, you guessed it, cruises. Together, Cruise.co.uk and Cruises.co.uk are what are known as category killers – domain names that define an industry or market. £560,000 may seem like a huge sum to pay for a domain name, especially when you already own a category killer, but it's likely to prove a very shrewd investment.

A little knowledge of the cruise industry, and the money it generates, explains all you need to know about the value of Cruises.co.uk to Cruise.co.uk. According to the Passenger Shipping Association, around one and a half million Brits take a cruise each year and that number is forecast to be nearer three million by 2012. Agents like Cruise.co.uk will be paid a commission of around 15% for each cruise sold. With a large slice of that passed on to customers by way of discounts, the net commission will usually be closer to 5%.

With the industry in the UK now worth over two billion pounds, there's a lot of potential commission to be earned. Indeed, with the average price paid for a cruise booked in the UK standing at £1,409 in 2009, an agent will be earning an average of at least £70 per cruise sold. Which means the new owners of Cruises.co.uk will need it to sell 8,000 cruises for it to pay for itself. It's currently used as a cruise forum with over 36,000 members, many of whom will be cruise regulars. Between them, I've no doubt that they will book thousands of cruises each and every year. That's a fantastic captive audience to sell cruise tickets too, and thanks to the soft branding of the website, a lot will be buying those tickets via Cruise.co.uk.

A successful forum also scores high in "stickiness", the ability of a website to not only attract visitors, but to keep them on the site for longer and to keep them coming back for more. The result in this case? More opportunities to sell cruises. Equally important, a popular forum means page after page of fresh content written almost exclusively by visitors completely free of charge. Each and every forum post will end up in search engine databases and will serve to attract others to the forum via the search results. Again, that will lead to more opportunities to sell cruises.

Talking of search engines, there is a huge marketing benefit to having two websites, one targeting the keyword "cruise" and another targeting the keyword "cruises". Enter both into Google and you will see that different results are returned for each search. To benefit from this, it's important that both sites have different content because duplicate content is not likely to rank well in search results. That happens in spades when one site is a forum and the other is an online travel agent (and in my eyes one of the best in terms of demonstrating a real understanding of internet marketing so it's well worth visiting from a Plan B point of view).

By bagging a second category killer, Cruise.co.uk were also denying a competitor the opportunity to buy it. A defensive purchase of this nature might itself be considered grounds for spending over half a million on a domain name. That might sound crazy, but the less competition, the more money you will make, and there's no doubt that a rival company trading as Cruises.co.uk would have been stiff competition.

Back in the late Sixties and early Seventies, the reggae music market in the UK was dominated by two record labels, Trojan and Pama. A big part of their success was directly down to the fact that they effectively crowded the market with sub-labels. Any rival wasn't just competing against Trojan and Pama for sales, but the myriad of labels that both companies used to release records - the likes of Attack, Harry J and Downbeat in the case of Trojan and the likes of Camel, NuBeat and Escort in the case of Pama.

A similar tactic can be used online today by defensively registering or buying domain names that relate to a particular market. I do it all the time. It's impossible to cover all bases, but if you are in control of key domain names relating to your industry or market it can only be to your benefit. Whether you develop them or not doesn't matter. The point is you are preventing others from doing so. It's also very easy to point multiple domains at one website (if your hosting comes with cPanel, look for the Parked Domains icon).

Could the buyers of Cruises.co.uk not have simply added a forum to their existing website and spent the money elsewhere in growing their business? Definitely, perhaps with equal success, but Cruises.co.uk was obviously central to their marketing strategy going forward.

Talking telephone numbers

Phones.co.uk is yet another category killer. It was bought by BuyMobilePhones.net, the largest independently owned web-based mobile phone retailer in the UK and a company with annual sales of over £30 million. Given that level of turnover, £175,000 isn't a large sum of money for a name that does exactly what it says on the tin (to borrow a phrase from Ronseal). I would expect the BuyMobilePhones.net website to be rebranded as Phones.co.uk at some point in the near future. The current name is something of a mouthful and easily confused with similar sounding domain names. I've seen it advertised on pitch side hoardings at football matches, presumably at a cost of thousands of pounds, and am always left wondering how many people who see it will remember it correctly after the final whistle blows. Probably as many as pop into the corner shop on the way home to buy some Rainham Steel.

An interesting thing about Phones.co.uk is that it was sold by James Dale who had himself bought the domain name six months earlier for £49,500. While you turn green with envy over the £125,500 he made by flipping a domain name, I'll just slip into the conversation that two other domains names that I mentioned previously, HorseRacing.co.uk and OnlineCasino.co.uk, were also sold by James. For every buyer, there has to be a seller, and domain names have made some fortunate people very rich indeed.

What about eBay, Facebook, Google?

What about the fact that the biggest online success stories use domain names that had no intrinsic value whatsoever when first registered? Names like eBay, Google and Facebook. When considering the success of a company like eBay, it has to be remembered that the idea and its execution were so brilliant that they would have enjoyed the same success irrespective of the domain name chosen. Truth be told, if you are about to launch the next giant of the internet, you too can afford to play fast and loose with your choice of domain name.

The vast majority of us are never going to be in that position however. Chances are that your website will be going head to head with others in your chosen niche (almost certainly from the off and definitely in the future) and you will have to use every trick in the book to not only differentiate your website, but to make it easy to find among all the noise. In the vast majority of cases, a good domain name can certainly bring some extra magic to the table. That's why you might find yourself paying a large sum of money for a domain name one day – or even be in receipt of a life changing sum by selling one.

What exactly is a domain name anyway?

For a website to be found on the worldwide web it will need to have a domain name. It's really a shortcut to a complex series of numbers (an IP address) that you'd need to remember if domain names had not been introduced. For example, it's much easier to remember Entrepreneur.co.uk than it is the corresponding ip address, 208.76.80.100.

Disney's web address or domain name is Disney.com. Everyone can find it simply by typing http://www.disney.com into their internet browser. You'll find the BBC's website at http://www.bbc.co.uk and *The Independent*'s website at http://www.independent.co.uk (incidentally, http stands for hypertext transfer protocol and it acts as a conduit between the server hosting a website and the internet browser on your computer so that pages can be downloaded for you to view them). Your domain name also allows e-mails to be sent directly to you - mickey@disney.com for example.

Little more than a decade ago, you could have had your pick of domain names. As recently as 1994, nobody had thought of registering McDonalds.com. Around this time, however, speculators who saw the potential of both the internet and the value of having a great domain name, started buying up names at ever increasing rates. This virtual goldrush was fuelled by news that domain names were changing hands for incredible sums of money. Individuals could register a domain for US$100 (it costs much less to do so today) and sell it on for many times that price. Compaq paid US$3.35 million in 1998 for the domain name AltaVista.com (before the days of Google domination, AltaVista was one of the world's leading search engines, but prior to the purchase of AltaVista.com, it was located at www.digital.com/altavista).

Business.com was sold for an amazing US$7.5 million in 1999 to eCompanies in a cash and stock deal. The seller, Marc Ostrofsky, had himself bought it in April, 1997, for US$150,000, a sum believed to be the most ever spent on a domain name at the time (eCompanies have since sold the name and the website they built on it for US$345 million). Wine.com sold for US$2.9 million, Autos.com for US$2.2 million, and so the gravy train rolled on until the domain name goldrush came to a temporary end when the dotcom stock market bubble burst in 2000.

Since then of course, the worldwide web has become an integral part of our way of life and the internet has gone on to justify the premature euphoria that defined the late Nineties. Even so, only a tiny proportion of the millions of domain names registered have ever been sold for six or seven figure sums. That hasn't stopped domain name buyers registering every single commonly used word in the dictionary - and then some. Evidently, there is still a lot of speculation going on. There are companies today with portfolios containing tens of thousands of domain names. A few with hundreds of thousands (seriously). I myself have over 3,000 currently registered.

Virtual real estate

Domain names are often described as internet real estate and that is certainly true to a point. As far as the Domain Name Edition of Monopoly goes, the likes of Sex.com would definitely be a Mayfair, while the likes of Bras.co.uk (which I paid just over £8,000 for in January, 2009) might be considered an Old Kent Road in comparison.

You can more accurately think of a domain name as a virtual plot of land, one lying undeveloped until someone builds a website on it. Like all undeveloped plots of land, a domain name will have a value ranging from worthless to millions. Any domain that does have value can be sold as is, just like a plot of land. Build a website on it and you will almost certainly add to its value.

Until building starts on your virtual plot, you can even use it to display the internet equivalent of advertising hoardings to anyone who passes by. You can do this either by building a simple one page website yourself and including advertising on it, or by listing the domain with a domain parking company, something I will talk a little more about later. That means that even undeveloped, a domain name can make you money.

What I find most exciting about domain names is that, unlike property or real estate, you can register a new one for a flat fee of just a few pounds or a few dollars. I don't know anywhere in the world where you can buy land or property for pocket change (although I understand you can buy an acre of land on the moon for not a lot more).

I can't think of any other investment that offers the returns that domain names do either. And I'm not just talking about the headline grabbing big money sales. I'll give you a very small example. I'm proofreading this page on the 26th of February, 2010. Yesterday, I registered the domain name, BettingChips.co.uk. I paid £5 to do so and I registered it with the sole intention of flipping it. Quickly. Today at 10.30pm I put it up for sale on a domain name forum for £30. It sold three hours later. That's a 500% return on my initial (albeit small) investment in three hours. Maybe I could have sold it as quickly for £50 or £100, who knows? Worst case scenario, I am certain I would have quickly found someone who would have paid me twice what I paid for it. At an asking price of £30, I could have waited six years for a buyer to come along (total cost to me for six years registration, £15) and would still double my money. Experience told me that it would sell quickly at that price and it did.

Indeed, a domain name would have to be absolutely awful for you not to find a buyer at £10 (approximately double what it would cost you to register). Don't get me wrong, hundreds of absolutely awful domains are registered each and every day, but if approached with even a modicum of common sense, such domains can be avoided for the most part.

Any that don't fall into the bastard category will double your money as sure as night follows day. Not that I'm suggesting this as a business model. Merely doubling your money each time you register a domain name would mean practically giving away names that someone might be willing to pay much more than £10 for. Much much more in some cases.

Squatter's rights?

Investing in domain names is not without its critics. There are those who feel that those who stockpile domain names are simply holding other internet users to ransom. Some people also wrongly confuse the offering of domain names for sale with cybersquatting. Cybersquatting is the term given to the practice of registering or using a domain name in bad faith, with the intention of profiting from the goodwill of a trademark belonging to someone else. Often the cybersquatter offers to sell the domain at an inflated price to the person or company who owns a trademark contained within the name.

I'm not advocating you do that, but there is nothing wrong – legally or ethically – with buying and selling domain names as a revenue stream. Nothing at all. The BBC for example bought bbc.com from Boston Business Computing for US$375,000 in 1999. Boston Business Computing had every right to register bbc.com and therefore every right to sell it to the BBC. When there is no trademark issue involved and the domain name is generic, it's usually a case of first come first served.

Any time, any place, anywhere

Unlike land or property, which by their very nature are place specific assets, domain names are also completely portable. You can store thousands on a memory stick, keep them in your pocket and take them with you on your travels. Or you could simply download a list from wherever you happen to be from the domain registration company you use.

The transfer of domain name ownership is also very simple. It can be completed online very quickly indeed, with the buyer and seller being at opposite ends of the world for all it matters. I regularly buy and sell domain names on specialist forums that bring buyers and sellers together. Many change hands for relatively small sums – under £100 in many cases. Often a deal is struck in real time while both buyer and seller are online. Payment is made instantly via bank transfer or Paypal, the transfer process is completed online, and the domain name changes hands in a matter of minutes.

Domain name investment must be an opportunity worth considering because if the name is good enough there is no doubt that one day it will find a buyer. It certainly meets my main criteria for the perfect business to run from home or indeed from anywhere. All you need is internet access - and that could be as basic as visiting an internet cafe once a week.

Here's why I love the domain name business.

portable – you can run a business like this from literally anywhere in the world which makes it ideal if you enjoy travelling or want to move to pastures new.

no physical stock - domain names won't fill your garage, don't get damaged in transit, and as long as you renew them and don't trade in "fad" names, they have no sell by date.

low initial investment – you can buy your first domain name for less than £10.

potential for high returns - pick quality names and returns can be hundreds and even thousands of times your initial investment.

work hours to suit - you can find suitable names while surfing the net in your leisure time and you can answer buyer enquiries at hours to suit you too as most sales will be conducted via the internet.

Turning fivers into thousands

The fact that domain names can have a value often many times the cost of registration should have your entrepreneurial juices flowing. Take Scott Brown for example. No doubt inspired by George Orwell's *1984*, he registered BigBrother.co.uk in 1997 for a company selling security systems, but the basic one page website only ever attracted a handful of visitors a day and the business soon folded. The website remained live though, all but forgotten until the reality TV show *Big Brother* was launched in the Summer of 2000. Suddenly, Scott's website was getting thousands of visitors a day, and he was soon earning an incredible £10,000 a month from advertising - all from the comfort of his bedroom in Lochwinnoch, Renfrewshire.

Scott chose to hang on to his valuable domain name and to make money from it, but he could have sold it to the highest bidder instead. Given the popularity of the TV show in the UK, a five or six figure sum might not have been out of the question (given that the show is to be ended after the eleventh series is aired in 2010, its immediate value will be a lot less now).

Or what about Lee Owen, an entrepreneur who currently lives in Romania and who buys and sells domain names for much of his income. One Wednesday in March, 2009, he registered KitchenAppliances.co.uk for £6. It had been registered before, but the previous owner had allowed the registration to lapse and the name was made available again. Lee sold it two days later for £9,500.

You can see the investment potential in domain names immediately. It costs just a few pounds to register a name and yet potentially it can be worth thousands. Quality domain names are certainly worth considering for any multiple revenue steam portfolio. You just might find yourself sitting on the next BigBrother.co.uk a few years down the line or the next KitchenAppliances.co.uk a few days down the line.

Let's forget the ones that sell for thousands of pounds for the moment though. There are countless others that sell for £100 or less. Such names often tick only one or two of the boxes that make for a great domain name (we will look at the qualities of a great domain name shortly), but are still able to find a buyer.

If you could turn the £5 or £6 it costs to register a domain name into £50 or £100 on a regular basis would you be interested? You'd be a fool not to be.

Let's take another example. The bodyguard industry. Once almost exclusively the preserve of those who had served in the police or military, the Government established the Security Industry Authority in 2003 to regulate the UK industry and since 2006 you must have a licence to work as a bodyguard or in what is called close protection. To obtain that licence you must complete and pass a training course.

Close protection training can be very lucrative. For example, a 14 day residential training course with Clearwater in the UK was £2,495 at the time of writing. Not only is it lucrative, but with dozens of training providers it is also very competitive. Therefore, anything that helps you stand out from the crowd has to be good.

Do you think that if I contacted every company involved in this business that I would be able to sell domain names like BodyguardTraining.co.uk and BodyguardCourses.co.uk for £10 each within 24 hours? I've no doubt I could, which would mean doubling my initial investment (the cost of registering them).

If you doubt that I could sell them both for £20 within 24 hours of contacting companies, humour me for the moment. What if I now tell you that bodyguard training firms are currently paying an average of £1 to £1.40 for each visitor sent to their websites via the sponsored links in Google search results relating to bodyguard training courses (they can do this via Google AdWords where their ad will appear in the Google search results either above the natural search results or to the right of them). Ten such clicks would cost a company at least £10. I think the fact that some companies will be spending hundreds if not thousands of pounds a year with Google makes my domain names at £10 each look very attractive indeed.

If you agree with me and you owned a bodyguard training company, would you pay £50 for both names? Again, I've no doubt that a savvy owner would pay me £50 for the pair without a second's thought. Whether used in conjunction with an established website or in their own right, the domain names would only need to attract a single customer for them to pay for themselves many times over (think how easy it is to remember BodyguardCourses.co.uk as opposed to a company's name).

Property development for the internet age

Now let's take it a step further. What if you built a small website that not only provided information about bodyguard training, but also included a directory of training companies in the UK? And what if that domain name ranked highly in search engines for searches relating to bodyguard training? It would involve very little work on my part to create such a website. If I did that and the domain name did rank highly. it would certainly add value to it.

Would someone then be willing to pay me £100 for the two names? Or £500? Or indeed more?

Again, I've no doubt that someone at sometime in the not too distant future would pay me at least £100 for the two names. Indeed, there's every chance I could sell them today for that sum without developing a small website.

What I have done here is register a pair of domains that cost me little more than £5 each and that are almost certainly worth £25 to £50 each to someone else, maybe more. Maybe a lot more. On a good day, with a motivated buyer, I'm sure I could get £500 for the pair. Maybe more still. True, I have to sell them to realise that profit, but at the asking prices we've been talking, I don't doubt my ability to do that.

Supposing you registered 100 such domain names in a year and were able to turn each and every one of them into a fifty pound note. Your initial investment of say £600 would become £5,000. In fact, you could wait five, even ten years, for those 100 buyers to come along, and still make a very healthy profit (renewal fees for .co.uk domain names are due every two years).

While you are waiting for that buyer to come along you could park the domains with a domain parking company – Namedrive.com for example – and share in any advertising revenue generated (offsetting the registration and any renewal fees). Even better, you could build a single page website for each domain name stating that it is for sale, and include some relevant links on the page to companies who will pay you a commission for sales generated or a flat rate simply to appear. Again any monies earned will offset the cost of registration and any renewal fees prior to a buyer being found.

Your own one page website will have a better chance of being ranked in the search engines than a parked page. Indeed, you could go further down that route, build a mini-website for each domain (five or so pages for example) and increase your chances of better search engine rankings, which in turn might earn you more commission and even find you a buyer. Get a niche website like that to the top of the search engine results for related search terms and you've also added value to the domain name because it's no longer a simple domain name: it's now a domain name with history, rankings and traffic.

Multiple mini-sites can be hosted on the one hosting account (what is usually called a reseller account). To host 100 such sites, I would expect to pay no more than £400 a year. Registration renewal fees on 100 .co.uk names works out at around £300 a year. So for £700 plus your time, you now have a portfolio of not only 100 domain names, but 100 websites too, most of which will be earning you money until the big day comes when you find a buyer. A couple you might decide never to sell. Maybe they make enough money to make you want to keep them and benefit from the passive income for years to come.

This business model is only limited by the availability of good domain names. It is still possible to register 100 available domain names a year and turn a profit on each and every one, but you will soon realise that once sold, that's a domain name gone forever. It can't be sold again (not by you anyway). That's when you start to think that at least one or two of those names might be worth a lot more than £50 or £100. The success of a minisite might lead you to increase the asking price many times over. Lee Owen, who we mentioned earlier, regularly sells domain names for under £100, but every now and then a KitchenAppliances.co.uk will come along to make his day. That's true for a lot of people in the domain name industry.

Bear in mind too, that internet marketing is still very much in its infancy. It may seem like the worldwide web has been around for forever and a day, so ingrained is it in much of our daily life, but the reality is quite different. Domain name values will continue to rise well into the foreseeable future simply because demand for them will increase with time. More people will want to work via the internet in the future than do now. There are kids at school today who will be the internet entrepreneurs of tomorrow. They will all be in the market for domain names when they set up shop - and they will have to pay good money for the best names simply because people have got there before them.

How to register a domain name

To register a domain name is as easy as falling off a slippery log. You don't need any expertise. You don't need to be an internet professional. You don't even need a website. Anyone can register a domain name. All you need to do is find a domain name registrar and away you go – and there are plenty of them out there. If you can think of a name that nobody else currently has registered, it's yours for a few dollars or pounds a year (you have to renew your registration every year, or every two years in the case of .co.uks - you never actually own a domain name outright).

All domain name extensions are preceded by a dot - hence the well known term, dotcom. The letters after the dot are called the TLD or top level domain and the letters (or numbers) before the dot are called second level domains (SLD). So for example, Microsoft.com: the top level domain is com and the second level domain is Microsoft.

As of 1985, anyone could register .com domain names (the extension was originally meant for purely commercial websites, but it quickly became a catch-all), .org domain names (originally intended for use by organisations) and .net domain names (originally for networks). Perhaps surprisingly, the original intentions for the top level domains' usage has never been enforced and that is true of UK domain names too where org.uk and even .me.uk domain names are regularly (and often clumsily) used for commercial purposes.

Today, there are well over 200 country code top level domains that you can also register, such as .fr (France), .uk (UK), .de (Germany), .in (India) and .us (USA). Some can only be registered by residents of the respective country while others only need the administrative contact (usually your registrar) to be in the respective country.

Most, including UK domain names, have no restrictions relating to residency or who can register them. Indeed, some smaller countries have made a lot of money by selling domain names worldwide. An increasingly popular extension is .tv, the country code for the tiny Pacific island nation of Tuvalu which has a population of 10,600 inhabiting just 16 square miles of dry land. Until very recently, the country relied heavily on selling fishing licences for its living, but its biggest industry today is the sale of domain names (accounting for about a third of the country's Gross Domestic Product).

When it comes to choosing a domain name for your own website you have to consider both a name (second level domain) and a suitable extension (top level domain). If you want to buy and sell names, you have to do the same thing because not all extensions are equally valued.

Let's look first at the extension. Simply because they have been around the longest, the .com extension is the most popular, most recognised and also most established in the public's psyche. If your website has worldwide appeal, I would seriously consider registering a dotcom domain name.

If however your website's target audience is largely within a specific country, then do not hesitate to register a country specific domain name. Say, for example, that you own a pizza delivery chain that operates exclusively in the UK. The domain name, Pizzas.co.uk, will be of more obvious value to you than Pizzas.com, certainly when the price difference of acquiring either is taken into consideration. As a very rough rule of thumb, dotcoms are valued at ten times their .co.uk equivalents.

As for other extensions, the jury is still out on that one. There is no doubt that .net and .org domain names are seen as secondary to .com domain names, but it is equally true that there are many successful businesses using other extensions, not to mention people paying big money for the best of them (Poker.org sold for a million dollars at the start of 2010 for example). My advice? If the .com is available, buy it and use it. If not, consider other extensions, but be aware that you will often be settling for second best by doing so.

For a website that specifically targets a UK audience, a .co.uk name is the most appropriate for commercial websites. The availability of good names is slightly better for country TLDs than it is for dotcoms so you have a better chance of getting a decent one. If the .com and the .co.uk domain names are both available, bullseye. There are other UK domain extensions, such as me.uk and org.uk, but with few exceptions, I seriously doubt their value, particularly for a website that you believe has long term commercial potential. Others disagree – not least those with large portfolios of such domains to sell.

Here's my thinking. The vast majority of UK internet users think primarily in terms of dotcom and .co.uk domain names for online shopping. Most have never even heard of org.uk and are likely to confuse it with .co.uk. Traffic leakage is inevitable when it comes to visitors looking to return to your .org.uk website and then ending up at the .co.uk version instead.

There is also the "fly by night" perceptions that can (rightly or wrongly) accompany anything but the leading domain name extensions and this may well impact on your business. You can also come across as amateurish by using anything but what the public expects to see from a commercial enterprise. You wouldn't expect a well known brand to be trading from a .me.uk domain name and you shouldn't set your own standards any lower. The worldwide web offers the closest thing to a level playing field for both David and Goliath websites so why anyone would start a business from the bottom of a hole dug by themselves in said playing field makes little sense.

There is an argument to be made for the lesser known extensions in that the availability of good names is greater. If you are buying one on the secondary market you will find that prices are much lower too. It is also true that a keyword rich domain name can help a website rank well in search engines, but a domain name's impact on search engine rankings is often greatly overstated. Rankings attributed to having a great domain name often have little to do with the name at all. For me, the disadvantages already outlined almost always outweigh any advantages, and so I prefer to stick with .co.uk domain names for my UK targeted websites. You can make your own mind up.

Domain names and local search

The choice of domain extension can have a major impact on your search engine rankings. 70-80% of internet users in the UK use Google.co.uk or Yahoo.co.uk, rather than Google.com or Yahoo.com. By using the local versions of search engines, the user has the opportunity to search through web pages either from just the UK or the entire world. It's therefore vital that a website targeting the UK market is included in the results returned for UK specific searches.

The interesting thing to note here is that a website owned by a UK based business or individual with UK specific content will not necessarily be ranked highly by the search engines for UK searches. It may not even appear at all. That's because it might not be sending the right signals to the search engines to tell them that it is indeed a website targeting a mainly UK audience.

Search engines decide what websites to include in country specific searches based on a number of factors. The most important is domain extension followed by the website's server location. If the website's domain name ends with .uk, it will normally be included in search engine results pages (SERPs) for th UK. Similarly, if the website is hosted on a server in the UK, it will normally be included in UK specific search results irrespective of domain extension (it could be a .com for example).

A third factor, the domain name registrant's location, is also said to be taken into consideration, but there is plenty of evidence that this is not always the case. What's more registrant details often exclude an address anyway, give inaccurate or incomplete information, or are hidden from public view (Nominet, the UK's domain name registry, allows private individuals to have their address omitted by way of an opt out option). Google actually says that it also uses information provided by webmasters via Google Analytics to determine the location of a website, but of course only a small minority of webmasters use what is a very useful and free way of analysing website traffic (http://www.google.com/intl/en_uk/analytics/).

This can be incredibly important to the volume of traffic you receive – or don't receive - from search engines. Bottom line, if you are primarily targeting the UK with a website, make sure it has a UK domain name or is hosted in the UK. There are UK companies with multi-million pound turnovers that use a dotcom domain name for a website hosted outside the UK and they do not appear in UK specific search results. It must cost them a fortune in lost sales. Don't make the same mistake.

Naming your new baby

Once you have decided on the most appropriate TLD to use, the real fun begins. As all proud parents to be will tell you, it's time to choose a name. Although it is true that virtually all generic words have already been snapped up, that doesn't mean that you can't come up with a great name. And as we'll discover soon, you may be a lot closer to owning a superb generic domain name than you think.

As we've already noted, the net's biggest success stories are the likes of eBay.com and not Auction.com, Amazon.com and not Books.com, and Google.com not SearchEngine.com. Such success stories are based on being first to dominate an online market and being seen by the wider public to be the best player in that market. The choice of domain name was and is largely irrelevant in such cases. If you too are aiming to be in a similar position, your choice of domain name might not be of great importance either, but the vast majority of websites do not fall into that category. Most are me-too websites, simply versions of what is already out there in what are often already crowded market places. Here, your choice of domain name can be very important, and in some cases crucial, in giving you an edge over your competitors.

The trick is to come up with a name that potential customers will remember. If you get them to your website once, you want to make sure that it is as easy as possible for them to find their way back again. In general, this means the shorter the name, the better. Longer, more complicated, harder to spell domain names are not going to be remembered, and even when they are, chances are they are going to be remembered incorrectly. For example, when you are looking at property online, you may visit umpteen websites, one after the other, following links and clicking on search results to reach them. How many times have you done a search similar to this, wanted to revisit a page days later, and completely forgotten the name of the website?

This is as good a point as any to list some of the features that make a domain name great. It's unlikely a domain name will tick all the boxes, but you'll know which ones are most important to the website you will be developing.

Memorable – A good domain name will always be easy to remember. If it isn't, customers might struggle to find you again and may end up at a competitor's site instead.

Unique – I know, all domain names are unique by definition, but some are more unique than others as pointed out elsewhere.

Descriptive – A domain name that tells you everything you need to know about the website behind it is right up there. A good generic domain will instantly identify you with the products and services you provide. The very best are truly category killers.

Trustworthy – Trust and confidence are all important for online success and any domain name must convey both. Where would you rather gamble, at Casino.co.uk or at Million-Pound-Casino.org.uk?

Short – Usually, a shorter domain name is not only easier to spell, it is also more memorable. But short has to be combined with memorable for it to work. Xgdj.com is short, but not a good domain name. If making a domain name out of keywords, try to avoid using more than two or three.

Spelling - Remember not everyone can spell. Say you decide on the name SuccessfulSpelling.co.uk. A good percentage of your potential customers won't even reach your homepage. They will be looking for sucsesfullspeling.co.uk and a hundred and one other variations. Avoid anything like this or be prepared to buy domain names that include the most frequent typing errors - before your competitors do. Slightly off topic, but think about spelling when constructing contact e-mail addresses too. There is a very good reason why most business use support@domainname.co.uk or info@domainname.co.uk. Most people can spell support and info. A more complicated e-mail address is likely to lead to spelling or typing errors, and if that e-mail subsequently bounces because of the error, a potential customer can be left confused.

Spelling Part Two - Remember not everyone can spell. And that might include you. Building a business on a domain name that contains a typo or a spelling error isn't going to make you look very good.

Radio Test - Would your domain name pass the radio test? If a customer heard it mentioned on the radio, would it be easily and correctly recalled later that day? And don't ignore the radio test on the grounds that you never intend to advertise on radio. For radio test read word of mouth.

Domain Extension – Stick to what your average man in the street understands. For most people in the UK that means .com. and .co.uk. You might want to consider .tv or .net and maybe one or two others, but avoid the more obscure extensions. Remember what I said about how a domain extension can affect what search engine results you turn up in too.

Infringement free – be careful you don't step on toes by registering a domain name that infringes trademark or other rights. Especially if you will be treading on very big toes.

What about hyphenated domain names?

There is also the question of hyphenated names. Is JohnSmith.com better than John-Smith.com? Everything else being equal, I would say yes every time. The reason being that hyphenated domain names are sometimes seen as second class citizens. A bit like lesser domain name extensions. People who use the internet have quickly learned to read domain names where words run together (in any visual marketing it's also easy enough to emphasise that two words are being used by using a different colour for each word for example). Owning both versions and directing both to your website is even better.

That said, there are times when a hyphen is a good idea. The National Lottery's website is at National-Lottery.co.uk (the domain name Nationallottery.co.uk redirects there). This makes sense because visually it is clumsy to have the last letter of the first word and the first letter of the second word – both Ls – running together.

As far as search engines are concerned, neither a domain name with hyphens or one without will by itself lead to higher search engine rankings. I have tested this and ranked highly for keyword phrases using first a hyphenated domain name and then the same two word domain, but unhyphenated.

A number of domain owners have started to buy longer domain names containing keywords that relate to their business in the belief that search engines will give them higher rankings - for example Buy-computers-and-printers-in-wales.co.uk. A domain name is just part of the overall package that you present to search engines in the hope of achieving a high ranking. If anything, a long domain name that features keywords separated by three or more hyphens is likely to be seen as an attempt to game the search engines, and you might end up being penalised for using one.

Even if you do get high search engine rankings for the hyphenated domain name, whether they would convert into visitors to your website is a different matter. For example, WelshComputers.co.uk sounds far more worthy of trust than the rather fly by night sounding Buy-computers-and-printers-in-wales.co.uk don't you think? I certainly know which one I'd rather visit.

Where to register a domain name

There are countless domain name registrar websites where you can register a domain name. For .co.uk domain names, I usually use either UKReg (http://www.ukreg.com) or 123-Reg (http://www.123-reg.co.uk). The prices are low and both include free e-mail forwarding and free website forwarding (this automatically redirects anyone who enters your domain name to any other web page). Support is generally good too.

When it comes to dotcom and similar domain names, I use GoDaddy (http://www.GoDaddy.com). Again good prices, and good support. I also like Go Daddy because I've got a lot of respect for its boss, Bob Parsons. A Vietnam vet and self-taught computer programmer, he founded software company Parsons Technologies in 1987 and sold it seven years later to Intuit for US$64 million. In 1997, he was back in business with Go Daddy, a young upstart domain registrar that had to compete head on with much larger companies in the internet domain registration market. By 2001, it had grown to be the same size as the likes of eNom and Dotster, largely thanks to aggressive pricing. Today, it is almost four times bigger than eNom and 30 times bigger than Dotster. In fact, it is now the biggest domain registration company in the world, managing an incredible 39 million domain names for customers like me.

In a video blog in September, 2009, Bob gave this piece of advice to would-be startups. "Start small and always have a fall back that allows you to fail time and again until you get it right". I couldn't agree more. Starting small is key. All too often I talk to people who want to start a business online and who think they will have to give up their day job and then spend thousands on development and marketing for it to be a success. That's not to say that won't work, but if it doesn't you are up shit creek without a paddle.

The reality is this. To register a domain name costs around £6. To host a basic website for a year should cost you £20 to £30 (obviously if the site is a huge success and you need more bandwidth, etc., you'll be paying more, but presumably because you are earning more too). So for well under £50, you can be up and running to see if your idea makes sense and can make money. Or as Bob puts it, to make sure there's water in the pool before you dive in.

True, you will have to build a website, but that is much easier to do than most people think – as this book has hopefully already demonstrated. The likes of WordPress and the incredible array of programs and scripts available make this a doddle even for technophobes like me. Everyone reading this should have basic website building skills – and if you don't, go and get them at a local college of an evening. It could be that once you see your idea has potential that you will want a professional web designer on board to help develop the site further, but again the money for that can come from the site's initial success.

The best thing about this approach is that it is more likely to work simply because you actually get started. The idea of giving up a job that pays the bills, and then investing thousands in a venture that may not work, quite rightly scares the living daylights out of most people. And that's when an idea remains just that. An idea. It's an entirely different ball game when you start small, work a few hours in the evenings and at weekends, and the most you've got to lose is fifty quid. That's a game we can all play.

So if you're currently in employment, don't give up the day job. That might be a surprising thing for me to say given that I view most forms of employment as wage slavery, but it's good advice. Use your job as your fall back. Then get busy building in your spare time, investing small sums to get your ideas off the ground. If they fail, write them off to experience and use what you've learned to try fresh ideas. Bob's spot on. Start small and always have a fall back that allows you to fail time and again until you get it right.

Back to domain names. Be wary of web hosting companies that offer to register your domain for free. Make sure the domain is being registered in your name and look out for having to pay for it anyway. Some hosting companies register it for "free" and you end up getting billed by the registrar for the one or two years' registration anyway. Better to do it yourself in the first place.

For new .com domain registrations, don't pay more than US$15 a year. For .co.uk names, don't pay more than £10 for two years (the minimum term for .co.uk domain names).

Some domain names are more unique than others

Every domain name by its very nature is unique. There can never be two domain names that are identical. In the tradition of *Animal Farm*, however, some domain names are more unique than others. Widgets.co.uk is unique. DirectWidgets.co.uk and WidgetsDirect.co.uk are less so.

There are also two distinct markets. The primary market, where domain names are initially registered for what is a flat fee (albeit a flat fee that can vary across registrars) and the post-registration market, or aftermarket, where domain names that have already been registered are bought and sold.

Every week, domain names change hands for thousands of pounds on the aftermarket. Others are bought and sold for pocket change. There is no correct price to pay for a domain name on the aftermarket – only a price that is agreed between buyer and seller. That price might have been more or less than the buyer would or should have paid. And it might have been more or less than the buyer would or should have accepted. Sellers will chance their arm. Buyers will hope for a bargain. You will come across the ones who want you to pay astronomical sums for domain names barely worth the price of a bus ticket let alone a journey into space. And the ones who "don't want to pay very much because I know it only cost you £5.90 to register" (actual quote from an e-mail received by me with regards to a domain name).

Putting a price on a domain name may not be the easiest of tasks, but it has to be done if you are in the market as either a buyer or a seller. If you are a domain name seller with no real idea of a name's value you are in danger of pricing yourself out of the market or giving away the family silver for the price of a cup of tea. Similarly, if you are buying a name without knowing its value to you, you are basically gambling on the unknown.

Valuations are as unique as the domain names themselves. One man's rubbish is another man's gold and all that. Take surnames for example. Unless we share the same surname, I would probably be more likely to pay more for Marshall.co.uk than you would – everything else being equal. Similarly, you are more likely to be interested in a domain name that matches your place of birth than you would be in the domain name of a similar sized town that you have never visited – again, all else being equal. We are after all only human.

If you visit domain name message boards, you will always find people asking for valuations and others giving them. Virtually all prices given are no more than stabs in the dark, often by people who aren't in the least bit qualified to be offering valuations anyway. Another common trait of such boards is that the owner is more than happy to accept high valuations, but is quick to dismiss any low ones. Human nature for you again.

You can of course pay to have your domain name valued by a domain appraisal company, but I would take such valuations with a very big pinch of salt in most cases. You can buy software to start your own domain name appraisal company for pennies. There's no saying that the company about to appraise your name didn't get into the business that way too.

So how do I go about valuing domain names that I am interested in buying? I start by mentally referring to the list we looked over earlier about what makes a domain name a good one. From that I develop a gut feeling for the domain name's worth to me. The more qualities it possesses in terms of being memorable, unique, descriptive, trustworthy, short, infringement free, easy to spell, able to pass the radio test, and having a domain extension that I value, the more interested I will be in acquiring the name.

Up to this point, I am making an educated guess as to the value of a domain name. And that valuation is personal to me. If I think a domain name is worth £1,000, it means it is worth that to me. A name that I see as having value, perhaps because of knowledge of the particular market for example, may mean nothing to you. Equally, I will not appreciate the value that you might attach to a domain name simply because I can see no profitable use for it where you might.

I then begin to look at the likely return I can expect on my investment. If the asking price is low, I often buy it there and then without any further thought, especially if the name relates to a niche market that I already know well and where I can immediately see the value. It's perfectly possible to pick up domain names that tick most if not all of the above boxes to a satisfactory degree for less than £100.

Otherwise, I have to work out whether the asking price is one that will give me a good return on my investment. Often there is no asking price. Sellers frightened of selling a domain name too cheaply will often ask for offers and some won't even give a ballpark figure when asked. It's something you will come across all too regularly with domain names. Then it's a case of working out what I'd be happy to pay and then trying to get the name for less than that amount. How much less? As much as possible!

How long is a piece of string anyway?

Knowing what to pay for a domain name that someone else has already registered and is selling is notoriously difficult and far from being an exact science. It's true of all unique products from works of arts to country homes. One of the UK's biggest domain name companies, Giant Games Ltd, sold Egg.co.uk back in May, 1998, to Prudential for £1,700. The Pru then launched the UK's first internet bank, Egg, that same year. Prudential may well have paid many times the agreed price to secure ownership of Egg.co.uk and no doubt Giant Games were kicking themselves when Egg launched. Lesson learned and barely two years later, Giant Games sold Taste.co.uk to supermarket giant Sainsbury's (who have since done nothing with it, at the time of writing anyway) for £110,000.

A domain name will ultimately sell for the price that the buyer and seller agree, but that doesn't tell you a great deal about its value to either party. Maybe the buyer would have accepted less, maybe the buyer would have paid more. In either case, another price would have been agreed. And again, maybe the seller would have accepted less still or the buyer paid even more – and another price would have been agreed.

As an example of how difficult it is to put a price on a domain name, I recently read a forum thread which mentioned the sale of Underdogs.co.uk for £2,750. Without any obvious use, it would have been a very difficult domain name to price for the seller, but in the thread he said he was happy with the price paid. Presumably his valuation of the name tallied with what the buyer paid. Do you think the buyer got a bargain, did the seller get the better of the deal, or was £2,750 a fair price for Underdogs.co.uk for both parties? Personally, I would have sold it for £2,750, particularly if I was happy with that sum and had no other information at hand to suggest it was worth more.

In fact, the forum thread was originally about the sale of Underdog.co.uk and not Underdogs.co.uk. The former was sold by a different seller to the same buyer for £15,000. In fact, negotiations to buy both names went on simultaneously, but presumably neither seller was aware of the buyer's interest in both names.

The singular Underdog.co.uk is more brandable than Underdogs.co.uk, and at £15,000 it looked like a good deal for both parties – assuming the buyer will earn that sum and more back on the strength of the name. It does make me think that Underdogs.co.uk could have sold for more though. £5,000 might have been achievable, maybe up to £10,000 depending on the depth of the buyer's pockets. Hindsight is a wonderful thing. Or maybe the buyer would have settled for just Underdog.co.uk, but bought Underdogs.co.uk simply because it could be bought for £2,750. If the asking price had been £5,000, it might still be for sale. Incidentally, the buyer of both names was National Accident Helpline who are currently usining the Underdog.co.uk domain name in a TV advertising campaign.

Here's another example from internet entrepreneur, Scott Jones, who buys names both for development and to resell. On his blog, SelfMadeMinds (http://www.selfmademinds.com), he posted a story of how he had offered £1,000 for DiningRoomFurniture.co.uk, but the owner had said that the offer was of no interest. Almost exactly a year later, the name was allowed to expire and Scott was able to register it for just £5.

In his very next blog post, however, Scott gave the flipside of the domain name pricing coin. He offered £750 for another name, TouringCaravan.co.uk, and finally agreed on a price of £1,000 plus VAT. Pleased with himself, he then went to the search engines to see if the domain name had any history attached to it – and discovered that the seller had been trying to sell the domain name on a forum without any success for just £50 plus VAT.

The truth is that there is no "correct" price to sell a domain name for or to buy one at. On both sides of the fence it comes down to a judgement call, and as with all judgements, mistakes are there to be made. What's more, domains are bought and sold in what is both an imperfect and inefficient market place. Even with a great deal of marketing effort (and in truth that rarely accompanies a domain name sale), the seller has no way of knowing whether all the someones who would be interested in buying a particular domain name even know it is for sale. And as mentioned before, no matter what best offer is on the table, it's unlikely the seller will know just how much a buyer is really prepared to pay. Like all buyers with an ounce of sense, he or she will play his cards close to his chest, hoping to get the domain name for the lowest price possible. Equally, a buyer doesn't know what a seller would really be willing to accept.

The price is right

There are a number of ways of putting your valuation of a domain name into some sort of context. One is to look at previous comparable sales prices. You'll find big ticket sales at DNJournal.com (http://www.dnjournal.com) and a large database of UK domain sales is available at DomainPrices.co.uk (http://www.domainprices.co.uk). Although I'm always interested in what others have paid for domain names, I actually don't let past prices influence my own judgement as much as others might. This is because I have no way of knowing how the buyer and seller arrived at the price paid. I don't even know if the reported price was the price paid.

Traffic is everything when it comes to successful websites, quality traffic that you can convert into money. Some domain names, particularly generic ones, benefit from having what is called type-in traffic. Type-in refers to how many people will enter a domain name into their internet browser in the belief that it will lead them to where they want to go. If you are looking for information on Glasgow Rangers Football Club for example, you might take a punt and type www.Rangers.co.uk into your browser to see if it takes you to the club's website. Other domain names have history, having been used in the past, and there may well be links to them from other websites left over from those past lives that still generate traffic.

The fact that a domain name can deliver traffic in its own right definitely adds to its value. An obvious example would be Sex.com. Another would be Cars.com. Or Cars.co.uk. All three will deliver large volumes of targeted type-in traffic to a website and are therefore of greater value.

If you have access to reliable statistics that show that a domain name comes with traffic you can determine what that extra traffic would be worth to you in terms of extra sales. For example, say you have a domain name that delivers 1,000 pairs of eyeballs to a website every month thanks to type-ins. And supposing, for every 100 visitors a website gets, it sells ten widgets at £50 a widget. If your domain name delivers 1,000 visitors on the strength of the name alone, you would expect an average of 100 widgets to be sold every month, adding £5,000 to the website's bottom line - without a penny being spent on marketing (beyond renewing the domain name's registration when required). And that's £5,000 a month for who knows how many years.

Men.com sold for US$1.3 million not because its new owner liked the sound of it, but because the vendor, Ricky Schwarz, could demonstrate its value in terms of the enormous levels of traffic it had generated over six or so years simply on the strength of the name. Interestingly, Ricky is known as the Domain King not because he sells domains (he sells relatively few), but because he has a portfolio of names that deliver traffic. And on the internet, traffic means money.

Car.com sold for a six figure sum in 2003 and was used to rebrand the car information portal that had been trading as StoneAge.com. As soon as the new domain name was put into use, traffic to the site shot up - without any advertising spend. According to an article in the *New York Times*, the domain name paid for itself quickly thanks to the increase in business that additional traffic generated.

Domains that have high in-built traffic-generating ability are usually common words or indeed phrases that people might type into their browser bar. Such domain names are also easily remembered, adding to their value further once attached to a live website. If I sell blue widgets and you're in the market for some, you would only need to hear or see BlueWidgets.com or even Blue-Widgets.com once to remember it. This is a hidden value, akin to goodwill, that may well be worth paying a premium for. What that premium is will once again be down to judgement, but it is a premium nonetheless on the domain's intrinsic worth.

Remember, traffic figures associated with domain names can easily be inflated. If those figures sound too good to be true then they usually are. Similarly, you will find sellers wanting you to pay multiples of parking revenue generated (often over ridiculously short times). Past earnings aren't a good guide to future earnings, especially in a rapidly changing environment such as the internet. Parking revenue has fallen across the board in recent times. Indeed, domain name parking in general in its most basic form has probably had its day.

Also be wary of domain names that are sold solely on the basis of figures pulled from the Google AdWords Keyword Tool. The implication is that because a keyword or two in the domain name gets a certain number of searches every month, it somehow justifies the asking price. Even putting aside for the moment that those figures aren't always accurate, a domain name alone won't guarantee that any of those searches will result in visits to your website.

Payback time

If you are considering investing a sizeable sum in a domain name, it will be important to know how long it will take for you to earn your money back. The basic payback period formula is very simple. Just divide the cost of the domain name by how much you realistically think it will earn you annually to arrive at the payback period. So for example, a domain name that will cost you £5,000, and that you project will earn you £2,000 a year, will pay for itself after two and a half years.

There is something in financial theory called the time value of money. It's business speak for a bird in the hand is worth two in the bush. Basically, a sum of money now is worth more than the certainty of receiving the same amount of money at some time in the future. What's more, that amount of money at some time in the future is worth more than the same amount of money at a date even further into the future. If you think about it, it is self-evident. If I offered you £50 in your hand today or £50 to be collected in a year's time, you would take the £50 now and eliminate the risk of what might happen between now and a year down the road. For a large investment in a domain name, bear this in mind because understanding the time value of money will extend the payback time – maybe even to the point of making the purchase financially unviable.

That said, a domain name is quite unlike most other capital investments. Unlike machinery for example, a domain name is more likely to appreciate rather than depreciate over time – so at the end of the payback period you may have not only earned your money back, but be in a position to sell the domain name for more than you paid for it.

Is there an optimum payback time? Not really – except the quicker the better. Textbooks often quote three years or less and I wouldn't really want to wait any longer than three years for a domain name to repay its purchase price. A quality domain name could pay for itself very quickly indeed, providing you get it for the right price in the first place. American entrepreneur, Rick Schwartz, has made millions out of domain names and it was one of his earliest domain name purchases that opened his eyes to the amazing value of a good domain name. Back in August, 1997, Rick bought Porno.com for US$42,000, despite knowing that the seller had paid just US$5,000 for it a week earlier. Those who knew about the deal thought he was mad – until the domain name paid for itself in a matter of weeks. Talking to DNJournal.com about this eureka moment, Rick said, "It was akin to buying real world property and paying off the mortgage not in 30 years but in 30 days!"

When working out payback time myself, I like to turn things on their head. I start with the price, select an arbitrary payback time based on how quickly I would like to see my money returned (for example two years), and then I work out how much the domain name would need to earn each year for that to happen. If the numbers stack up, I'll go ahead. If I know the domain name itself will retain or see an increase in its market value over that period it becomes a no brainer because then I will have an asset that is both appreciating and one that acts as a revenue stream for me while it is appreciating.

For example, I paid just over £8,000 for Bras.co.uk as stated previously, knowing nothing about the bras market beyond the fact that half the UK's population buys them. I quickly found out that commission on sales varied from 2-10%, with the average basket value being between £20 and £40. For every sale made, I didn't stand to make a great deal – perhaps a pound or three. This in turn meant I would need to make around 4,000 sales to see my investment returned.

Was that likely to happen in year one? From a standing start with no marketing budget, I didn't think so. In year two? Well, that would equate to 2,000 sales a year over the two years or 40 sales per week. Again, the realist inside me told me that was possible, but still unlikely. By the end of year three though, I did think the Bras.co.uk website would be firmly established in the search engines and would be delivering at least 150 sales per month 1,800 sales over the 12 month period) based on my traffic projections and a low 1% conversion rate. Worse case scenario was that it would take four years to see my money repaid in full (as things turned out, I recouped the purchase price within 18 months). That was good enough for me, not least because I thought that, if marketed properly to bra related companies, I would be able to resell the domain name for more than what I paid for it initially anyway. In my eyes, it is definitely a £10,000 domain name and it might be worth £50,000 to the right buyer. With traffic maybe more.

Location location location

Geo domains, names that refer to a geographic location and most commonly towns and cities, are often valued by population. Leading domainer, Rick Latona, values U.S. City domain names at 10 to 25 cents per citizen. If a town or city has additional opportunities, because it is a tourist destination for example, that figure would be higher.

I like to value UK geo domains on a similar basis. For a UK geo domain to be viable it will need a population of at least 10,000 to 50,000, depending on other factors such as tourist visitor numbers.

As a rough rule of thumb, paying 5p per head of population would value London.co.uk at a very conservative £360,000. I think you would definitely need to factor into the equation the 15 million visitors the Big Smoke attracts each year, and the fact that they spend close to eight billion pounds, to get a better handle on its potential worth.

A name like Carlisle.co.uk would come in at £10,000 at 10p per head of population. Is a domain name like Carlisle.co.uk worth £10,000? It obviously depends on how you can monetise it and earn your money back. If you built a site dedicated to the city of Carlisle on the domain name that then had proven levels of monthly traffic, do you think you could attract 100 local businesses to pay you £99 a year to advertise on the site? Hotels, restaurants, shops, pubs, plumbers, taxis, takeaways? If you could, there's your £10,000 back in year one. If you could charge them £199 a year, or attract 200 businesses at the original price of £99, you've doubled your initial investment in year one. Plus you have a developed domain name and a profitable business that has value too should you choose to sell it.

(Almost) free to a good home

One hurdle you'll come up against time and time again when looking for domain names to register is that the vast majority of the obviously good ones have already been registered. Some because they have been developed into fully fledged websites, but most are simply gathering dust. having never been developed or having once been developed, but since failed. Some are in the hands of people who simply have no idea of their value. Others are held by individuals and companies who buy and sell domain names and who are waiting for a buyer to come along and make them an acceptable offer.

Potential buyers can either approach the domain name owner direct or there are numerous sites dedicated to buying and selling domain names, sites like GreatDomains.com, Sedo.co.uk, AcornDomains.co.uk and Afternic.com. Established domain name traders often have their own websites listing hundreds of domain names that are for sale or rent. Long-time domain name investor, Edwin Hayward, has an excellent one at MemorableDomains.co.uk for example. Another respected investor, Colin Edwards, has a site listing his domains for sale at FCDomains.co.uk.

I talked earlier about how domain names are not unlike land or property. There are also differences between them too and there is one that I haven't mentioned in anything but passing yet that can make investing in domain names incredibly lucrative. It stems from the fact that you never actually own a domain name and therefore have to renew its registration on an annual basis (or every two years in the case of a .uk domain name).

For various reasons, thousands of domain names are simply not renewed. When that happens they are once again made available for anyone to register. According to the Domain Monster website (http://www.domainmonster.com), an almost unbelievable 400,000 or so domain names are made available again EVERY DAY simply because they are not renewed. Equally unbelievably, some of those domains are potentially worth thousands of pounds. That doesn't happen with land or property. Nobody forgets to live in their house.

We have just been talking about geo domain names. What price Liverpool.co.uk? Liverpool is the UK's fourth largest city with a population of just under half a million people. In October, 2005, the Liverpool.co.uk domain name was not renewed and was allowed to drop. Seeing that it had been suspended, I contacted the then registrant asking if they would sell it rather than let their registration expire. Unbelievably, they said no. Presumably they didn't need the thousands of pounds a name like that was worth.

One domain name that I had wanted to own for some time was Entrepreneur.co.uk. I have always considered myself an entrepreneur rather than a business person and as a kid there was only one thing I wanted to be when I grew up. An entrepreneur.

When I first tried to register the domain name in 1999, it had not surprisingly been taken. It was then the home of an online magazine aimed at small entrepreneurs and so I didn't even bother enquiring about its availability. Had it been up for sale, I'm not sure what I would have been willing to pay for it. At £1,000 I'd have snapped it up. £5,000 wouldn't have been out of the question, but at £10,000 I'd have probably walked away. I simply didn't have that money to spend on a name, especially when I had no master plan in mind to develop it. Amazingly enough, four years later on the 10th of June, 2003, I became the proud registrant of Entrepreneur.co.uk. Even more amazingly, I paid just £25 for it. I still can't believe my luck.

In the UK, domain names are administered by Nominet UK (http://www.nominet.org.uk) which acts as a central registry of UK domain names. Nominet UK has performed this role since 1996 and as of the 31st of January, 2010, its database of registered names contained 8,209,451 domain names, the vast majority of which are .co.uk domain names. The English language by comparison consists of around half a million words according to the University Of Birmingham's *Bank Of English*.

When you purchase a domain name you are actually purchasing the right to use that domain name for a specified period - two years in the case of .uk domains. You normally register a domain name through a company that specialises in registering domain names rather than directly from Nominet UK themselves (you can actually register names directly, but to do so is much more expensive unless you are also a Registrar).

Once you have purchased your domain name, it will be assigned the Tag of the company that registered it on your behalf. A Tag is simply a one word code in upper case letters that uniquely identifies your Registrar's account with Nominet. These Tags allow your domain name to be managed.

The time will come when your domain name comes up for renewal. If you do not pay your Registrar by the agreed date, the Tag is removed so that the company is not charged by Nominet UK for the renewal period. This stops any services associated with the domain name, such as a website, from working. It doesn't however mean that someone else can register the domain name and use it. Not yet anyway.

Nominet has a duty to contact the registrant of a domain name due for renewal to confirm that they do not want to renew the domain name before the registration can be cancelled. Once a registrant has confirmed that they no longer require their domain name, or have not paid the renewal invoice by 30 days after the expiry date, the domain name will then be suspended for 60 days. After the 60 day suspension period the domain name will be cancelled and will then be available for anyone to register.

Although Nominet do not give a specific date or time for a domain name's release, a suspended UK domain name is typically released 92 or most commonly 99 days after its renewal date. When this happens, it is said to have "dropped" from Nominet UK's database and it once again becomes available to be registered. There is a website called DropDates.co.uk that allows you to enter the renewal date of any suspended .uk domain name and it will tell you the most likely drop date for the domain.

If you go to Nominet's website (http://www.nominet.org.uk), you'll see a WHOIS box near the top of the homepage that allows you to check whether a UK domain name is available to register or not.

If the domain name is available, you will be greeted by a message saying, "No match for XXXXXXX.co.uk. This domain name has not been registered."

If the domain name has been registered, you will be given the WHOIS information for the domain name: who registered it, when it was registered, and when it is due for renewal. If the renewal date has passed, the domain name will be marked as "Suspended". The current registrant can renew it right up to the moment Nominet cancel the registration and make it available again.

Here's an example. On the following page is the WHOIS record for LoanDoctor.co.uk (with registrant details removed). As you can see, the domain name was originally due to be renewed on the 12th of February, 2010. 92 days on from that date would be the 8th of May and 99 days on would be the 15th of May.

Although not set in stone, those two dates are the likely release dates for the domain name, and more often than not Nominet release names after 99 days. True to form, LoanDoctor.co.uk was made available to register on the 15th of May, 2010, at 12:36pm (I know this because I registered it as soon as it became available).

Domain name:

     loandoctor.co.uk

Registrant:

     XXXXXXX

Registrant type:

     Non-UK Individual

Registrant's address:

     XXXXXXX

Registrar:

     XXXXXXX

Relevant dates:

     Registered on: 12-Feb-2008

     Renewal date: 12-Feb-2010

     Last updated: 07-May-2010

Registration status:

     No longer required

     *** **This registration has been SUSPENDED.** ***

Name servers:

     ns1.fastpark.net

     ns2.fastpark.net

A similar thing happened to the domain name, Entrepreneur.co.uk. At the end of May, 2003, I visited Entrepreneur.co.uk and was surprised to find the website gone. Through Nominet UK's whois facility it was possible to check the registrant details and it emerged that Entrepreneur.co.uk had not been renewed and was actually suspended awaiting release.

A large proportion of suspended domain names have little real value, but it almost beggars belief to see some of the names that people have let slip from their grasp for the want of a renewal fee of less than £10. Names that on the open market can be worth many thousands of pounds are dropped or released after a period of suspension and anyone can register them and then attempt to realise their true value. Not surprisingly, a number of people have cottoned on to this fact and a cottage industry has developed to "catch" dropped names. People involved in the industry are known as dropcatchers. A dropcatcher's aim is to register a domain name as soon as the name is released, either for him or herself or on behalf of a client. When I say as soon as it's released, we are talking within a fraction of a second.

This is exactly how I managed to obtain Entrepreneur.co.uk. As soon as I saw it was suspended, I booked its catch with a dropcatching service which was operated at the time by Dark Marketing Ltd. I simply paid them the £25 monitoring and catching fee, sat back and waited for any news. Within a week, I received an e-mail from Dark to say that they had successfully caught Entrepreneur.co.uk for me. It was that easy.

Catch me if you can

If you try to manually register a name that is dropping, you will first need to know that a name has dropped by repeatedly entering a domain name into the whois, often for hour after hour, in the hope that it suddenly shows as available. Then you will need to hot foot it over to a website that registers domain names, fill in any forms, enter your payment details, and hope that nobody else beats you to the draw. We are talking one or two minutes for the process to complete, maybe longer.

If a dropcatcher is monitoring the same name you haven't got a chance. Without even needing to be at a computer screen, an automated script will be trying to register the domain name within a fraction of a second following its release. In fact the time between a name being made available and it being caught can be less than a tenth of a second. It just isn't possibly to manually register a domain name that fast so if you can't beat them, join them, by becoming a dropcatcher or by using dropcatching services.

Dark Marketing Ltd no longer offer a dropcatching service unfortunately, but there are other dropcatching services available. The most established UK dropcatching service is run by CHC Internet and can be found at Dropcatcher.co.uk (http://www.dropcatcher.co.uk). For £29 plus VAT (2010 price and less if you order in bulk), they will monitor the status of a domain name for you (providing they are not already monitoring it for someone else) and if it drops they will attempt to register it for you before anyone else does. Should they succeed, the domain name will be registered in your name for two years as part of the price already paid. Should they fail, you can simply apply your credit to another domain name. Basically you cannot lose because the time will come when they do catch you a name that you want.

As well as Dropcatcher, another dropcatching service I can recommend is Chris Bowler's Caught (http://www.caught.co.uk). Again, for a flat fee of £30, they will monitor a suspended domain name for you and attempt to catch it on your behalf the moment it becomes available. They operate on a no win no fee basis so again you cannot really lose.

Two others worth mentioning at this point. Dale Hubbard's Dropcatch (http://www.dropcatch.co.uk) offers a £30 no catch no fee dropcatching service with a full refund for unsuccessful catches, while another company, Domain Monster (http://www.domainmonster.com), charges £19.99 plus the registration fee, payable only when a domain is successfully caught.

Domain Monster also offer a dropcatching service for non-UK domains such as dotcoms, but there are much bigger players in this wider market including the likes of Snapnames (http://www.snapnames.com), Pool (http://www.pool.com) and Namejet (http://www.namejet.com). Unlike their UK focused counterparts, the big American companies have adopted an auction system whereby more than one person can backorder a domain name, and if this happens, the name will be auctioned. In fact Snapnames has recently adopted a business model whereby all expired domain names that it handles are sold by auction. This ultimately means that the chances of acquiring a dotcom for much less than it would normally sell for on the aftermarket are reduced, but the chances of actually getting it are increased (funds permitting).

To date, all the dropcatching services that catch expired UK domain names operate on a first come first served basis and do not catch the same name for two different people. So if you have a domain name in mind that is due for renewal and that has not been renewed, book it with one or more of the UK dropcatching services as soon as possible to increase your chances of getting a slot and then getting the name. If you really want a name, book it with as many dropcatchers as you can.

As well as the above dropcatchers who offer domain catching services to businesses and individuals, there are dozens of dropcatchers who usually only catch names for themselves – either for their own use or to resell. Some will offer to catch names on an irregular basis for others, however, and you will find them offering their services from time to time on forums like Acorn Domains (http://www.acorndomains.co.uk).

Do it yourself

You could of course become a dropcatcher yourself, either by using one of the ready made catching solutions on the market (where you pay a monthly fee to use a catching script hosted on a server) or you could set up your own dropcatching system, developing your own script and hosting it on your own server.

For off the shelf solutions, look for relevant forum posts at the likes of Acorn Domains.

As a dropcatcher, you will need to become a Nominet Registrar and a Nominet Member (the latter costs an initial £400 plus VAT plus £100 a year, but does entitle you to register domain names for £5 plus VAT instead of the non-Member rate of £80 plus VAT). You will also want access to Nominet's Domain Availability Checker (DAC) which enables you to make high volumes of queries about the real time availability of domain names. You will need to be a Nominet Registrar with Nominet membership to be eligible to use the DAC and there is a fee of £25 per year plus VAT for its use. If this is the way you want to go, you'll find more information on the Nominet website (http://www.nominet.org.uk). Nominet staff are also incredibly helpful should you have any questions.

To give you some idea of the costs involved in becoming a dropcatcher, in year one it will probably cost anything from £2,000-£3,000 in terms of Nominet fees and the cost of a ready made script hosted on a server. Beyond year one costs are lower because Nominet membership renewal is less expensive in subsequent years. Then there's the registration cost of each domain caught. That's quite a financial commitment and not to be rushed into. It's also worth thinking about what £2,000-£3,000 will buy you in the domain name aftermarket, particularly today when economic uncertainty means forced sales aplenty.

Domain name catching services basically use dedicated servers that query Nominet's database of domain names on a continuous basis, looking for any changes in the status of a domain name being monitored. You are basically asking Nominet over and over again if a name is available until you get a positive response. As soon as a suspended domain name is made available, the dropcatcher will attempt to secure it for their customer or himself by registering it.

Nominet do not publish lists of suspended domain names or names that are about to be dropped, but such lists do exist. One of the most successful dropcatchers of UK domain names in recent years has been Denys Ostashko, with valuable names like Liverpool.co.uk (yes, that is where that name ended up), Radio.co.uk and plenty more besides being caught by him since he started catching in 2005. He now runs a domain name auction website called DomainLore (http://www.domainlore.co.uk) where you can bid on domain names, mostly recently dropped ones. It's free to join and members have access to lists of UK domain names that have not been renewed and are due to be released by Nominet the following day. It's worth joining just to see the lists of dropping names and to judge for yourself the quality of names being released every single day of the week. Incidentally, DomainLore is a fantastic place to buy because it is still relatively unknown outside of domainer circles and prices aren't what they will be when the site becomes more established.

Dropcatchers also compile their own lists, and some spend hours every day querying Nominet's whois database to see the status of domains they are interested in buying (you'll find the search facility on Nominet's home page). Because of the time involved, it's often a good idea to specialise in a certain field - for example sports names - so that you can focus your searches on selected keywords. Software exists to help you do this. The most widely used is Domain Name Analyzer (available free from www.domainpunch.com) and it works with top level domains like .com as well as country level domains including .uk.

Lists do come up for sale on the domain name forums. Sometimes a partial list will even be posted to a forum free of charge so it's worthwhile checking them regularly. They won't differ very much from those published on DomainLore, but may give you more notice of domain names that are expiring (DomainLore only publishes lists a day in advance). Some dropcatching services also make lists available to their clients so it is worth asking.

Domain name fever

When developing multiple streams of income, as you will be urged to do throughout *Get Out While You Can*, I would recommend that you seriously consider domain name investing, even if your portfolio only consists of one or two good names. It's not a guaranteed passport to success, but domain name trading can offer the potential for big returns for anyone with an eye for a good name and the willingness to look at the long term potential of quality domain names.

A word of warning though. There is a danger you will develop domain name fever. It afflicts all domain name speculators at some point, usually early on in their careers. The temptation is to go on a buying frenzy, with every name you see or think of exploding in your mind's eye with potential.

You can learn as much from people's successes as you can their mistakes. Learn from one of mine. About eight years ago now, I had an idea for a series of websites that would trade under the one general banner, 24Seven, but would be operated independently on a franchise basis. So for example, one website would sell flowers online and would be operated by a florist and another would sell gifts online and be operated by someone who sold gifts. All of the sites would benefit from cross-linking so that anyone buying flowers would be told that they were only a click away from gifts or any of the other websites that franchisees had developed. I even had plans for more general content sites under the same 24Seven banner - football for example - which would help direct targeted traffic to related websites within the group.

Even now, while I'm writing about it, I can see the potential the idea had, but it was never going to work for one simple reason. I didn't have the time or resources to get it off the ground properly. That minor detail didn't stop me going on a spending spree that saw me buy every single domain name that was even vaguely related to my forthcoming internet empire.

Within a week I had spent £4,000 on registering domain names, all of which oozed massive potential as far as I was concerned.

In the cold light of day, most of those names were of no value whatsoever - either to me or anyone else. They were never going to develop into viable websites. Out of hundreds of domain names, I have only ever renewed half a dozen of them. An expensive lesson for me and a warning to you.

That warning aside, I don't know of a better online opportunity than domain name investing. Don't think you've missed the boat simply because you didn't take part in the initial goldrush. The boat is still taking on passengers. Opportunities abound both in selling domains and developing them simply because every website has to start with a domain name, something that will remain true for the foreseeable future.

Google is your new best friend

"If we value the pursuit of knowledge, we must be free to follow wherever that search may lead us. The free mind is not a barking dog, to be tethered on a ten-foot chain."
Adlai E. Stevenson Jr.

A website without visitors is like a telephone that never rings and yet far too many businesses think that all they have to do is build a website, put it on the worldwide web, and the world and his dog will beat a path to its door. If only life was that simple.

And yet in a funny sort of way life is that simple. That simple thanks to search engines and online directories. Search engines really are amazing pieces of technology. They allow us to find the proverbial needle in the haystack, and without them, the web just wouldn't be able to function.

Billions of pages are currently out there in cyberspace. Without search engines and their kin, finding your way around the web would be an impossible task. According to figures I came across recently, around 90% of internet users rely on search engines and directories to find what they want. I can only assume that the remaining 10% aren't online very much or tell lies to people conducting surveys.

For the owners of websites, the search engines are a gift from the gods. They drive targeted traffic direct to your door, bringing potential customers who, through their search criteria, have already expressed an interest in what you have to offer. And the search engines do this for you for nothing. Zilch. Nada. It's quite incredible that some of the biggest companies on Planet Earth – Google, Yahoo, Microsoft with Bing – will drum up business for you 24 hours a day, 365 days a year, and you don't have to pay them a penny.

I've already explained how little it can cost to get a website up and running. You can start an internet business for less than £50. That includes the cost of registering a domain name and an entire year's worth of hosting for your website. Now you know that some of the world's best salespeople can be out there working for you come rain or shine, day and night, and they won't charge you a penny for their services! With zero marketing costs, it's perfectly possible for you to make hundreds, thousands, even millions of pounds online thanks to the search engines. Nobody knows how to pull a crowd quite like Google!

In the UK alone, over 18 million households had internet access in 2009 according to the Office For National Statistics. That's 76% of all households - and rising. Of those, 90% have broadband. Add in those people who access the internet from work or school or college or the library or by mobile phone or via other devices like an iPod Touch or an iPad, and there must be close to 50 million internet users in the UK. Every day, these same millions of people use search engines to find what they are looking for on the web. Into a search box they type the one or two or more words that they think best describes what they are looking for and within a blink of an eye their favourite search engine has returned page after page of results. Not only that, it has kindly ranked what can be thousands of web pages in order of relevance.

Nobody remembers who came second

Given that thousands of results are returned for all but the most obscure of searches, we just don't have the time to trawl through them all. Instead, we tend to trust the search engine's judgement and look at the first one or two pages at most, only venturing further into the results if we haven't found what we were looking for on those first couple of pages (in fact we are as likely to start our search again as go much beyond page three).

Every day, any one (or any ten or hundreds or thousands) of those people might be directed to your website by the search engines, but the sad truth is that if you don't rank highly in the search engine results, you're simply not at the races. Those visitors are being sent to someone else's website.

You can be selling the best widgets in the world, but if you're not on the first two or three pages returned by the major search engines, forget it. In fact, let's cut to the chase. If you're not on the first page, forget it. Nobody is that bored or desperate to stumble across your website on page 102 of the search results. And if your website isn't even included in the search engines' results, you are not only sitting next to a phone that doesn't ring. You've been disconnected.

The flipside to this coin is that if you do rank highly in search engines for certain keywords and keyword phrases, you can cash in big time. Recent research by on-line advertising network, Chitika (http://www.chitika.com), revealed just how important it is to be ranked highly in Google's natural search results. Based on data taken from over eight million impressions across the Chitika advertising network during May, 2010, it was discovered that 34.35% of people clicked on the website ranked number one in the natural search results (in 2006 a similar study by AOL concluded that 42% of people clicked on the number one spot). So, if your website is ranked number one for keywords or keyword phrases, you can expect roughly a third of all searchers to visit your site. Obviously the more often that particular keyword or set of keywords is searched for, the more traffic your site will get.

The Chitika research goes on to show that websites that fill the second place slot received a 16.96% share of natural search traffic, while those in third, fourth and fifth place, get 11.42%, 7.73% and 6.19% respectively. This means that the number one spot gets nearly as much traffic as the number two to five spots combined. The research also shows that the number one spot gets more traffic than all the websites ranked from number five to number 20 put together (20th place is generally at the bottom of page two of the search results).

The upshot of this research is that if you're not on the first page, don't expect to benefit from much Google juice in terms of traffic. The higher you are up page one the better. If you make it to the top five, you're in business. And if you make it to number one, you are the business!

Given what is at stake, it's not surprising that an entire industry has grown up around what is called Search Engine Optimisation (or simply SEO). Search Engine Optimisation is the use of various on page and off page techniques to improve a website's ranking in search engines in a bid to attract more visitors to a website.

There are some excellent SEO companies that can do wonders for any business, but there are also plenty who promise much more than they will ever deliver. Nobody can guarantee to get you to the top of the search engines. Not unless they are talking about obscure search terms or even more obscure search engines. My advice? Do your own SEO, at least initially. This will not only save you money, SEO is so fundamental to running a successful website that it's something you should understand and implement yourself from day one. Should you then decide to employ an SEO company at some point down the line, you will have the basic knowledge and understanding to not have the wool pulled over your eyes. This chapter will hopefully point you in the right direction.

VIP entry to the very best search engines

The first thing that needs to be done is to make sure that search engines know that your website exists. You need to be in it to win it as the saying goes. And when I say search engines, there are barely a handful that you need to concern yourself with, particularly if you are in the UK.

Google currently stands head and shoulders above all the other search engines put together. Indeed, nine out of ten internet users in the UK use Google, making it in many ways the only game in town. As a rough rule of thumb, Google will deliver ten times the traffic that any other search engine does when comparing like for like rankings.

That said, that still means that 10% of the UK's internet population, around five million people, are using other search engines – not far off the entire population of Scotland. Yahoo accounts for around 5% of the UK's search market, MSN's Bing 3% and the likes of Ask (formerly and still known by many as Ask Jeeves) make up the remaining 2%. It's often the case that the likes of Yahoo or Bing will include a new website in its rankings months before Google does, and that, coupled with the fact that millions of people do use these search engines, means that you will want to be included in their search results too.

So that leaves us with four search engines who account for 99% of all searches conducted in the UK – Google, Yahoo, Bing and Ask. Since there are only four, it's not difficult to make sure that each one considers your website for inclusion in its search results.

One way to do this is to directly submit your website to the search engines for consideration. It's as simple as entering your website's URL (http://www.yourwebsite.co.uk) into the appropriate box and waiting for the search engine's robots to crawl and index your website's pages.

Google kindly provides a page for you to do this, but it does state that it cannot make any predictions or guarantees about when or if your website will appear in its search engine. It can be weeks, even months, before your website gets that all important visit. Here is the link anyway:

http://www.google.co.uk/addurl/

Bing also provides webmaster with a submit url page:

http://www.bing.com/webmaster/SubmitSitePage.aspx

Perhaps surprisingly, neither Yahoo or Ask make it as easy to suggest a site for inclusion. That's because search engines have their own way of finding and adding new sites, as Ask explains best. "Like most search engines, Ask Jeeves finds new sites by following links from others. Provided your site has authoritative incoming links, our crawler will pick it up automatically once it is live. This is an automated ongoing process, so we do not need to be made aware of your new site or any changes to it once it is live."

Knowing this is the key to not only getting your website indexed by the search engines, but to getting it indexed quickly. In fact, I know of several SEO companies who charge extra for this "express" submission and listing service when it's not costing them anything to do this for you. They simply provide a link from an established website to your new one and the search engine crawlers obligingly follow that link – usually within a couple of days.

Search engines have a picture of the worldwide web that they are continually monitoring for changes so that they can provide their users with the most up to date results possible. You want your website added to that picture. To get that done quickly, you simply need to get a website that is already being visited by the search engine robots to link to your new website.

It really is that simple. Instead of joining a massive queue along with all the other new websites, get an established website to link to you and bingo. The next time the search engines check the established website's page with your link on it, they will follow that link and add your website to their databases. And the likes of Google visit established sites every day looking for changes - so your website should appear in Google's index within days too. The link will only be to one of your pages, usually the homepage, but the search engine spiders will then follow your website's own internal links (links between the pages of your website), and in time those other pages will be indexed too.

Please don't confuse this technique with companies who offer to link to your site for a fee. These so-called "link farms" are well known to search engines, are universally disliked, and many don't even appear in the search results themselves. Adding your link to them is pointless. No, you need a genuine quality link from an established website, preferably in the same field as you, but not necessarily so. The more established and reputable the website, the better too.

Don't know anyone with an established website that will link to your new website? Yes you do. Me. Providing that your website is at least partly developed (no "coming soon" one page sites please), and is worthy of a link, I'll provide one from the Get Out While You Can website as part of a showcase of what people are doing to get their Plan B off the ground. Just e-mail me at info@entrepreneur.co.uk when you're ready.

The Hawthorn Effect and SEO

Getting indexed by the search engines and included in search results is a necessary first step, but the Holy Grail of SEO is to be sitting pretty at the top of the search engines (and Google in particular) for keywords and keyword phrases that will bring visitors to your website.

Three things about Search Engine Optimisation that you should bear in mind before we get down to the nitty gritty.

First, it isn't an exact science - doing X doesn't always lead to Y despite what you may read elsewhere. There are perhaps 200 or so factors that come into play when deciding how best to rank web pages, with search engine companies constantly tweaking their algorithms in a bid to deliver the best possible search results to their users. The precise nature of those algorithms is never divulged and what might be an important factor today might be irrelevant tomorrow. It's all too easy to attribute movement in ranking to changes that you recently made to your website, but any movement could as easily be attributed to unknown algorithm changes or indeed changes made to websites that rank above or below yours.

Following on from this, SEO is a job in progress. You have to keep at it, constantly defending your rankings from competing sites and continually aiming for those top spots yourself. Subtle changes in the algorithms can send you to cloud nine or knock you for six. Further down the line, it might be wise to employ an SEO company to manage this for you, especially in very competitive markets where it should be considered a full-time job. Just be aware of the fact that there are an enormous number of charlatans in the industry as well as otherwise well-meaning individuals who have most certainly risen to their level of incompetence. I won't be popular for saying that, but I see evidence of it every day.

Last but not least, every website is different. Every niche market that websites operate in is different. There is no one size SEO solution that fits all. General rules do apply generally, but it's specific action relating to a specific website that pays real dividends.

Back in the 1920s and 1930s, a series of productivity experiments were carried out at the giant Hawthorne Works in Cicero, Illinois. Employing as many as 45,000 people at the time, the factory produced telephones and other consumer electrical goods. The most famous of the experiments involved varying the amount of light available to workers on the factory floor. When the amount of light was increased, a rise in productivity was noted, leading to the initial conclusion that light had a beneficial effect on output. However, when light levels were reduced, increases in productivity were also noted. It turned out that it wasn't so much light levels that were affecting productivity, but the fact that the workers were responding to the attention received for being part of an experiment.

Although many SEO professionals might disagree, getting your site ranked highly by the search engines has a touch of the Hawthornes about it. I say this because not only is SEO not an exact science, but doing practically anything at all to your website is going to have a positive effect in terms of your rankings, providing that it's not something frowned upon by the search engines. Simply adding fresh content to a website on a regular basis will increase your search engine derived traffic many times over as the months tick by. Simply ensuring that your website is live year after year will boost your traffic. Search engines love websites that hang around. Maybe, just like the workers at the Hawthorne Works, websites like being part of experiments.

One piece of very good news though. Simply by employing even the most basic of SEO techniques, your website will quickly overtake the vast majority of websites that don't employ them. And by vast majority, I mean everything from hobby sites to those of multi-national behemoths because there are plenty of big cheeses out there that don't understand search engines either.

Straight from the horse's mouth

Although there is incredible secrecy surrounding the precise algorithms that Google and other search engines use to rank sites, what they are looking for in general isn't a secret at all.

Here's the highlights of what Google says in its webmaster guidelines:

Design and content guidelines

• Make a site with a clear hierarchy and text links.

• Every page should be reachable from at least one static text link.

• Create a useful, information-rich site, and write pages that clearly and accurately describe your content.

• Think about the words users would type to find your pages, and make sure that your site actually includes those words within it.

• Try to use text instead of images to display important names, content, or links. The Google crawler doesn't recognize text contained in images. If you must use images for textual content, consider using the "ALT" attribute to include a few words of descriptive text.

• Make sure that your <title> elements and ALT attributes are descriptive and accurate.

• Check for broken links and correct HTML.

• If you decide to use dynamic pages (i.e., the URL contains a "?" character), be aware that not every search engine spider crawls dynamic pages as well as static pages.

Quality guidelines - basic principles

• Make pages primarily for users, not for search engines. Don't deceive your users or present different content to search engines than you display to users, which is commonly referred to as "cloaking".

• Avoid tricks intended to improve search engine rankings. A good rule of thumb is whether you'd feel comfortable explaining what you've done to a website that competes with you. Another useful test is to ask, "Does this help my users? Would I do this if search engines didn't exist?"

• Don't participate in link schemes designed to increase your site's ranking. In particular, avoid links to web spammers or "bad neighbourhoods" on the web, as your own ranking may be affected adversely by those links.

• Don't use unauthorised computer programs to submit pages, check rankings, etc. Such programs consume computing resources and violate our Terms of Service.

Quality guidelines - specific guidelines

• Avoid hidden text or hidden links.

• Don't use cloaking or sneaky redirects.

• Don't load pages with irrelevant keywords.

• Don't create multiple pages, subdomains, or domains with substantially duplicate content.

• Avoid "doorway" pages created just for search engines.

• If your site participates in an affiliate program, make sure that your site adds value. Provide unique and relevant content that gives users a reason to visit your site first.

Bing will tell you much the same :

• The best way to attract people to your website, and keep them coming back, is to fill your webpages with valuable content in which your target audience is interested.

• In the visible webpage text, include words users might choose as search query terms to find the information on your website.

• Limit all webpages to a reasonable size.

• Make sure that each webpage is accessible by at least one static text link.

• Don't put the text that you want indexed within images.

• Links that are embedded in menus, list boxes, and similar elements aren't accessible to web crawlers.

• Keep your website hierarchy fairly flat. That is, each webpage should only be from one to three clicks away from the default (home) webpage.

And here's what Bing doesn't like:

• Attempting to increase a webpage's keyword density by adding lots of irrelevant words. This includes stuffing ALT tags that users are unlikely to view.

• Using hidden text or links. Only use text and links that are visible to users.

• Using techniques, such as link farms, to artificially increase the number of links to your webpage.

So there you have it – straight from the horse's mouth. Follow those guidelines and you won't go far wrong. In fact, if you do produce a website full of quality, informative content, and follow a few simple Search Engine Optimisation tips, your website will be welcomed with open arms by the search engines and it will rank highly.

Of course there will always be those who look for short cuts to the top. Those who produce poor quality content, offer little if anything of value to visitors, and who still want high search engine rankings. Those looking for a magic bullet to the top. It's those webmasters who will be most tempted by activities that seek to boost search engine rankings, but that run contrary to the search engine guidelines outlined above (hidden text, pages stuffed with keywords, etc.,). Techniques that are collectively known as Black Hat SEO. They are used primarily by people from the dark side. They aren't messiahs. They're just very naughty boys. Black Hat SEO can and does work – until it is found out and then the damage caused can be extremely costly indeed. Don't think you'll be caught? It just takes one of your competitors to tip Google off and all hell breaks loose.

SEO techniques that work with the search engines to accurately reflect the content of a web page are collectively known as White Hat SEO. It all sounds very Harry Potter, with references to wizardry only encouraging the widely held belief that SEO is some form of magic. It isn't. Put very simply, SEO works best when it acts as signposts for search engines to that fantastic content of yours. Think of SEO in those terms and you are halfway there.

Content is king

I've been writing about Search Engine Optimisation since 2003. Much of what I advocated as true back then is still true today. Yes, SEO is a constantly shifting landscape, but the core values remain more or less constant. One of those core values is that written content is king. You'll be sick of hearing that content is king by the end of this book, but it's as true for human visitors as it is for search engines.

When search engine robots visit your website, the information they take away with them is text – and it's that text that they will use to decide what each page on your website is about and how it should rank compared to other web pages about the same subject.

Search engine robots love plain old text on a web page. They can lap it up all day long. They cannot read text that is part of an image. You need eyes to be able to do that and search engine robots don't have eyes. Similarly, when it comes to designing websites using frames, scripts and fancy programs like Adobe Flash, it's largely lost on the search engine robots. They just want text, text, and more text. It therefore makes sense to give the search engine robots exactly what they want so that they can return to their masters, bellies full of good news about your website.

The search engine robots don't see your web pages as human visitors do. Instead, the robots crawl the source code that makes up the page. That source code contains not only the text on a page that is visible to human visitors, but also some vital text that for the most part is never seen by humans (unless they are particularly nosey). This vital text can be found in what are called Meta Tags and it represents manna from heaven for search engine robots.

If talk of Meta Tags is starting to sound like the kind of techie stuff you normally avoid like the plague, don't throw in the towel just yet. It is not only very easy to understand, it's very important too in terms of Search Engine Optimisation. So bear with me for two minutes. Your top spots in Google might depend on it.

Everything you need to know about Meta Tags, but were afraid to ask

Meta Tags are lines of code that appear at the top of the html code of web pages between the <HEAD> and </HEAD> section. Apart from the Title Tag (which isn't really a Meta Tag, as I'm sure the purists will be quick to point out), the information that appears here isn't normally seen by visitors to your website - unless they choose to look at your source code.

Instead the Meta Tags provide information that can be used by browsers, spiders and crawlers, to find out more about your web page. I say web page and not website because every page on your website has its own code and therefore has the potential to have its own Meta Tags too. Since every web page has the ability to rank in the search results in its own right, it's well worth remembering that.

Below is a short sample source code for a simple HTML web page (HTML stands for Hypertext Markup Language and it is used to publish content on the Web).

```
<html>

        <head>

        text here is visible in the source code,
but not visible on your web page because it
appears in the head of the html  code - this is
where your Meta Tags go

        </head>

        <body>

        text here is visible in the source code
        and on your web page because it appears
        in the body of the html code - this is
        where your page content goes

        </body>

</html>
```

Search engines, like everything else in this wired world of ours, don't stand still long enough to pin them down precisely. What works one month, might not work another. What doesn't work this month, might be back in the equation next month. It's important to know this because a lot of what passes for gospel on the internet regarding search engines is often out of date. And that's particularly true of Meta Tags. Indeed, it's true to say that their overall importance to search engine rankings has diminished with time, but that's not to say that they don't still play a significant part in the overall SEO and indeed wider Search Engine Marketing (SEM) game.

Here's an example of what Meta Tags look like for one of my websites, Bras.co.uk:

```
<html>
      <head>
      <meta name="Description"
content="Bras.co.uk - The Bras Website, the
best designer bras and brand name bras at the
best prices in bra sizes A to K with news,
special offers, bra sizing help and
lingerie" />
      <meta name="Keywords" content="Bra, Bras,
Brassiere, Lingerie, Underwear, Designer, Plus
Size">
<title>Bras - The Bra Website</title>
      </head>
      <body>
      Website content that is visible to human
visitors goes here
      </body>
</html>
```

Other Meta Tags often appear such as Copyright and Distribution Meta Tags, but they are optional and not relevant to SEO. The three Tags you want to focus on are the Title Tag, the Description Meta Tag and the Keywords Meta Tag.

When I say most visitors to a web page never see the Meta Tags, that's not strictly true. If they find the web page via a search engine, chances are they have seen your Meta Tags. That's because search engines generally use Meta Tags to provide the short piece of information that people see in the search results.

Take Bras.co.uk. If you use Google to search for the word bras, at the time of writing you would find Bras.co.uk at around the fifth spot in the rankings (obviously my plan is that one day someone will read this, go to Google and find Bras.co.uk sitting pretty in the number one slot).

Here's exactly what you would see:

Bras - The Bra Website
Bras.co.uk - The Bras Website, the best designer bras and brand name bras at the best prices in bra sizes A to K with news, special offers, ...
www.bras.co.uk/ - Cached - Similar

The underlined top line, Bras – The Bra Website, is taken directly from my Title Tag. The description that follows is taken word for word from my Description Tag. By providing Google with both, I can more or less control what Google shows in its search results with regards to my website. The idea is to make both the Title Tag and the Description Tag attractive enough for the person doing the search to want to click on the link to my website and not a link to another website that is also vying for their attention above or below my entry,

The Title Tag

For me, the most important element of Search Engine Optimisation at the moment is the page's Title Tag. You may not have realised that each web page has a Title because it's only visible in the very top left-hand corner of the browser bar and a lot of people don't even look at it. The point is, search engines do look at it and they look at it very closely indeed. It's also used as the title for when your page is added to favourites or bookmarked.

Imagine you were opening a new shop in your nearest town and for arguments sake let's say you were going to sell dog bowls. Just dog bowls. To make it even more interesting let's pretend your name is John Smith. Unfortunately, because of lack of money you can't afford to rent anything with a shop front and so your new enterprise in confined to a room above the fish and chip shop. You do however have the money to erect a sign on the wall outside to alert potential customers of your presence. What would you put on that sign? Hopefully the two words "dog" and "bowls" appeared in your answer.

The Title Tag is a lot like that sign. It will tell potential visitors what's on the page before they see it. More importantly, it will be used by search engines to label that page and define its content. If you have a website that sells nothing but dog bowls, the title tag of your website's homepage should say just that. Dog Bowls. With just those two words you have made a giant step towards a high ranking for the search phrase "dog bowls".

Unfortunately, or fortunately for you, a lot of website owners do not realise just how important that sign can be. Instead of Dog Bowls, they will put something like Home Page or Index or John Smith's Website. There are literally hundreds of thousands of web pages out there whose Title Tag reads "Your Title Goes Here" (check it out by searching for that phrase at Google). "Welcome To My Website" is another one in this category. Such websites are wasting a golden market opportunity. Their Title Tags say nothing. The sign outside the fish and chip shop might as well be blank.

Use your Title Tag to sum up your web page in one to six words. Keep it short and focused so that search engines know exactly what the web page is about. Think hard about what people will enter as their search term. Your website is about dog bowls so Dog Bowls is a great Title Tag for the homepage. If you then have a page for pink dog bowls say as much in the Title Tag for that page: Pink Dog Bowls.

Don't try to be all things to all men. Keep the title tag short, and sweet. Cut out any unnecessary words. Title Tags should be clutter free. Be specific – because by being so you will attract very targeted traffic to your website. If your page is a review of a Porsche Cayman S, your title tag should be as simple as:

<title>Porsche Cayman S Review</title>

Another big mistake is putting your company name - as in Acme Services - when it means absolutely nothing except to people who know who you are already. It's okay for the Ford Motor Company to do it or Amazon or British Airways, but it's not a good idea if you're not a household name. One exception would be if your business has some local or niche recognition or your business name says everything anyone needs to know about you - as in Lockerbie Locksmiths.

A bad Title Tag would be:

<title>Joe Smith's Porsche Cayman S Review</title>

Unless of course Joe Smith was well known in Porsche circles and his opinion was in great demand. If that was true and people were specifically searching for Joe's reviews, I would definitely include his name in the Title Tag. Otherwise you are just confusing the search engines. Is this a page about Joe Smith or a Porsche Cayman S?

If your title tag matches a search term that's likely to be used, and your web page also contains that search term, you're on your way to high rankings. So for example, your company is called Acme Ltd and you organise fishing holidays in Scotland. Your Title Tag should simply read "Fishing Holiday In Scotland" or even "Fishing Holiday Scotland" because that is what people will search for if they are looking for a fishing holiday in Scotland.

<title>Fishing Holiday Scotland</title>

Don't put Holiday Scotland in the hope of drawing a bigger crowd. It won't happen. You'll just be lost in the huge scrum surrounding those two keywords. Even if you did succeed in drawing a larger crowd, few of those extra eyeballs would be interested in a fishing holiday of any kind. Meanwhile, a more savvy webmaster is going to be targeting your niche with the precision of a sniper and cleaning up by doing so.

Fishing is obviously key to your offering. You only want those interested in a fishing holiday in Scotland visiting your website. Let the search engines know precisely what your page offers and the search engines will pass on the good news to the appropriate people.

Don't cut out important words. Chinese Restaurant for example might describe your business, but Chinese Restaurant Dublin is far better because someone looking for a Chinese meal in Dublin's fair city will include the word Dublin in their search. In this instance it's probably a good idea to include the restaurant's name too. So you might go for:

<title>Chinese Restaurant Dublin Lucky Star</title>

Always place the words in your Title Tag in order of relevance. The most important words must come first. Ditch any words that you don't really need, but don't ditch the wrong ones. Always put yourself in your visitors shoes. What is it that they are searching for? Does my page help satisfy that need or want?

And if so how can I use my Title Tag to tell the search engines that my page is what their users are looking for?

You can use the Google Keyword Tool discussed earlier in the chapter, *You Don't Need No Rich Dad*, to find keyword phrases that people actually use to find things online. You'll find it here:

https://AdWords.google.com/select/KeywordToolExternal

Put in a keyword or keywords relating to your website and a string of search queries will be shown. Each one not only gives you an idea for content. Each one will make a great Title Tag too.

The Description Tag

You can think of your Description Tag as your elevator pitch – 15 to 25 words that sum up your offering to someone you meet between floors in a lift. Again, webmasters (including me more often than not) don't use this tag to its full potential. If you have no Description Meta Tag, Google will take a random sentence from your web page that it feels is relevant, and it will use that in the blurb about your website in its search results. Not the end of the world, but you lose control over what Google shows to potential visitors. At the same time, your competitors may be using that blurb to full effect, simply by having a Description Meta Tag.

It's actually a very good idea to take the time to write a short description that perfectly captures the essence of what the web page offers potential visitors. In fact make it so good that it can be the opening paragraph of text on your page so that every visitor knows exactly what you're offering them.

Again, each page of your website is unique and so deserves its own description tag, even if it is derived from your "master" version.

For our Chinese restaurant's homepage we might have:

<meta name="Description" content="Lucky Star Chinese Restaurant, Any Street, Dublin, offers the best Chinese food seven days a week – takeaway and home delivery also available" />

For a page that featured the menu we might have:

<meta name="Description" content="Lucky Star Chinese Restaurant, Any Street, Dublin, restaurant menu and takeaway menu – open seven days a week" />

The Keyword Tag

The third Meta Tag that's worth discussing in the Keyword Meta Tag. Once upon a time this was a very important Tag - it basically told search engines what keywords related to your web pages. It was abused from day one though. To increase traffic, webmasters would stuff this Tag with popular search words like Sex and Elvis when they were irrelevant to the page's content. And so search engines more or less gave up on them.

Should you bother including a Keyword Tag? It costs nothing and as long as the keywords are genuinely relevant to the page's content, it's not going to harm you. You also never know if or when they will once again play even a small part in the ranking formula. So my answer would be yes.

How many keywords should you include? No more than 20 keywords AND keyword phrases (if you are a window cleaner the keyword phrase "window cleaner" is more relevant than "window" and "cleaner" apart). Separate each keyword and keyword phrase with a comma.

I wanted to mention it because the Keyword Tag has not only been misused, but as with keywords in general, it has been misunderstood. Webmasters tend to list words that they would

LIKE to be ranked for – and not what their content says they SHOULD be ranked for. Make sure that the content of the page is accurately reflected in your Title Tag, Description Tag and Keywords Tag and you won't be going far wrong.

WordPress and Meta Tags

If you are building websites using a software program like Adobe Dreamweaver, SeaMonkey or KompoZer, it is easy enough to add or change Meta Tags. Simply toggle between the WYSIWYG page view (known as Design in Dreamweaver, Normal in SeaMonkey and KompoZer) and the Code or Source view respectively and you will be in a position to edit the page's code. If you are using WordPress or another content management system, it isn't quite as easy to look under the bonnet unless you are confident enough to hack away at the code provided. WordPress by default uses the title of your blog post as your Title Tag, but doesn't generate other Metatags by default. As always though there are plenty of Plugins ready to ride to the rescue – the popular All In One SEO Pack Plugin, for example, promises to automatically optimise your WordPress blog for search engines. Job done.

Content is (still) king

When search engines rank pages, they are more accurately ranking the content of those pages. Through their algorithms, they aim to provide their users with the most relevant content for their search enquiries.

Some websites will always have an advantage over others. For someone searching for the keyword "Porsche", the official Porsche website quite rightly should be top of the pile in any self-respecting search engine. You could write page after page of content regarding Porsche cars and I've no doubt it would help you rank highly, but toppling the official Porsche site would take some doing – even if you had more or better content. Other algorithm factors, such as the authority nature of the official site, high quality inbound links, and the age of the site, will conspire against you and assure that the official Porsche site maintains the number one slot (I say that with the proviso that no site is guaranteed the number one spot, whether an official site or not, and there are countless examples of "official" sites ranking below "unofficial" ones).

For someone searching for "Porsche Maidenhead", the website of a Porsche dealership in Maidenhead, or classified ads for Porsches for sale in Maidenhead, are probably more relevant than the official Porsche website. That's a completely different search to "Porsche" and not surprisingly produces different results. In fact the official Porsche website isn't in the top 20 results for "Porsche Maidenhead" in Google UK at the time of writing. Why would it be unless Porsche had some sort of connection with Maidenhead, was promoting a dealership in the town that incidentally boasts the widest brick-built arch bridge in the world, or was otherwise specifically targeting the "Porsche Maidenhead" search result?

For someone searching for "black leather handbag", well that's where it gets interesting because it's not so obvious which website should rank above all others. Unlike the brand name, Porsche, "black leather handbag" is a generic term used by purveyors of handbags the world over. This is where it's game on for you to convince the search engines that anyone searching for a black leather handbag should be sent in one direction only. To your website dedicated in whole or part to black leather handbags. Get it right and you could well be in the money.

As a small fry in a big pond the best weapon at your disposal is content. The key to creating good content is to write first and foremost for your visitors. They are the ones who are going to make you money. Write naturally, as if you are having a conversation with each reader, one at a time. Create the best content possible about black leather handbags, make sure your Meta Tags are singing from the same hymn sheet as your content, and good things will surely follow.

There will always be those who want to cut SEO corners by continually repeating a keyword on a page, a technique better known as keyword stuffing. Not only does keyword stuffing not make for a great reading experience (in fact it makes the writer look illiterate), it is a black hat SEO technique that went out with the ark.

If your web page is about sailing for example, rather than squeeze in the keyword "sailing" umpteen times, use it only when you would anyway, as if search engines didn't exist. Better for the word to appear naturally alongside other words relating to sailing such as sail, sailed, yacht, yachts, boat, sea, skipper, man overboard, and so on.

Search engines know all about keyword stuffing. They know full well that it is a clumsy attempt to game the rankings. Equally, they know that content written for humans would be full of related words, and they are increasingly ranking pages not just on specific words found on them, but in what context those words appear, their meaning in that context, and their relationship with other words that appear with them.

For example, the word "Essex" on a page is likely to be related to the county of Essex in England. When that same word appears on a page with the word "David" before it, it's likely to be about the man who sung such pop classics as *Gonna Make You A Star*, *Hold Me Close* and *A Winter's Tale* (I thought I'd list three of David's hits in case it helps someone win Radio 2's *PopMaster* quiz one day). Search engines know that someone searching for "David Essex" has no immediate interest in the county of Essex and so will rank only those pages related to the actor and singer.

Search engines do this by using what is called Latent Semantic Indexing (LSI), a technique which allows pages to be indexed and ranked in terms of identified word patterns and the relationships between important terms and concepts contained in text. It's no secret that LSI is playing an ever increasing role in the ranking of web pages and that's where naturally written content comes up trumps. It's exactly what LSI is looking for.

Follow that blog

At the start of the Noughties, blogging emerged from the shadows of the Web to go mainstream, spurred on by the release of easy to use blogging services and software such as Blogger, Movable Type and WordPress. A blog is short for weblog, a diary style website that can cover any subject you care to mention. You can blog about politics, current affairs or nuclear physics or you can blog about handbags, chocolate or your sex life. It's a free world or so they tell me.

Blogging quickly came to the attention of the SEO community when blogs started to appear all over the search results. This shouldn't have been that much of a surprise. After all, a blog is simply a website by any other name. The leading blogs were often very well written, they were updated very regularly (often several times a day), they were often dedicated to one specific topic, and they attracted inbound links because of the quality of the content. In short, everything a good website should be (blog or not). They deserved to rank well.

The success of blogs in terms of their ability to rank well was based on the fact that content is king – and that content written for humans is the king of kings. Rather surprisingly, this point was often overlooked in SEO circles where it was decided that the success of blogs must be down to the platforms that they were built on.

This led to a rush for the door as everyone and his dog started a blog for no other reason than to game the search engines. Instead of the articulate, passionate and entertaining blogs that inspired this stampede, literally hundreds of thousands of "splogs" - spam blogs – were created with poor, stolen or recycled content from the likes of Wikipedia, and then plastered with Google AdSense and affiliate links. Splogging became the new spam.

Not so surprisingly, splogs didn't automatically rank highly simply because they were built on blogging platforms. Indeed, the vast majority didn't rank at all. Those that did find their way into the rankings didn't stay there very long. Indeed, splogs fared no better than the countless blogs that also never rank well. Only the best of blogs rank highly. The sheer volume of blogs simply meant that there were lots of very good ones in what is a very big sea of mediocrity. I would guess that the vast majority of the writers of those blogs that did (and still do) rank well had never even heard of SEO. It didn't matter because the natural semantic quality of the content and the frequent addition of more content (a characteristic of a diary driven website) was exactly what the search engines were looking for.

The missing link

There is another characteristic of blogging that helped it on its way to the top of the search engines. Links. Linking to other websites is a big part of blogging. Or at least it is when you are blogging for no other reason than to entertain and inform your readers.

Many moons ago, a link was considered by the search engines as a vote for another website. The thinking behind this was that a link from one website to another was a recommendation to visit it. The more links a page received from other websites, the more recommendations or votes. Search engines, and particularly Google with its PageRank, used this information to help rank web pages.

PageRank is part of the Google algorithm that is based on link analysis. Each web page is assigned a PageRank of between 0 and 10, with a higher PR indicative of the importance of that page within its field. The commonly held belief was that by increasing the number of links to a web page from other websites, your PageRank would increase and so would your search engine rankings.

Cue a similar rush for the door. The race was on to get links. Webmasters became obsessed with their PageRank, feverishly seeking out link after link that would (fingers crossed) propel them up the search results. Link building quickly became the Holy Grail of SEO, and I believe that just as quickly, Google and the other search engines took note. Links were no longer about recommendation. Links were being used and abused to game the search engines.

The search engines couldn't have been any clearer about their change of direction as to the value of links. Link stuffing forum posts and blog comments were among the first casualties. Google even removed its beloved PageRank from Webmaster Tools in 2009, with the comment, "We've been telling people for a long time that they shouldn't focus on PageRank so much; many site owners seem to think it's the most important metric for them to track, which is simply not true."

I would advise the squeamish to stop reading now because I am about to tell you something that few believe and even fewer want to hear. Link building as a SEO tool in 2010 is dead. That's my personal opinion and it certainly isn't one shared by the majority of SEO professionals. Not publicly anyway because there is a good deal of easy money to be made from link building campaigns and probably will be for years to come.

Create a website yourself and you will quickly become the target of link building campaigns. You will start to receive link requests from webmasters who have visited your site, love its content and want to swap links with you. All very flattering, unless you know that the very same link request is being sent out to as many webmasters as the link builder can find e-mail addresses for. I have around 50 live websites and many more holding pages with a contact e-mail on them. Every week I receive literally hundreds of link exchange requests, all from webmasters who have visited one of my sites, love the content and want to swap links. I am obviously so good at what I do that these webmasters even love the content on my holding pages that are by and large content-free.

If I am receiving hundreds of requests a week, I can only guess at the millions of link requests that must be flying around on a daily basis, all sent with the sole aim of gaming the search engines. You are welcome to join in if you want, but don't for one second believe that a link from one mediocre website to another counts for something in this day and age because it doesn't.

Link builders think they are being very clever by setting up triangular link exchanges. Instead of the very obvious direct link between websites A and B, a third website C is introduced. Website A is asked to link to website B, but so that the search engines don't suspect anything underhand is going on, website C will link to website A instead of B linking to A. Indeed, why stop at three? You could be really clever and introduce D, E and F to the link building coven. That would really fool the search engines. Not.

Just as links in forum posts and links in blog comments are virtually worthless as far as SEO goes, so too in my opinion are links gained via such link building strategies. I am not quite a lone voice in believing that, but if SEO people were a football crowd, I would be among the away fans who must have come in a taxi.

The baby hasn't been thrown out with the bath water, however. Genuine links are a valuable clue to the popularity of a page and should play a role in determining quality search results and indeed they do. Search engines today, and Google in particular, place great emphasis on the origin of the link. If it comes from what is known as an authority website, a website such as the BBC or a sport's governing body or any other site that Google has earmarked as an authority in its niche, then that link will carry a great deal of weight. If it comes from "just another website", it will carry very little. Indeed, my guess is that a link from a website such as the BBC is worth hundreds of links from websites that command no authority whatsoever.

Why should this be? Authority websites are seen as trustworthy. If the BBC's website links to your website it does so for no other reason than to enhance its own visitors' experience. The BBC won't link to another website without good reason. It certainly doesn't link to you because it wants a link in return.

How do you get links from authority sites? Build websites full of great content and useful information. That's right. Content is king yet again. Great content always does and always will attract quality links from other webmasters without you having to ask for them. There is nothing wrong with making others aware of that great content by commenting on related blogs, posting in same niche forums, issuing press releases, gaining entry to quality directories like the Open Directory Project (http://www.dmoz.org) and so on. The point is you should be doing this anyway, not simply to gain some sort of SEO benefit.

It is also worth noting that links to authority websites can help your search engine rankings. Outbound links to relevant content improves your visitors' experience and can increase your credibility in your visitors' eyes, so even without SEO benefits, it is worth doing. Yes, visitors will leave your website, but if your content is good enough, they will be back. The SEO benefits are not clear, but my own take on this is that relevant outbound links, especially to authority sites, help the search engines see where your website fits into the jigsaw. If you have a new website dedicated to widgets and your outbound links are to relevant and authoritative widget websites, it helps reinforce what your website is about.

As I said earlier, my take on link building is far from the madding SEO crowd in terms of orthodoxy. Most SEO gurus will tell you different. Not only should you be link building like there is no tomorrow, you should be using their services to do so. This despite the fact that Google explicitly states in its guidelines, "Don't participate in link schemes designed to increase your site's ranking." What part of "don't" do they not understand?

SEO in a nutshell

If you want Google to be your new best friend, here is what I want you to do.

• Read over the guidelines provided by Google and Bing earlier in this chapter relating to websites. Do as they ask.

• Build websites full of great original content. Add new content on a regular basis. The more competitive your niche, the more often you will need to add fresh content.

• Remember that search engines love text. They can't get enough of the stuff.

• Make sure that each web page can be reached via a link from at least one other page on your website. Keep your site architecture as flat as possible: no page should be more than two or three clicks away from your home page.

• Ensure that your Title Tag sums up the content of your page accurately and concisely.

• Make sure that the words used in your Title Tag, as well as keywords and key phrases relating to it, appear in you content, but do not go down the route of keyword stuffing. Write primarily for humans.

• Ensure that your Description Tag does the same in an elevator pitch style so that you stand out in the search engine result pages (SERPs).

• Use the Google AdWords Keyword Tool and your own site statistics to see what people are actually searching for and build more great content around that.

• Never forget that content is king and that unique well written content will always be linked to by other websites. You too should link to great content.

That's what works for me. My websites consistently rank well for related keywords. With no marketing budget and having never spent a second of my time "link building", my humble collection of niche websites attracted around half a million unique visitors in 2006. That gave me half a million opportunities to make money. In 2009, that figure had risen to over 1.25 million unique visitors. Maybe I'm doing something right. It has been known to happen on occasion. Or maybe I just like being part of experiments.

How to earn money by asking visitors to leave your website

"You'll never leave where you are, until you decide where you'd rather be."
Robert Brockman

Back in 2001, I was selling CDs and related music products both by mail order and online. I concentrated my efforts on niche markets – punk, reggae, Seventies rock and so on – and had lots of ideas for expanding what was really one of several part-time businesses I filled my days with at the time.

My biggest problem was getting record companies to supply me. Small independent record labels were happy for me to sell their CDs, but the majors and their distributors were only interested in supplying me if I had retail premises and would commit to buying so many thousands of pounds worth of product per month (a favourite trick of big companies who want to monopolise markets through the back door is to have a minimum order requirement that leaves you with little or nothing to spend with other companies).

Frustrated, I contacted CDNow, one of the biggest internet music retailers at the time, to ask if they would be willing to supply me with what I needed. CDNow was started in 1994 by twin brothers, Jason and Matthew Olim, in the basement of their parents' home in Amber, Pennsylvania, and it was one of the first big retail success stories of the dotcom boom. It transpired that CDNow didn't supply other websites, but to my surprise they were more than happy to put me in touch with their own main supplier. That supplier quickly agreed to supply me with practically any CD then available in the USA, including releases from all the major labels. Overnight I had access to a truly huge catalogue of music including hard to find imports.

I then began importing CDs from the States and selling them to my customers in the UK. Often I was able to supply current best selling albums for less than UK retailers, even after taking into account the cost of transportation from the USA, currency fluctuations and custom duties. A week wouldn't go by without DHL turning up at my door with boxes of CDs that I'd unpack, sort, and then send on to my customers.

What was quite a successful enterprise came to a rather abrupt end, however, when the British Phonographic Industry (BPI) starting accusing the likes of Amazon, Play.com and CD Wow (no relation of CDNow) of breaching copyright laws by buying CDs meant for overseas markets and selling them in the UK. I was doing exactly the same. I didn't really want the BPI coming after little old me so I moved on to pastures new.

CDNow is no longer trading either. After struggling financially, it was bought by Bertelsmann in 2000, and shortly after helping me find a supplier, the rights to the CDNow name passed to Amazon. Even today, if you visit CDNow.com you are redirected to Amazon's website.

The birth of affiliate marketing

In its day, CDNow was a very innovative business. It was the first internet company to offer a huge range of albums, making full use of the fact that internet stores do not have the limited shelf space of their bricks and mortar counterparts (virtual shelves can be as long as you like). It was also among the first to realise the importance of website "stickiness", attracting and retaining visitors by adding record reviews and music news to its site. In short, giving customers a reason to come back often and hang around longer. And as early as 1995, it was using the RealAudio format to allow visitors to "sample" music before they bought it.

CDNow was also one of the first online retailers to operate a program whereby other website owners could earn money simply by linking to the CDNow website. It launched its Cosmic Credit program in March, 1997, and by the end of the year it had 10,000 Cosmic Credit members. By September, 1998, it had passed the 100,000 member milestone, and by the Summer of 2000 there were more than 250,000 members in the program.

Think about that for a moment. Over 250,000 members who were sending visitors to the CDNow website on a daily basis. And only if those visitors became customers did CDNow reward the referring members with either credit to spend at CDNow or cash in the form of commission based on a small percentage of the order value. A quarter of a million (sales)people driving traffic to a website and they only get paid if someone buys something. No wonder CDNow said that its Cosmic Credit program was the company's most successful method of acquiring new customers online.

Another early pioneer of what is now most commonly known as affiliate marketing was Amazon. Its Amazon Associates program was launched in July, 1996, and today boasts almost a million members. In the UK, Amazon Associates can earn up to 10% commission on sales resulting from sending visitors to Amazon's UK website (http://www.amazon.co.uk). If your website's main audience was in the USA, you could do the same by sending visitors to Amazon.com (after signing up to its Associate program) and if you had a French language website you could become a Partenaire at Amazon.fr (you will need a separate Associate account for each Amazon program that you join as they are run independently of one another).

Amazon provides Associates with text links, banners and other tools including a self contained online store called aStore. As an Amazon Associate, you use these tools to link to the Amazon website from your website, visitors follow the links, and if a sale results you earn a commission. It's that simple. You can log in to the Amazon Associates website to see how much you have earned on any given day and every month any commissions earned are transferred directly to your bank account.

Anyone with a website could and should be earning money via the Amazon Associates program. It's free to join and you can sign up simply by going to the foot of the Amazon.co.uk homepage and clicking on the link named Join Affiliates. I know of people who earn full-time incomes from the Amazon Associates program alone, but even for those earning less, it's likely to be only one of many revenue streams you can develop.

To give you an idea of the money I make as an Amazon Associate, I earned £231.85 for the month of January, 2009. Not enough to retire on admittedly, but a welcome contribution to my overall online earnings, nonetheless, and for very little work. That commission came from me selling 288 items during the month with a retail value of £2,819.70. By comparison, in January, 2010, I earned £317.34 as an Amazon Associate from selling 415 items with a total value of £5,007.40.

Around half of the items I sell as an Amazon Associate are books, about a third DVDs, and the remainder toys, games and so on. Not big ticket items, but regular sellers. Given the huge range of products that Amazon sells – books, DVDs, jewellery, clothing, toys and games, electrical goods, computer hardware and software, even adult sex toys – you too are bound to find products that you can link to that will interest visitors to your website(s) and that will make you money. At certain times of year, Christmas for example, you find customers following your link to one product and then buying it and other (often unrelated) items too. You earn a commission on everything that they buy.

Up to 10% commission on the sale of a book might not sound like a lot, but compare it to what the publisher of the book might earn on that same sale. Amazon will take 60% of the cover price of the book for starters if the publisher trades with Amazon via their Advantage program. Around 10% (often a shade or two less, but let's keep things simple) will go to the author, leaving 30% of the cover price for the publisher. Out of that 30%, the publisher has to pay the printer and related production costs (perhaps 15% of the retail price) and will have to store and send the book to Amazon (5%). For taking all the risk, the publisher may well walk away with just 10% of the cover price of any book sold – and that's not accounting for the copies of the book that he or she has paid for as part of a print run that will never sell. By comparison, as an Amazon Associate, you can earn 10% with no risk whatsoever and without even so much as touching the book in question.

According to The eConsultancy Affiliate Marketing Merchants Report, affiliate marketing generated sales worth over three billion pounds during 2009 in the UK alone, and yet the vast majority of affiliates (the general industry term for what Amazon calls Associates) work from home. One affiliate, Chris Frost, wrote on his blog (http://www.webaffiliate.co.uk) that he had generated £4,910,305 worth of sales for merchants during

2008 working from a computer in his house – and he still managed to hold down a full-time job.

The Amazon Associate program is just one of literally thousands of affiliate programs that you can join today and earn money from every sale that you generate for them. Within minutes you could be working with some of the biggest names in British business right down to the smallest of specialist retailers that you have probably never heard of. The likes of Vodafone, Asda, British Airways, Marks & Spencer and Apple, all have affiliate programs paying various levels of commission to people who sit in front of a computer screen at home.

Why would some of the biggest (and smallest) companies in the world want to partner with little old you though? Done properly, affiliate marketing is a no risk marketing strategy for them, that's why. Not only will the brand appear on yours and potentially thousands of other websites run by other affiliates, thereby raising the company's online profile, commissions are only payable on confirmed sales (and sometimes agreed actions: for example when an affiliate is paid on a per lead generated basis rather than per sale). "No sale no fee" should be music to the ears of all businesses.

Affiliate marketing therefore minimises the downside at the same time as maximising the upside – the fact that thousands of entrepreneurs will be promoting your products and services at their own expense, while only being paid when a sale is made, really is as good as it gets. With merchants factoring in the cost of paying a commission to affiliates, the more sales affiliates can generate the better. True, you personally might only be able to generate one or two sales a month, but if another thousand affiliates are doing the same, that's a lot of extra orders.

Under one roof

Here's more good news. You don't have to do a tour of countless websites to join the affiliate programs of all those companies wanting to partner with you either. Retailers who have affiliate programs are usually called merchants, and although some do run independent programs like Amazon does, the vast majority of merchants are members of one or more of what are called affiliate networks.

The affiliate networks make life incredibly easy for affiliates. The leading networks are home to hundreds of merchants and that in itself can be your passport to opportunities to work with affiliate programs you might not have considered or known about otherwise. After joining a network, signing up to any number of merchants' programs can be as easy as clicking a Join This Program button. Your application to join a particular program may show as pending until the merchant in question manually approves it, but many programs automatically accept new affiliates. Meaning you could be earning money within minutes of applying.

It's also the network's responsibility to collect any commissions you earn across all of the merchant programs you sign up to. So rather than receiving umpteen small payments from a myriad of merchants (not to mention the time and effort you would spend monitoring and chasing individual payments), the network consolidates your earnings across merchants into one (typically monthly) payment.

There's maybe two dozen affiliate networks that currently operate in the UK, although I work with less than ten. Here's a quick guide to the ones I do work with – details of the others can be found at Affiliates4U (http://www.affiliates4u.com), an excellent website for all things affiliate marketing and a very rich source of information, advice and help for anyone new to the game as well as old-timers. Remember too that merchant programs can change networks or indeed close down altogether, so the following information regarding merchants on networks may have changed by the time you read it.

Affiliate Future (http://www.affiliatefuture.co.uk)

An affiliate network with over 750 merchants to choose from including Blockbuster, Sun Bingo, Virgin Atlantic, Thomas Cook and some excellent niche offerings too. Big on travel related merchants. Has a good range of tools you can use to promote merchants beyond the standard banners and text links. Once you join the network, approval to join nearly all of the merchant programs is automatic. Currently has over 65,000 affiliates signed up.

Affiliate Window (http://www.affiliatewindow.com)

The biggest affiliate network in the UK with over 750 merchants, and over 75,000 registered affiliates. Blue-chip merchants include Dixons, Boots, Early Learning Centre and Vodafone, and there are plenty of niche specialist retailers too. Excellent user interface and tools including a deeplink building widget for use with the Firefox web browser.

Buy.at (http://www.buy.at)

Once part of AOL's online advertising services subsidiary, Advertising.com, the Buy.at network represents around 200 merchants including Butlins, Carphone Warehouse, John Lewis, Thorntons and Sky. Again very easy to use site with good tools, although all merchants need to manually approve affiliate applications and this can take weeks in certain cases. Now owned by the people who own Affiliate Window.

Commission Junction (http://www.cj.com)

One of the first affiliate marketing network companies, CJ has its headquarters in California, but also has offices around the world including one in London. It offers opportunities to work with over 700 merchants, both in the UK and worldwide, including Best Western, Kodak, Match.com and Homebase. Its website takes a bit of getting used to.

Linkshare (http://www.linkshare.co.uk)

Launched in the UK in late 2006, LinkShare is now one of the UK's fastest growing affiliate marketing networks, having partnered with some leading brand advertisers in the retail and travel sectors. Big in fashion with the likes of Ted Baker, House Of Fraser, Miss Selfridge, Liberty, USC and more as merchants. First class affiliate support.

Paid On Results (http://www.paidonresults.com)

Established in 2002, Paid On Results has been making a name for itself in affiliate circles through its technological excellence. I only started working with POR in 2010, but already it is one of my favourite networks to work with for its ease of use. Merchants include Dobbies, Daily Express Bingo, Prezzybox, LoveHoney and around 150 others. Superb user interface and excellent range of affiliate tools.

Tradedoubler (http://www.tradedoubler.com)

Founded in Sweden in 1999, Tradedoubler now has offices in 18 countries, including the UK, and employs 650 people. It is home to hundreds of merchants including Apple, Disneyland Resort Paris, Figleaves, American Express, Hertz and the Post Office. It also boasts 128,000 plus affiliates worldwide.

Webgains (http://www.webgains.com)

Launched in 2004, Webgains is currently home to just under 500 merchant programs including CAT Footwear, Maplin, Viking Direct, Debt Line and some very good niche merchants too. Another network with a wide range of tools and creatives ready for affiliates to use to promote merchants.

You can join one or more of the above networks free of charge.

buyer

your website

merchant's website

purchase made

merchant takes payment,
fulfills order

network (or merchant) track sale

commission paid

Joining the dots

So how exactly does this affiliate marketing malarkey work? It's actually very simple. There are three or four players in the game. The customer, the affiliate, the merchant and (if the merchant doesn't run their own independent affiliate program) the network. And here's what happens in a typical transaction:

1 The customer will visit an affiliate's website.

2 The customer will leave the affiliate's website to visit the merchant's website via a link that contains tracking information that identifies the referrer as the affiliate.

3 The customer buys a product or service from the merchant's website.

4 Tracking software records the sale and informs the network.

5 The merchant fulfils the order and deals with any customer service issues.

6 The merchant pays the commission to the affiliate either directly or via a network.

Worth noting at this point is that the customer doesn't necessarily have to buy something immediately for you to earn a commission. The tracking software records sales made for a defined period of time, with the most common tracking cookie length being 30 days. This means that if a visitor that you refer to a merchant's website buys something within that 30 day period, you will earn a commission. The tracking period can be anything from one day (Amazon's tracking cookie only lasts 24 hours for example) to the maximum cookie length of 9,999 days as offered by some merchants like Buyagift, (not that I expect too many people will still be using the same computer after 27 years, but I regularly earn commission months after sending a customer to the Buyagift website via an affiliate link).

There are a number of affiliates who refuse to promote Amazon because of their very short cookie period. Big mistake. Amazon's conversion rate will more than make up for the short life span of its tracking cookies. I've promoted DVDs and books using other well known merchants who offer longer lasting cookies, but in terms of converting visitors into customers, Amazon blows them out of the water. I actually know of no other affiliate program that converts quite like Amazon.

Tools of the affiliate trade

To help affiliates achieve sales, the affiliate networks and merchants provide an arsenal of weaponry that you can use. Most require no technical knowledge to employ on the battlefield (simply copy the code supplied and paste it into your page's code), while others involve learning curves of varying gradients and length.

Banner Ads

One of the most basic tools is the banner ad. Each merchant will provide you with a selection of banner ads, usually in various shapes and sizes, for you to place on your website. The code for the banner ad includes both the information required for it to display on your website and the tracking information required to record any click-throughs and subsequent sales.

Generally speaking, banners on web pages do not enjoy a high click-through rate. The most common reason for this is banner blindness, where visitors to a website ignore banner-like information either consciously or sub-consciously. Banner blindness is most common in those who are internet savvy and who have learned to ignore advertising in much the same way as you do when reading a newspaper or when you put the kettle on during TV commercial breaks. Similarly, if you are familiar with a website's page format, and know where to find the relevant information on a page, chances are you may well ignore whatever appears elsewhere on the page – and that will include advertising.

Ironically, banners that desperately try to attract our attention (bright colours, flashing dollar signs, you know the ones I mean) are usually regarded with most suspicion, their gaudiness only serving as a reminder of the last time you clicked on such an ad only to end up in a maze of pages and pop-up ads that refused to go away. It's equally true that plastering numerous banners on a web page is counter-productive. Doing so does nothing to improve the web user's experience and simply amplifies banner blindness.

Above: typical banner used by affiliates. This one is for Laptops Direct whose affiliate program is on Affiliate Window.

Another problem with most banners is that they are general in nature. This is inevitable given the wide variety of websites that they are likely to appear on. Many therefore seek to promote a brand (Debenhams, Boots, Sky) rather than a particular product or service. What's more, the vast majority will only take a visitor to the homepage of whatever website they are promoting. For such a click through to end in a sale requires extra legwork from the potential customer – and that's assuming they are in buying mode and are not just window shopping.

That's not to say banner ads aren't worth using. I use them on virtually every web page I create. It costs me nothing to add one to a page and they do deliver sales, even if not in the quantities other forms of marketing do. I always try not to overdo it though. I add them to enhance the visitor's experience and so I avoid any that flash annoyingly or could potentially cause offence (a banner from Play.com advertising Disney DVDs would work well on a toy website, a Play.com banner for X rated horror movies wouldn't).

Banner ads can also add colour to an otherwise plain web page, but for me the main reason for displaying banner ads is to add credibility to a website. Few visitors to a website will know anything about affiliate marketing. If they see a banner ad advertising a High Street name or well known brand, they may not click on it, but at the same time it lends credibility to whatever else in on that page. If my page features a review of a new television set for example, the fact that a big company like John Lewis or Currys is "advertising" on it (because that's what it looks like to the untrained eye) can only add kudos to both the review and the website.

Text Links

Another basic tool is the humble text link. By inviting your visitors to leave your website via an affiliate link, you are in with a chance of making money, and what a text link lacks in glamour, it more than makes up for in impact. In terms of click-throughs and conversions, a little old text link beats the fanciest of banners time after time after time. There ain't no such thing as link blindness. Life online involves looking for and clicking on links. That's what surfing is. Using links to surf from one page to another, one website to another.

Another huge advantage of a text link is that it can be incorporated right bang in the middle of your written content. Banner blindness happens partly because banners tend to be at the periphery of a page's main content. Readers can't help, but notice a link placed in the text that they are reading – and that means there is a good chance of them clicking on it. When a reader does click on an affiliate link, it will take them through to the merchant's website and any purchases they make will be subsequently tracked and commissions paid.

At the top of the next page is a short article that appeared on the Bras.co.uk website announcing that Kelly Brook had become the new face and body of Ultimo. The article goes on to say what bra Kelly is wearing in the picture and that you can buy it from Debenhams. If you were looking at that article online, Kelly would be in glorious colour and the word Debenhams would be blue – the colour most commonly used to distinguish a link to another page on the Web. All the reader sees is the word

Debenhams underlined and assumes that if he or she clicks on that link, it will take them through to the Debenhams website.

Kelly Brook is the new face and body of Ultimo
8th April 2010

Kelly Brook, who FHM readers voted the World's Sexiest Woman, has replaced Mel B as the new face and body of Ultimo. The 30 year old model has signed a two year deal, with Ultimo's boss Michelle Mone describing Kelly as "effortlessly sexy" and "the perfect choice" for the label. Kelly, who wears 32E bras, is pictured left wearing the Rio Underwired Plunge Bra with its embroidered floral and spot design and removable gel pads. It's available now from Debenhams in sizes 30 B-D and 32B to 38D price £26 and sizes 30DD to 38FF price £28. The matching Rio Thong in sizes 8 to 16 is £12.

The Debenhams' website can be found at http://www.debenhams.com. If I was just linking to that website as a non-affiliate that is the web address that I would include in the link's code. The code for the link would look like this:

```
<a href="http://www.debenhams.com">Debenhams</a>
```

However, as an affiliate of Debenhams, I not only want to link to the Debenhams website, I want to be rewarded if any visitors I send buy anything.

You can find the Debenhams affiliate program (at the time of writing) on the Affiliate Window network. As with every program on the network, you will be given the code to use for banners and text links.

Here's the code that you would use to link to the Debenhams website:

```
<a          href="http://www.awin1.com/awclick.php?
mid=2194&id=XXXXX">Debenhams</a>
```

The XXXXX at the end would normally be a five digit number that would be your affiliate id. By using that link in the article with your affiliate id, that little one word link to the Debenhams website has the potential to make you money for as long as you remain a Debenhams affiliate and that article stays online. Most visitors will click the Debenhams link and go about their business, oblivious to the fact that the link took them to the Debenhams website via the Affiliate Window network. All they see is the word Debenhams and they know that they can click it to reach the Debenhams' website because it is underlined and blue.

Deep Linking

Basic text links generally deliver visitors to the merchant's home page which is far from ideal in most cases. It is better to link to the actual product or service you are promoting. If you are in a supermarket and ask where the butter is, you expect the shop assistant to tell you exactly where it is - or better still to take you there. That's what deep linking is all about. It allows you to (deep) link to a particular page on a merchant's website so that you can take the customer directly to the product or service you are promoting. In the Kelly Brook example, that would mean not linking to the Debenhams website homepage, but to the actual page on the Debenhams website where visitors could buy a Rio Underwired Plunge Bra by Ultimo.

The vast majority of merchants support deep linking. Creating deeplinks is generally very easy, although how you do it will vary across networks and sometimes merchants. Each network shows you how to do it and most provide you with deep link generator tools to make life even easier. The best networks even provide tools that create deeplinks simply by visiting the page you want to deeplink to and then clicking a button.

Deep linking does involve a wee bit of extra work, but it is nowhere near as scary as it might sound and it will definitely lead to better conversion rates and more money for you. As I'll say more than once in this book, content is king. Well, content that contains deeplinks to products and services is royalty with knobs on as far as affiliate marketing goes.

Datafeeds

Datafeeds or Product Feeds are basically files that contain a list of products together with information for each product (typically including price, description and so on). Going back to Debenhams, they provide a datafeed of products that they sell that you can access via Affiliate Window. Last time I checked, the Debenhams Datafeed contained close to 30,000 products that are available to buy on the Debenhams website.

What this means is that as an affiliate you could build a site that sells all of those 30,000 products just by making use of the Datafeed. It gets better. Datafeeds from merchants on the same network (and even across networks) share the same values and can be merged to give you a Datafeed that includes products from more than one merchant. Or you could just select all of the products in one category – women's clothing for example – and create a Datafeed that included products from one or more merchants. Instead of trawling numerous websites, your visitors could find an array of little black dresses from leading online retailers all under the one roof. Your roof.

To take another example, I sell fancy dress costumes on a commission basis via the website, FancyDressClothes.co.uk. I work mainly with two merchants, Angels Fancy Dress and Jokers Masquerade (both currently with Affiliate Window). By combining the Datafeeds of those two merchants, I can offer a bigger selection of fancy dress clothing than either of those two leading fancy dress merchants do individually.

Unlike text links and banners, working with Datafeeds does entail some technical knowledge. Once downloaded, it is up to the affiliate to convert the Datafeed files into a format that can be used on a website.

To be totally honest, I haven't got a clue how to do this so won't even pretend that I do, but as with so much on the internet, that doesn't actually matter. There are always plenty of people who do know – and that means there will always be off the shelf solutions for things like Datafeeds that even an idiot like me can use.

With the FancyDressClothes.co.uk website, I have an online shop that brings together the Datafeeds of both Angels Fancy Dress and Jokers Masquerade so that my visitors can view a huge range of fancy dress clothing. I do this by using software called Datafeed Studio (http://www.datafeedstudio.com) that costs just £79 (2010 price) and can be used on any number of websites.

Once installed, Datafeed Studio imports and organises multiple Datafeeds and then creates the pages that will become your online shop. Datafeed Studio can be used to create online stores, price comparison sites, and even single pages, quickly and with minimal knowledge (when you do run into problems, the support offered by its creator, Martin Wood, is first class too).

Remember that site we built in just an hour using WordPress? Well, Datafeed Studio even comes with a WordPress Plugin, meaning that you can quickly integrate Datafeed Studio into any WordPress based website. So not only do you now know how to build your first website, you also have a way of incorporating an online shop featuring Datafeeds from some of the biggest names in online retail.

I was recently asked what percentage of sales from FancyDressClothes.co.uk were actually generated by the Datafeed Studio Shop by someone interested in using it. I checked the stats and month after month it transpired that roughly 80% of all orders were placed via the Shop. It is only a small site so I wouldn't read too much into that statistic. What's more, it is the content rich pages that attract most of the traffic to the website in the first place and not the shop pages. But even with those two provisos, it is clear that Datafeed Studio works and works well. There's certainly no question that it has paid for itself many times over.

Above: The Fancydressclothes.co.uk online shop powered by Datafeed Studio and incorporating Datafeeds from Angels Fancy Dress and Jokers Masquerade

Discount And Voucher Codes

To help you convert visitors into sales, a large number of merchants issue discount codes (also called promotional codes and voucher codes). When the customer gets to the online checkout, he or she will enter the code into the relevant box and qualify for the stated discount on their order. So for example, at the time of writing, if you shop at the hosiery website, Tightsplease (http://www.tightsplease.co.uk), you can get 5% off any order over £25 (excluding postage) by using the voucher code TP5 at the checkout.

Some codes don't expire, others are time sensitive and have to be used by a certain date. Merchants will usually e-mail affiliates whenever a discount or promotional code is issued and it is also possible to arrange exclusive and bespoke codes, particularly if you work closely with a merchant and can guarantee a certain level of promotion or sales. Most networks also have a section on their website listing all current discount codes that you can use to encourage sales.

It's very important that you do make your visitors aware when a discount code is available. It will save them money and might just be the nudge they need to get them over the finishing line in terms of buying. Online shoppers now actively look for such codes in the hope of saving money and so it is therefore in your interest to serve these codes to them on a plate rather than have them look elsewhere for the code and you lose the sale.

The use of discount codes in affiliate marketing is unfortunately seriously flawed thanks to poor implementation of this marketing strategy by the vast majority of merchants. Virtually all checkout pages have an "enter your discount code here" box - whether or not a discount code is actually available. Any internet savvy shopper worth his or her salt will wonder if a code is available though and will use Google to find out. Google will no doubt point them in the direction of one of the numerous discount code websites out there. Such websites are designed to give the impression that they have codes for every merchant (including those that don't even issue codes). Whether a code exists or not, if the shopper follows a link from a discount code site back to the merchant's site, a new tracking cookie will overwrite your tracking cookie. The result? In most cases, you will lose the sale to the discount code website.

This has caused a great deal of controversy in affiliate marketing circles, with affiliates calling foul over what they see as lost commissions. Merchants and networks have been slow to respond to such concerns, no doubt because of the huge volume of sales that discount code websites deliver. Hats off then to Red Letter Days who were the first merchant to display a voucher code box for code traffic, but hide it for non-code traffic. Let's hope other merchants follow suit.

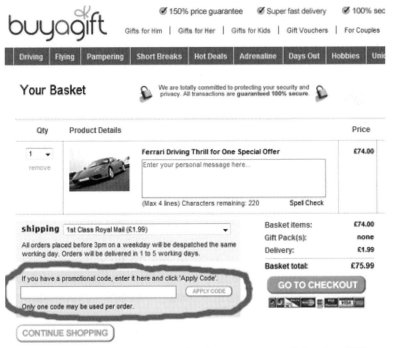

Above: The Buyagift.co.uk checkout page with the "If you have a promotional code, enter it here" box circled

Like them or loathe them, discount code websites exist. There's no getting away from that fact. That means that it's important that you give your visitors access to any discount codes that are available so as to minimise commission leakage caused by them having to go elsewhere. And if no code is available? Where practical, I'm now stating that fact so as to discourage customers looking for one when they are confronted by a code box on a merchant's checkout page.

Incidentally, a website dedicated to discount codes is yet another example of how information can make you money. People want to know something – in this case what discount codes are available. You provide a service by providing this information via a website. If those people then visit a merchant via your discount code website and buy something, you will earn a commission. It's now a very crowded and competitive market, but it has made millions for the likes of 29 year old Mark Pearson who started MyVoucherCodes.com in 2006 and quickly turned it into a multi-million pound concern.

More affiliate marketing tools

The affiliate networks also provide a whole range of other tools that you may be able to use to drive sales. Amazon's aStore allows you to quickly and easily create an online store selling your choice of Amazon products. Affiliate Window has its ShopWindow suite of tools that uses product data for 4.5 million items supplied by over 800 retailers. Affiliate Future provides search boxes that return results from multiple merchants so that your visitors can search for flights, accommodation, holidays and car hire. Webgains has a mobile phone recycling comparison tool for you to use. These and other tools can quickly and easily be implemented to enhance your visitor's experience and hopefully lead to increased sales for you.

Are you sitting comfortably?

Here's a real life example of how affiliate marketing works. On the 9th of November, 2008, I came across an article on the Existem-AM website (http://www.existem-am.com) entitled "Why Beanbags Make Excellent Christmas Presents". Existem-AM are one of a number of companies that manage affiliate programs on behalf of merchants and this article was a promotional piece to encourage affiliates to promote beanbag sales during the festive season for a company called Beanbag Bazaar.

Being the owner of two giant beanbags myself, I thought a beanbag would indeed make an excellent Christmas present. It also struck me that beanbags were an ideal product for an affiliate to promote. Anyone who visits a website after Googling "beanbag" is almost certainly looking to buy one. With an average basket value of over £85 and an average conversion rate of 7-8%, it's the kind of product that is well worth pushing.

I had never promoted beanbags before so I decided to take a look at Beanbag Bazaar's website to see what they had to offer (http://www.beanbagbazaar.co.uk). One thing that struck me immediately was the large number of big beanbags that were available. This got me thinking about building a small niche website that sold nothing but big beanbags. The next step was to see what domain names were available around this idea. I didn't have to look far. Bigbeanbags.co.uk was available so I registered it immediately.

I then signed up to Beanbag Bazaar's affiliate program at Affiliate Window. At the time of joining, Beanbag Bazaar were offering a basic 7% commission on sales, rising to 10% if you made 30 or more sales in a month. 7% commission on an average basket value of £85 works out at £5.95. With a 7% average conversion rate, that meant that I stood to make about £42 for every 100 visitors I sent Beanbag Bazaar's way (incidentally, stats on average basket value and conversion rates are available on the affiliate networks' websites). They also offered a 365 day tracking cookie which meant that if any visitor I referred to the Beanbag Bazaar website made a purchase within 365 days, I would earn a commission (assuming the cookie hadn't been deleted).

The next step was to build a simple website that would feature the biggest beanbags that Beanbag Bazaar had to offer. Each beanbag would have a small introductory paragraph with a small image on the Bigbeanbags.co.uk homepage. Visitors who wanted to know more about a particular beanbag could follow a link to the relevant page that I'd created for that beanbag. From that page they could follow another link that took them to the Beanbag Bazaar website where they would hopefully place an order.

I could have missed out one of the stages above. I could have simply had a one page site with the introductory paragraphs and images. Instead of then creating further pages, I could have linked directly to the relevant Beanbag Bazaar page instead. I prefer to create my own information pages because a multi-page website is likely to fair better in the search engines than a single page website, if for no other reason than every page you create has the ability to rank, not just your homepage. The more lines in the water, the more fish you can catch.

It took perhaps three hours to build what was a very basic website consisting of half a dozen pages. Not particularly big by any stretch of the imagination and not very clever either – just text, a few images and hyperlinks. The old marketing principle, Keep It Simple Stupid, works very well when it comes to websites. The idea is to give visitors the information they need and then to politely ask them to leave (via an affiliate link).

I created the pages using basic HTML code using Adobe Dreamweaver, but I could just as easily have used WordPress to create my beanbag website just as I did when showing you how to start your first internet business in less than an hour. WordPress might be best known as blogging software, but in reality it is content management software and can be used for a wide variety of websites.

All of the information I needed was on the Beanbag Bazaar website – I just had to rewrite it so that the content would be unique to my website rather than simply being a straight copy. Unique content is the key to successful search engine marketing and the lack of it is the reason why so many affiliate based websites fail. Search engines are more likely to rank your site highly if you actually bring something different to the table so think about adding reviews, price comparisons across different merchant websites, that sort of thing. Remember what Google told you. If your site participates in an affiliate program, make sure that your site adds value. Provide unique and relevant content that gives users a reason to visit your site first.

Apart from the time invested, it had cost me just over £5 to register the domain name and then there was the cost of hosting the website (this was negligible because I simply added it to an existing multiple hosting package that I had already paid for).

For a site like this to be successful in my eyes, it doesn't need to become the world's biggest beanbag website (not that I would complain if it did). It simply needs to contribute to my Plan B. This means recouping the time I had invested in it plus my costs. Around £100 within the first year would do that given the time spent on it, and with a little updating from time to time I'd expect my initial investment in the site to pay off again in years two, three and hopefully subsequent years. To get that £100, I would be looking to send around 250 visitors in the direction of Beanbag Bazaar, based on the average basket value and conversion rate figures we've already discussed. That's not a lot of people over a period of a year.

The marketing budget for my beanbag website was zero so I would be dependent entirely on search engine traffic for any visitors. I was assuming there would be others out there who shared my love of big and who would use the search engines to search for and then buy "big beanbags" (and "big bean bags"). I was also assuming that although my new site was very unlikely to rank for the broad search term "beanbags" given the large number of better, older and frankly more deserving websites out there, I would (sooner or later) rank well for specific long tail search terms relating to big beanbags.

My assumptions were based on past experience of building similar niche websites. As far as I'm concerned, if something is only going to take me a few hours to make and very little money to execute, I won't waste any time on market research. With small projects like this you can't do any better than simply throw it at the wall and see if it sticks.

Softly, softly catchee monkey

To get my new site indexed quickly by the likes of Google and Yahoo, I linked to it from the homepage of one of my other sites, Entrepreneur.co.uk, which is crawled at least daily by the search engine gods. Getting a link from an existing website to a new site is the quickest way to get it indexed and the first step towards appearing in the search engine rankings for searches. I can't stress the importance of this enough so remember my offer of a link to the first site you build if I think it is worthy of one.

The first week that the site was live, it attracted just 21 unique visitors. Most of those visitors had followed the link on Entrepreneur.co.uk, no doubt to see what I was doing rather than to buy a beanbag. On the 17th of November, Beanbag Bazaar announced a Christmas incentive for affiliates. Deliver 15 or more sales between the 20th of November and the 20th of December and you would win a beanbag. 15 sales in 30 days seemed a tall order for me with a brand new site and next to no traffic, but it certainly spurred me on to add a few more beanbags to my website.

My first sale during those 30 days came on the 21st of November and by the end of the month I had made four sales in total. All thanks to search engine traffic. In fact those four sales came from the 261 unique visitors who arrived at the site during November via Google and Yahoo for the most part.

Here's the ten most popular search terms that delivered visitors to the site via search engines during November (stats like this are nearly always available to website owners as part of their hosting package):

bean bags	53
gaming bean bags	13
big beanbags	9
gaming bean bag	9
bigbeanbags	6
gaming beanbags	4
bean bag gaming	4
maternity bean bags	4
giant bean bags	3
big bean bags price	3

Below is a screenshot of a Google search for "big bean bags" with BigBeanbags.co.uk starred. It is actually ranked number one in the natural results for the search term "big bean bags" – the three entries above it are paid for Sponsored Links. A similar search for "bean bags" and my site is nowhere to be seen. Google seemed to reward the niche nature of my site almost immediately while ignoring its general relevance to bean bags.

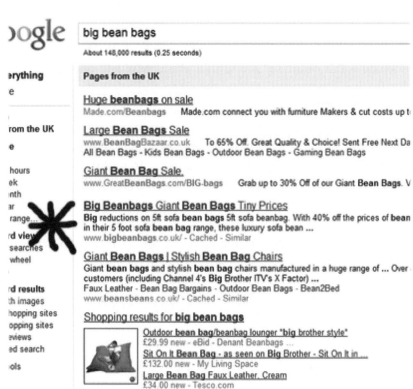

By the 10th of December, I'd sold a further three beanbags, taking my total to seven with just ten days to go. At any other time of year I know I would have fallen short, but this was Christmas, everyone and his dog was using the internet to find presents, and I knew I was in with a chance. Fingers crossed!

Traffic during December was averaging around 25 unique visitors a day and by the 15th I had made a further six sales - 13 in total during the qualifying period. On the 16th I sold a Whopper Gigantic Solo Beanbag, meaning I needed just one more sale to win a beanbag. By now I was checking my sales stats about ten times an hour, hoping for that one more sale.

I had previously posted a comment on the Affiliates4U website to say that I was moving into beanbags, and as something of an update, I posted another message on the 16th to say that I needed just one more sale to win a beanbag.

And that's when a fantastic thing happened. After seeing my message on Affiliates4U, and then without me knowing, Chris Clarkson of Sunshine (http://www.sunshine.co.uk) contacted Hannah Swift, who at the time did a great job of looking after Beanbag Bazaar's affiliate program through Existem-AM. Chris asked Hannah for my affiliate code so that he could buy a beanbag and get me that 15th sale. I would never have known this if I hadn't been chatting to Hannah on IM as that 15th sale came in and she then mentioned that Chris had been in touch. There are a lot of good people like Chris who are involved in affiliate marketing and you will be surprised how far many will go to help a fellow affiliate.

So by the 16th of December I had my 15 sales and I was guaranteed an XL Faux Leather Bean Bag - not to mention the commission I'd pocketed by making those sales! So how much commission did I earn? I've just checked the sales statistics on Affiliate Window and I made £90.11 commission on £1,287.07 worth of sales. Not a bad return for a few hours work, but it didn't stop there. During 2009, and with very little additional time invested in the site, I earned a total of £689.17 in commissions from Beanbag Bazaar on sales of £8,951.86. 2010 sales are 25% higher and I expect to make closer to £1,000 in commission from this website during 2010 by the time Christmas comes and goes.

All this from a website that only needed to earn me £100 to play its part in my Plan B. It just goes to show that from a standing start, and with no budget much beyond the time it took me to build the site, it is possible to make money from affiliate marketing.

Life is a rollercoaster

You probably don't go to sleep at night dreaming of beanbags, but let's suppose you are one of those crazy people who actually enjoys rollercoaster rides. You could very easily build a website dedicated to the best rollercoaster rides in the world and the theme parks that house them – just like I built a site for large beanbags. There is nothing stopping you from then earning a commission on theme park ticket sales (at the time of writing Attractiontix have an affiliate program on Affiliate Window and pay up to 6% commission on ticket sales for everything from Disneyworld to the London Eye). Or flights to Florida (Virgin Atlantic on Affiliate Future, British Airways on Tradedoubler for example). Or airport parking (BCP, Purple Parking or Holiday Extras on Affiliate Future). Or travel insurance, guide books, car hire, package holidays and so on.

And if you know your visitors like theme parks, there's every chance they will enjoy other adrenaline-soaked activities like bungee jumping (Red Letter Days on Affiliate Window) or even a balloon flight over the Valley Of The Kings in Egypt (Do Something Different, again on Affiliate Window).

If such a website formed part of your business and was shown to be generating an income, any visits you yourself made to theme parks would be tax deductible too. It would be very easy to make a case for needing to actually experience the parks for yourself to give visitors to your website the best information possible.

Whatever it is you enjoy filling your days with, think about ways to turn them into multiple revenue streams by working with companies already serving the market. Affiliate marketing offers you the opportunity to do just that. The idea of having to compete with some of the biggest names in business may have put you off starting a website before now. The answer isn't to beat them, it's to join them – as an affiliate.

Two things to always bear in mind. To be successful your site needs traffic. Provide unique and relevant content so that search engines rank you and so that visitors benefit from coming to your site. Equally important, don't promote merchants just because they offer the best commission rates. Visit the merchant's site yourself, see how easy it is to use, go through the buying process at least to the point of payment. There is little point sending visitors to a site that will never convert them into sales. A golden rule of making money online is to make it fantastically easy for people to buy. Not everyone gets that.

Little acorns . . .

You might think that unless you have a website that can generate huge number of visitors that there isn't much money to be made in affiliate marketing. If you're only earning a few pounds a week it can seem like a waste of time. Stick with it. As you'll discover over time, patience is a real virtue when building multiple revenue streams.

In September, 2008, Buyagift announced a competition for its affiliates to win one of eight places on a holiday of a lifetime – a road trip from San Francisco to Las Vegas. You could win a place through a variety of ways that gave big and small affiliates a chance of going, but basically success depended on your sales for the fourth quarter of the year. I decided to see if I could win a place and spent a week or so preparing websites to promote Buyagift's experience days and related products. Despite my efforts, I didn't win one of those places. On £718.60 worth of sales made, I earned £69.83 commission, but no cigar as they say. I was actually really disappointed by the low sales figures, given the work I'd done.

In what is an annual incentive, Buyagift announced a similar competition in September, 2009, to win one of six VIP trips to Monaco. Again, I wasn't one of the lucky winners, but the work that I had done the previous year was to bear fruit 12 months on. The content that I had created in 2008 was now ranking well in search engines and driving targeted traffic to my websites. With little more than some updating of the previous year's work, I made £7,011.22 worth of sales and earned £701.55 commission. Ten times what I made in 2008 through the Buyagift affiliate program for next to no extra work. I've talked before about snowballs. This particular one I started rolling down the hill in 2008. Although no longer pushing it, it kept on rolling right through 2009 all by itself, gathering more snow as it went.

With time your earnings will grow too. Earning an average of £1 a day in commission equates to about £30 a month, £365 a year. That'll get you a new laptop.

Earning £5 a day equates to £150 a month and £1,825 a year. That's Christmas paid for.

Earning £10 a day, equates to £300 a month, £3,650 a year. That'll pay for a dream holiday.

Earning £33 a day equates to £1,000 a month, £12,000 a year. That's your mortgage taken care of.

Earning £100 a day equates to £3,000 a month, £36,000 a year. That'll buy you a brand new Mercedes Benz M Class 4x4.

And so it goes on. You don't need much growth in your daily sales figures for it to make a big impact on your annual income. Add the money you make from affiliate marketing to your other revenue streams and it's quite surprising how quickly your income can snowball. And when those snowballs are rolling down the hill, they take some stopping.

The SeaMonkey that builds websites

"Every time I learn something new, it pushes some old stuff out of my brain. Remember when I took that home wine-making course and I forgot how to drive?"
Homer Simpson

If a journey of a thousand miles starts from beneath one's feet, your tootsies must be aching given the ground we have covered thus far. Don't worry if much of it has gone in one ear and out the other. What may seem like a mountain to climb today will be like a stroll in the park once you have one or two multiple revenue streams under your belt.

I make money online by gathering information (anything from news of a sale at M&S to why dogs eat grass), making that information available via simple websites, and then monetising those websites. What I want to do in this chapter is to provide a walkthrough of how I build a website from scratch and at the same time introduce you to free software that will allow you to do exactly the same.

We have already seen how easy it is to create a website using WordPress. It could be that you create a Plan B using nothing but WordPress – and in fact you could do a lot worse than go down that road. Jason Calacanis spotted the money-making potential of blogs back in 2003 when he founded the blogging network, Weblogs Inc, with fellow American, Brian Alvey. They quickly developed a stable of blogs covering everything from cars (Autoblog) to gadgets (Engadget) and went about monetising them in ways we have already discussed: Google AdSense, selling advertising space, Amazon's Associate program. Two years later, AOL bought Weblogs Inc for a reported US$25 million.

Calacanis' latest baby is Mahalo.com, a "human-powered search engine" which was launched in 2007. How is he making money from that? You guessed it - Google AdSense, selling advertising space, Amazon's Associate program. At the start of 2010, Jason posted a short piece with screenshot to his blog (http://calacanis.com) saying that "Mahalo sold US$250k+ in Amazon product in 2009 without trying" and made US$18,823.30 in commission. For a multi-millionaire, US$18,000 is not much more than pocket change, but I know what excites Jason. He knows that in a year or two that one revenue stream could be ten times, twenty times bigger, as Mahalo grows. You can also make money "without trying" just by adding relevant ads to your web pages and blog posts.

Blogging is just one route you can go down to get your information online and to start earning money. There may be times though when the blogging format doesn't suit what you have in mind and often a simple website is more appropriate. HTML (HyperText Markup Language) was developed to allow internet browsers to display web pages correctly, and today HTML provides the building blocks for practically every basic website you visit.

HTML is actually very easy to learn. HTML elements or "tags" are surrounded by angle brackets - < > - and are used to tell the browser how to display each page. For example, if you wanted a sentence to appear in bold, you would surround it by the HTML element for bold text - your sentence goes here. If you wanted it to appear italicised you would surround it by the element for italicised text - <i>your sentence goes here</i>. Learning HTML is simply learning what is no more than 100 such elements, and most of them you will only use once in a blue moon anyway.

With What You See Is What You Get (WYSIWYG) web page editors, you don't even need to have any knowledge of HTML. Not to begin with anyway. There will be times when you do want to look at the code to see why something isn't quite as you want it to be and that's when a little knowledge of HTML will go a long way.

If you have never built a website before and all this talk of HTML elements and WYSIWYG editors is causing heart palpitations, relax. Let your inner geek come out to play. You are more than capable of handling what's coming.

Did you ever own Sea Monkeys?

I used to love reading comics as a kid. I wasn't particularly loyal to any one title. A free gift stuck on the front cover and I was anybody's. No matter what comic I picked up, however, one thing could be almost guaranteed. It would contain an advertisement for Sea Monkeys.

Sea Monkeys are the most amazing creatures on the planet. Sold in "instant life" packets, Sea Monkey eggs survive in suspended animation for up to two years until you add water. Then they miraculously hatch and come to life. And boy do they come to life! According to the advertising that appeared in my comics, Sea Monkeys not only looked like tiny water monkeys, but soon after hatching would be performing circus tricks, racing bicycles, and living as families in little castles! How could you not want to own Sea Monkeys?

Always the entrepreneur, I had visions of being able to breed and train the little creatures before selling them to friends as pets, but when I did finally get my hands on a packet of Sea Monkeys, I quickly discovered that they weren't exactly as described. When you mixed the sachets in water, the "Sea Monkeys" did indeed come to life, but look like monkeys they did not. They couldn't ride bicycles either. In truth, they were tiny brine shrimps that floated about the tank, slowly filling my bedroom with the pungent smell of stagnating water.

Incidentally, the man who brought us Sea Monkeys, Harold von Braunhut, also invented X-Ray Specs ("see through your hand, see through clothes!") and Invisible Goldfish (complete with glass bowl, invisible goldfish food and a cast-iron guarantee that their owners would never see them). Before his death in 2003, he was allegedly working on the world's first "instant frog". I like people like Harold.

I am going to introduce you today to another SeaMonkey that also can't ride a bike, but can make you money. It also has quite an interesting history. Nowadays, every computer that has a Microsoft Windows operating system comes with an internet browser, Microsoft Explorer. A lot of people think that Internet Explorer is "the internet" and at its peak it enjoyed a market share of 96% simply because it was pre-installed on virtually every PC sold. Once upon a time though, back in the mid-90s, another browser enjoyed almost total dominance in the browser market place, Netscape's Navigator. Part of the Netscape Communicator Internet suite, it rapidly lost ground to Internet Explorer because it had to be bought (until 1998 anyway) and then installed, whereas Internet Explorer has always been free and was "already there". By 2002, Navigator had all but disappeared from the online landscape, but Netscape's parting shot had been fired four year earlier when it released most of the code base for its Netscape Communicator suite under an open source license and entrusted it to the newly formed non-profit Mozilla Foundation.

Mozilla has gone on to develop the increasingly popular Firefox web browser and Thunderbird, an alternative to Microsoft's Outlook e-mail application. It has also kept the idea of an internet suite alive too by fostering the development of the less well known, but equally free to use, SeaMonkey. You are going to become better acquainted with SeaMonkey very soon because it includes a powerful yet simple HTML editor called Composer that was once part of the Netscape Communicator suite.

Composer is a WYSIWYG editor and so you basically create each page as it will look to readers, not unlike a Microsoft Word or similar document. You don't need to know any HTML because the most used HTML elements are only a click away on toolbars and drop down menus (Composer does let you edit the HTML source - simply select HTML SOURCE from the VIEW menu at the top of the screen or click the HTML SOURCE at the bottom of the screen).

You can download SeaMonkey from the official SeaMonkey website (http://www.seamonkey-project.org/). Once downloaded and installed, you can launch SeaMonkey and use it like any other internet browser. Don't start surfing the Net just yet though. Instead, look along the top tool bar until you find the word WINDOW. Click on it and a drop down list will give you access to the box of tricks that is SeaMonkey, including Composer. Click on COMPOSER and it will open in a new window.

You can access Composer's documentation by clicking HELP on the top toolbar, selecting HELP CONTENTS and then reading the notes under "Creating Web Pages". Rather than regurgitate them here, let's jump in at the deep end (don't worry, you can swim!) and complete a walkthrough of how to build the first few pages of a simple website.

The first thing you will want to do is create a Folder on your computer that will house all of your websites. Inside that Folder, each website should have its own Folder to keep things neat and tidy. The obvious place to create your Websites Folder is in My Documents.

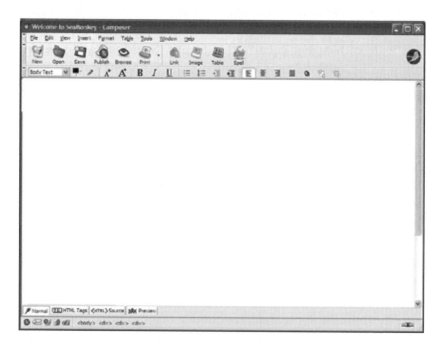

Above: Screenshot of Composer page that will greet you when you launch the program via SeaMonkey

Most PCs have a shortcut to My Documents on the Desktop or on the Start menu. To add a new Folder for your websites:

1. Navigate to your My Documents Folder.

2. From the FILE menu, select NEW and then select FOLDER.

3. Give the new Folder the name Websites.

Every time you start work on a new website, navigate to the Websites Folder in My Documents, select NEW from the FILE menu and then select FOLDER. A new Folder will be created. Give it the same name as the new website.

Sea Monkeys for sale

Appropriately enough, the website we are going to be working on in this walkthrough is one dedicated to Sea Monkeys (http://www.sea-monkeys.co.uk). I have already registered the domain name and have arranged hosting through one of my reseller accounts that allows me to host a number of websites on the same hosting account (you actually won't need either to use SeaMonkey to start building websites, not until you are ready to go live anyway). I have also created a Folder for it within my Websites Folder and all files relating to this website will be saved to this new Folder.

Believe it or not, even if you have never built a website before, you have a big advantage over most professional web designers. That is because you don't have clients to pander to. Instead of filling pages with the assorted bells and whistles that nearly all clients love, that some designers include to justify their fees, and that most visitors largely ignore, you can get straight down to business. The business of making money.

Every page of a website should have a purpose. Apart from housekeeping pages (About, Contact, Privacy Policy and so on), the purpose of every page that you make should be focused on satisfying visitors' wants and needs because by doing so you will make money. In fact, everything you do should be geared towards attracting visitors (including repeat visitors) and converting those visitors into sales by satisfying their needs and wants. If you find yourself doing anything else while building websites, you are basically wasting your precious time.

The Sea Monkeys website has one purpose in life. To sell Sea Monkeys. It is not going to be a general website that sells Sea Monkeys alongside 1,001 other things. It will just sell Sea Monkeys. As such, it will only attract visitors who have an interest in Sea Monkeys. As far as the old marketing acronym,

AIDA (Awareness – Interest – Desire – Action) is concerned, my work is half done without me having to lift a finger. Visitors will be by definition aware of Sea Monkeys and will almost certainly have an interest in them to – or why visit a Sea Monkey website? All that is left for me to do is encourage the desire to buy some Sea Monkeys and supply the opportunity for my visitors to act on that desire.

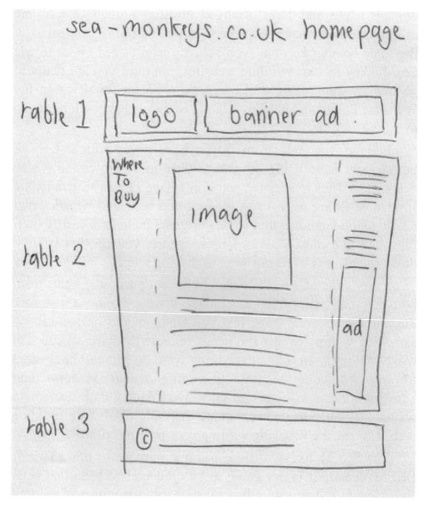

Above: Sketch outline for Sea-Monkey.co.uk homepage

Before I start building a website, I like to do a quick sketch or two of what I have planned in my mind's eye for the site's basic design. It doesn't have to be a work of art (as you can tell, I am no artist) and nothing is set in stone just because I have committed a few thoughts to paper, but it helps to quickly crystalise ideas, sparks off new ones, and gives you an outline to work to. As you can see from the quick outline sketch I did for sea-monkeys.co.uk, the homepage is quite simple. It consists of just three tables:

• Table 1 which will consist of two columns and house the website's logo and a banner ad.

• Table 2 which I have mentally divided into five equal width columns, and then merged the three columns in the centre to leave me with two narrow columns on either side of a wider central column. This Table will house the main content that I want to appear on the homepage. Column one will be devoted to links to where visitors can buy Sea Monkeys, the central column will feature a big image and information about Sea Monkeys, and the third column links to other yet to be created pages, perhaps another banner ad, that sort of thing.

• Table 3 is going to be used to house the copyright notice and any other debris that usually sits at the bottom of web pages.

The homepage is also going to provide the basic design for all internal pages too. There is certainly no reason why Tables 1 and 3 can't be used without any changes on other pages, something that will save us a lot of time when creating new pages. Only Table 2's content will differ on every page.

Why not just use one big table divided into rows and columns instead of three? You could do that, but working with a number of smaller tables makes for a better visitor experience.

Content will appear on your page faster, with each table loading in turn rather than visitors having to wait for one big table to load.

I know for a fact that there will be purists reading this who are wincing at my use of Tables to layout web pages. Sorry! I know it is not the done thing in polite circles, but the reality is that Tables are a fantastic way to organise text and images into rows and columns. When I first started to build websites myself, I always wondered how people managed to put content in columns. When I discovered that Tables could do exactly that, quickly and easily, it was like the curtains had opened on a new dawn. The "correct" way to arrange content is via Cascading Style Sheets (CSS), but the good news is that either way gets you to where you want to be and I still like using Tables.

How to create a Table

Creating a Table is easy peasy Lemon Squeezy. At the top of each Seamonkey Composer page, you will find three tool bars, the middle one of which houses a series of icons. To create a Table you simply click on the TABLE icon (circled above). As with most software programs, there is more than one way to do tasks with Composer and you could select TABLE from the top toolbar and select INSERT from the dropdown list of choices.

When you click on the TABLE icon in the middle toolbar, a dialog box opens so that you can specify the size of the Table and the size of any border. First you input the number of rows and columns you want the table to have. My first Table requires two columns – one for the logo and one for a banner ad – and just the one row.

The width of the Table can either be a percentage of a window or a fixed number of pixels. If for example you choose to have a Table that fills 100% of the browser window, your Table will stretch to fit the width of whatever computer screen it is viewed on. The biggest advantage of opting for a variable width design is that visitors will never need to scroll horizontally to view your web pages, but you also have less control over how your website's pages will be displayed. On a browser at its maximum size on a big monitor, websites can look stretched and what was designed to be a neat easy to read paragraph can appear as one long line of text.

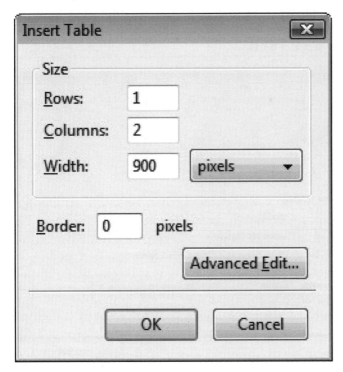

Using a fixed number of pixels gives you far greater control over how a website is displayed on a computer monitor. On small screens this may mean visitors having to scroll horizontally and on large screens it may result in acres of white around each page. There are those who champion either fixed or variable width designs, but both are of value in different circumstances. For the Sea Monkeys website, we are going to choose a fixed width of 900 pixels.

The final option is the size of the Table's borders. A rule of thumb here is that if you are using Tables to display data on a web page, then select an appropriate border size. If you are using Tables as a layout tool as we are here, set the borders to zero for a more professional-looking result.

Once done, your new Table with two columns will appear on your screen with a red outline. This outline is only there as a guide while you work on the page and will not appear on your actual web page.

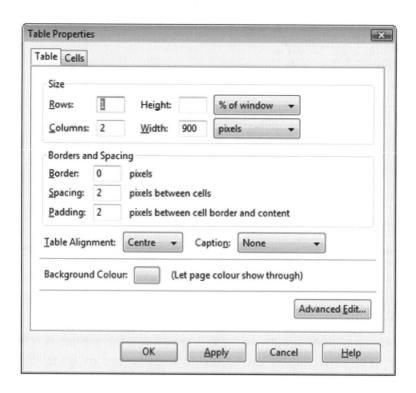

At the moment, your new Table is placed to the left of your screen and consists of two columns of equal width. We can change this by first clicking inside the Table itself to select it and then selecting TABLE PROPERTIES from the TABLE dropdown menu on the top toolbar. At the top of the Table Properties dialog box are two tabs, one marked Table and the other Cells. The first allows you to adjust the Table's properties, the second an individual Cell's properties.

The Table's size is as required – one row, two columns and a width of 900 pixels. The Border setting of 0 is also correct. By default, the Table Spacing between Cells is set to two pixels, as is the Padding between the Cell border and content. Usually, two to five pixels is fine, but you can adjust either to suit your web page's overall design.

We do want to change the Table Alignment from Left to Centre if we want our Tables (and web page) to appear in the centre of visitors' computer screens. If you want it to appear to the left, leave it as Left.

Once done click the APPLY button at the bottom to save your changes and to keep the dialog box open or OK to save your changes and close the dialog box. In this instance, click APPLY and then click on the CELLS tab at the top.

The first option allows you to select the Cell you wish to change. Click the Previous and Next buttons and you will see a different Table Cell highlighted on your Composer page. Make sure the second cell (the right-hand one) is highlighted.

In this Cell we are going to put a banner advertisement. The standard size for an ad that would best fit that space is 468x60 pixels so the Cell needs to be at least 468 pixels wide – I have chosen 480 pixels to give it some breathing space (see screenshot on the next page). Notice that I have chosen not to set a height for the Cell – I rarely do unless vital for a web page's design.

The Content Alignment options allow me to determine how the content will appear in a Cell. I have selected it to be aligned to the top and to the left. Nothing else needs to change so we can click OK. Now our Table should be sitting pretty at the top and in the centre of our web page.

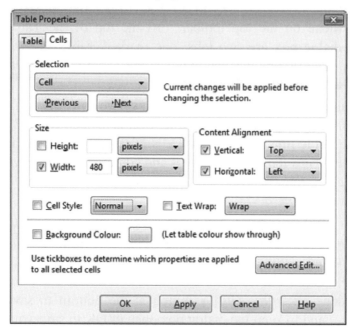

Adding content to a Table Cell

To add content to a Table Cell, start by clicking inside the Cell. We need to add a logo to the first Cell and a banner ad to the second.

To add a logo we first need to create one and save it to the Folder for the Sea Monkeys website. You can create a logo using any graphics software like Adobe Photoshop or Selteco Bannershop (more about this software in the *How Does Your Garden Grow?* Chapter). If you don't have any graphics software installed on your computer, consider downloading the free image and photo editing software, Paint.NET (http://www.getpaint.net/). I downloaded and created a simple logo using Paint.NET in a matter of minutes.

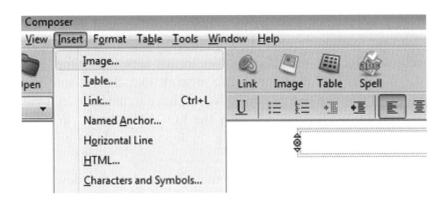

Above: To add an image, click INSERT on the top toolbar and then click IMAGE from the dropdown menu. A dialogue box will appear.

To place the logo into the Table Cell, select INSERT from the top toolbar and then select IMAGE. This will open another dialog box, Image Properties.

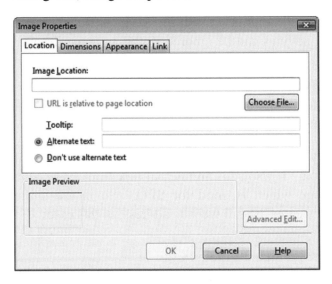

Above: The Image Properties dialog box which lets you tell SeaMonkey where it can find the image on your computer

I saved my logo as logo.jpg to the Folder I created for the Sea Monkeys website earlier (always save images for use with websites as a .jpg - a .gif is another format specifically for Web use, but it is best used for simple artwork like clip art and line drawings that use few colours). Now, I have to navigate to it via the CHOOSE FILE button under the LOCATION tab. When I am in the correct folder, I click on logo.jpg to highlight and select it, and then click OPEN.

I also need to add some Alternate Text – text that describes the image. In his instance, I will simply enter into the box:

`Sea Monkeys website`

Clicking on the DIMENSIONS tab, I then make sure ACTUAL SIZE is selected (I created the logo to measure 299 pixels wide by 60 pixels high to comfortably fit inside the Cell). I can then click on the APPEARANCE tab where the only thing I will do is to set the Solid Border to 0 as I don't want the image to have a border (if the border is set to 1, the image will appear in a box). The other settings can be ignored in this instance because the only thing that will be in this Cell is the logo.

The fourth tab, LINK, allows you to link your image to a web page and it is a good habit to link your logo to your homepage on every single page of your website. Some of your visitors will assume that by clicking on your logo, they will be taken from the page being viewed to your homepage so there is no point disappointing them. It also adds an internal link from every page to your homepage which is good for SEO. So in the space provided I usually enter the full website address, in this case:

`http://www.sea-monkeys.co.uk`

That's all we need to do so I can click the OK button and the logo will be inserted into the Cell. That may seem like a lot of work just to insert an image, but once you have done it a few times, it will literally take you seconds to add an image to a Cell.

Saving your work

Now that we have the beginnings of a web page, it makes sense to save our work rather than risk losing it to a power cut or a computer crash. From the top toolbar, select FILE and then select SAVE from the dropdown menu. This will open a dialog box asking for a title for the page. This is the same Title that we discussed earlier in the chapter on Search Engine Optimisation and it is vital that we get it right. The Google Adword Keyword Tool comes in handy here to see what keywords and phrases people actually use when searching for Sea Monkeys. The results for Local Exact Monthly Searches are as follows:

```
sea monkeys 5,400
triops 1,600
sea monkey 1,300
sea monkeys uk 480
what are sea monkeys 210
buy sea monkeys 91
```

As you might expect, there are also a small number of searches relating to Sea Monkey food, tanks and related products, but the interesting one for me is searches for "triops". I will make a note of that and make sure that my Sea Monkeys website contain references to Triops as well as a page dedicated to Triops in the hope that search engines will rank me highly for that keyword. If they do, those searching for Triops may well end up buying Sea Monkeys from my website.

The home page's Title Tag is going to be simply:

```
Sea Monkeys
```

Just those two words. Other pages on my website will target the other search phrases, but I want the search engines to know that my homepage (and by inference, my website) is about one thing and one thing only – Sea Monkeys.

After adding a Title, click OK and another dialog box will open asking you to save the Page. There is a golden rule to remember here. A website's homepage is ALWAYS given the file name of index. Any valid file extension can be used with the file name, but in most cases when building basic websites the extension will be .html or .htm (HTML is just a later version of HTM). So for my homepage, I'll enter the following in the dialog box before pressing the SAVE button:

```
Name: index

Type: HTML Files
```

That will save the homepage as index.html.

Incidentally, you can change the Title Tag at any time by clicking FORMAT on the top toolbar and by selecting PAGE TITLE AND PROPERTIES from the dropdown menu. This not only allows you to enter or change the page's Title, but also allows you to enter a Page Description and this is the Description Tag also discussed earlier. For the Sea Monkeys website I am going to enter the following under Description:

Sea Monkeys - What Are Sea Monkeys And Where To Buy Them In The UK

Adding a banner advertisement to a Table Cell

Work saved, we will now add a banner advertisement into the Table's second Cell. It could be that a merchant has designed a banner specifically for a product or service, but as I have never seen one for Sea Monkeys, I will add a banner that is at least in keeping with the website. Sea Monkeys are generally bought for children as a gift so a banner ad relating to children, gifts, and gadgets, would not be out of place here. I have opted for one for Prezzybox who run their affiliate program via Affiliate Window, paying a 10% commission with a 60 day cookie.

By logging into Affiliate Window, I can see all of the banners available to me to promote Prezzybox and the most appropriate one was for birthday gifts and presents. I can also get the code that displays both the ad on my page and tracks any click-throughs so that the visitors I send Prezzybox are recorded as are any sales made. The code for that particular banner is:

```
<!--START MERCHANT:merchant name Prezzybox from
affiliatewindow.com.-->
                <a
href="http://www.awin1.com/cread.php?
s=196548&v=164&q=103326&r=XXXXX"><img
src="http://www.awin1.com/cshow.php?
s=196548&v=164&q=103326&r=XXXXX"
border="0"></a>
                <!--END MERCHANT:merchant name
Prezzybox from affiliatewindow.com-->
```

It looks fairly complicated, but our only real concern is that it works and you will be pleased to hear that it does. That is the code we now need to add to our web page. Since it is code, we can't just paste it into a Table Cell like we could do text for example. If we did, it would be treated as text and shown on the page to visitors as the gobbleydegook you see above. Text and images can be placed onto a web page while in WYSIWYG Normal view mode, but code has to be added to the page's code.

Above: Tabs at the bottom of the screen allow you to toggle between views: Normal, with HTML Tags, as HTML Source, and in Preview (what it will look like to visitors)

At the bottom of the SeaMonkey screen, you'll see four tabs that allow you to view your web page in four formats.

Normal – the What You See Is What You Get (WYSIWYG) format that makes life easy for creating web pages and the one we use most of the time

HTML Tags – The WYSIWYG view, but with the HTML Tags included

HTML Source – this is your page's source code

Preview – this is how your page will look in an internet browser like Internet Explorer or Firefox, but it isn't a substitute for actually checking your website in commonly used browsers

With the likes of Adobe Dreamweaver, if you click somewhere on a page when in Normal view and then switch to HTML Source view, the cursor blinks in exactly the same place in the code. This makes inserting code in the right place very easy. Unfortunately, SeaMonkey doesn't do the same. This can make life a little difficult if you switch to HTML Source view and aren't quite sure where to insert the new code.

One way around this is to view the page in Normal view mode and click inside the Table Cell where you want to place the banner ad's code. Then write the word "INSERT" so that it appears in the Table Cell. Now switch to HTML Source view mode and search for the word INSERT in the code. When you find it, you know that is where the code has to be pasted. Paste the code there and then delete the word INSERT. Return to Normal view and you should see the banner ad on your page.

First table completed, it's time to save our work again. Either click the SAVE icon on the middle toolbar or select SAVE from the FILE dropdown menu on the top toolbar.

Above: The index page with the first Table completed showing both the logo and banner ad

The next step – Table 2

Table 1 completed, we can now start work on Table 2. For this we need to create a Table with three columns, with the middle one wider than the left and right columns. To insert this new Table, click on the page just below Table 1 so that your mouse cursor is flashing on the screen. Then repeat what we did to insert the first Table:

1. Click on the Table icon in SeaMonkey's middle toolbar

2. When the dialog box opens, enter:

Rows: 1
Columns: 3
Width: 900 pixels
Borders: 0

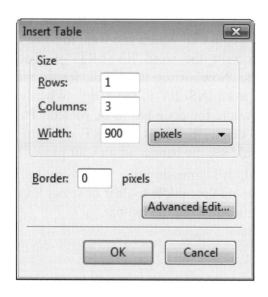

Above: Dialog box for Table 2

3. Then press OK

    That will insert Table 2 into our web page, but we still need to centre it on the page and also adjust the column widths.

    To centre the Table, click anywhere inside the Table and then press the TABLE icon on the middle toolbar. A new dialog box will open with two tabs at the top that will allow you to edit the properties of both the Table and each Cell.

1. Click the Table tab and change Table Alignment to Centre

2. Click OK

3. Table 2 should now be centred under Table 1 on your web page

Now we need to adjust the widths of the columns. My plan is to have a narrow column on either side of a wider central column. The width of each of the two narrow columns is going to be 125 pixels – this allows me to use the popular 120 pixels wide banner ads in either. The central column doesn't need to be any particular width. So to adjust the width of Column one:

1. Click inside the first Column and then click the Table icon on the toolbar

2. This will open a dialog box

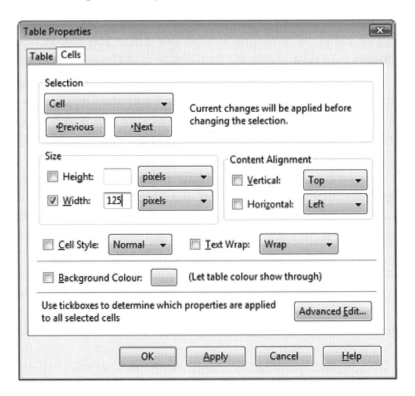

3. The only thing we need to do is set the Width to 125 pixels and to make sure Content Alignment is set to Vertical – Top and Horizontal – Left

4. Then click OK to save those changes

Now click inside Column 3 and repeat the above so that it too has a width of 125 pixels. That should give us the three column Table that we want.

Adding content to a Table

Next, we want to add some content to the Table, starting with Column one. In this column I want to give visitors links to where they can buy Sea Monkeys, the idea being that when they do I will earn a commission.

The easiest way for me to find out where you can buy Sea Monkeys is to do a search for Sea Monkeys at Google.co.uk.

Amazon dominates the natural Search Engine Results Pages (SERPs for short and not to be confused with the UK pension of the same name), but the Shopping Results also show that Tesco, Play.com, Toys R Us and John Lewis also sell Sea Monkeys. Further down the SERPs, I see Zavvi sell Sea Monkeys too.

Having been involved in affiliate marketing for a number of years now, I know that each of the above companies has an affiliate program that will pay me a commission on every sale generated. If you are not sure if a merchant has an affiliate program or not, there are a few ways to find out:

● Visit the merchant's website and look for a link to an affiliate program (it is usually in the footer at the bottom of the home page)

● Google the merchant's name with the words "affiliate program" after it (eg Asda affiliate program)

● Visit the Affiliates4U website (http://www.affiliates4u.com) and search the Forum for the merchant's name

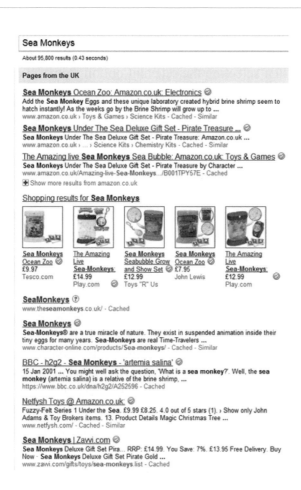

Above: The first page of Google SERPs for Sea Monkeys

Now all I need to do is enter details of where you can buy Sea Monkeys into that first Column. Just click inside the Cell and start typing, just as you would if writing an e-mail or creating a Word document. I like to keep things very simple so will just be listing the name of each product, its price, and the name of the retailer.

The text will appear in a plain default font (usually Times Roman) and will be at a default size too. You can change the text's size, font, colour and appearance, either by using the third toolbar, which is for text, or by selecting FORMAT from the top toolbar and then selecting the relevant option from the dropdown menu.

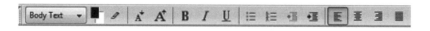

Above: SeaMonkey's text tool bar

The text toolbar is more or less self-explanatory. It is very similar to the type of toolbar found in word processing software like Microsoft Word.

If you want to change the font you will need to use FORMAT from the top toolbar, but remember to keep to fonts that are common to all computers – Helvetica, Arial, Times and Courier.

I am going to change the text in that column to Arial by first highlighting it (with your mouse, click the left mouse button just before the first letter of the text you want to highlight, keep it held down, then drag the mouse over the text to be highlighted, releasing the mouse button when you have finished highlighting). Once highlighted I go to FORMAT, select FONT and then choose Arial.

I also want the first lines of text to be in bold and a size bigger than the rest of the text. To do this I use the text toolbar, highlight the required text as before, press the BOLD icon and then the INCREASE SIZE icon (hover over any of the icons with your mouse cursor for a short description if you are unsure of their function).

Adding affiliate links

The next task is to add affiliate links. When possible, I want to deliver visitors to the exact page on a merchant's website that is selling the product I am promoting. Deeplinking leads to a higher conversion rate and more money for me. How you do this varies across the affiliate networks, but most provide tools that enable you to create deeplinks quickly and easily.

Amazon for example has a Site Stripe that allows you to quickly link to any page on its site. If you first log into your Associates account and then visit Amazon's actual website, the Site Stripe will automatically appear at the top of each web page (unless turned off). The first thing you will notice on the Site Stripe is a button marked "Link To This Page". Go to any page on Amazon's website, click that button, and the affiliate link you require will be automatically generated.

Above: Amazon.co.uk's homepage with Site Stripe and Link To This Page button circled

I want to link to the page on Amazon.co.uk that is selling the Sea Monkeys Ocean Zoo set so I navigate to that page, click the "Link To This Page" button, and a dialog box opens.

The dialog box gives me the option of creating three types of link: Text and Image, Image Only and Text Only. In this instance I only want a text link and so I select that. I also only want the word Amazon to appear in the link and so I enter that in the box labelled Link Text. The only thing left to do is to copy and paste the HTML code provided to my web page.

Customise and Get HTML

Link to a specific product on Amazon and show some information about that product. The Product Links tool lets you build customised Text Links, Text and Image links, and Image only links to Amazon products.

Signed in as barnsetc-21 ▾   Tracking ID seamonkeys-21 ▾

1. Select Link Type	Preview
○ Text and Image ○ Image Only ◉ Text Only	To create this link, cut and paste the HTML code in the lower left textbox into your web page. Amazon
2. Customise Link	
Link Text Amazon	

3. Get HTML Code For This Product Link

Highlight and copy the HTML below, then paste it into the code for your Web site.

```
<a href="http://www.amazon.co.uk/gp/product
/B001CBZXEE?ie=UTF8&tag=seamonkeys-21&linkCode=as2&
camp=1634&creative=19450&
creativeASIN=B001CBZXEE">Amazon</a><img
src="http://www.assoc-amazon.co.uk/e/ir?t=seamonkeys-
21&l=as2&o=2&a=B001CBZXEE" width="1" height="1" border="0"
```

[Highlight HTML]

Note: Your Associates ID, **seamonkeys-21**, is already embedded in the code.

Above: Dialog box that opens to give me the code I need to link to a page on Amazon.co.uk

Since it is code that I do not want to appear as is on my actual page, I will need to go to the Source code again (by selecting the HTML Source tab at the bottom of the page) and paste all of the code provided in the appropriate place.

If I view my page in Normal view mode, the first Column of Table 2 has details of where to buy Sea Monkeys. Taking the first entry – Sea Monkeys Ocean Zoo £7.14 Amazon – I want to link the word Amazon to the page on Amazon.co.uk's website that is selling this set. I therefore need to switch to HTML

Source view, find the first entry, highlight the word Amazon, and then paste the HTML code provided by the dialog box over that one word. When I return to Normal view mode, the code itself won't appear, but the word Amazon will, in blue and underlined, and it will have been transformed into the link I need to track any sales I make.

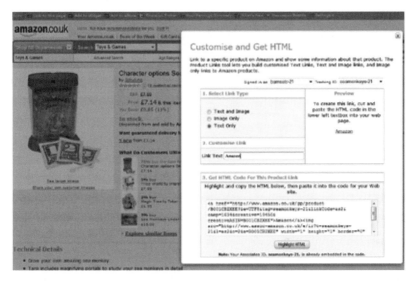

Above: The Site Stripe dialog box

Again, what has filled a few pages of this book will soon take you seconds to accomplish. I have just added the tracking links to the other two products available from Amazon in less than a minute.

I now just need to create links to the products available from Play.com and John Lewis. At the time of writing, the affiliate programs for both were on the Affiliate Window network, and as per all of the networks, deeplinking instructions are provided on their website. Remember, you have to join each affiliate program, not just the network, to earn money from it.

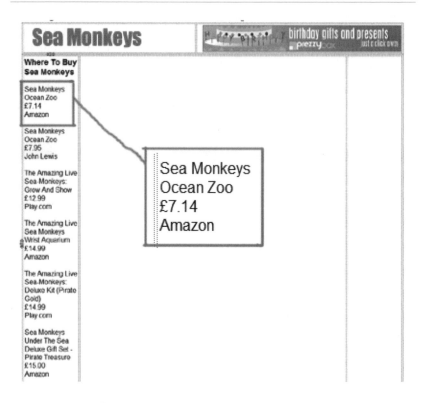

Above: The Sea Monkeys homepage so far with logo and banner at the top and details of where to buy Sea Monkeys in the first column of the second Table.

After logging in to your Affiliate Window account, the navigation menu on the right includes a section headed Linking Methods and one of those is a link to the Deep Link Builder.

Follow that link to the Deep Link Builder and it is then just a case of filling in the information required and copying the code generated.

Select Merchant: Select the merchant from the dropdown menu – if the merchant you want to link to isn't included it will be because you have not joined its affiliate programme

Click Ref: This is for you to add a reference so that you know exactly where the traffic is coming from. I will add Monkeys as the click reference

Deep link url: This is the full url of the web page you want to like to (copy it from your browser)

Choose format: You can choose "html" and get the code in a format that can be pasted into your source code or just the "url" link

Link text: If you choose the html format you can enter the words you want to appear in the link eg John Lewis

Open in window: you can choose for the linked to page to open in the current browser window or a new one (normally I select current because I think it delivers a better user experience)

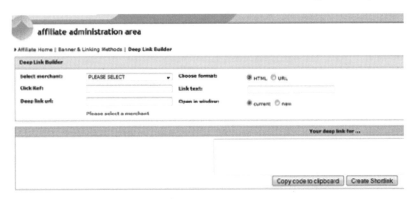

Above: The affiliate Administration Area of Affiliate Window and The Deep Link Builder

All filled in, I just need to copy the code that has been generated. I have opted for the url format rather than the html format so that I can show you how to work with affiliate links that come in the form of a web address. The url generated is as follows (the XXXXX is where your affiliate ID would be):

```
http://www.awin1.com/cread.php?
awinmid=1203&awinaffid=XXXXX&clickref=Monkeys&p
=http%3A%2F%2Fwww.johnlewis.com
%2F230646810%2FProduct.aspx
```

With an url, we don't need to edit the HTML Source code and can remain working in Normal view mode. To add the url link to my page, I go to where I want the link to be - Sea Monkeys Ocean Zoo £7.95 John Lewis – and I highlight the words John Lewis. I then click on the LINK icon in the middle toolbar at the top of the page and paste the url supplied by Affiliate Window into the dialog box. Click OK and the link will be added to your page.

Above: Affiliate Window's Deep Link Builder with the information required to deeplink to a page on the John Lewis website

The John Lewis link is actually one of two links to the same product, the Sea Monkeys Ocean Zoo. Above the John Lewis one is the Amazon link we created earlier to the same product. The reason I do this is to not only give my visitors a choice of where to buy the product, but to present them with a price comparison in the hope that they won't feel the need to scour the Net for a lower price. I want the sale. If buying on price alone, nobody would click the John Lewis link, but that underlines its value in being included because it encourages visitors to buy from Amazon (on another day, John Lewis might be cheaper).

Above: SeaMonkey toolbar with LINK icon circled

I can now create links to the Play.com Sea Monkeys pages in exactly the same way to complete the first Column. I now have six options for my visitors to choose from if they want to buy Sea Monkeys. I am now officially in the Sea Monkey business.

How to add an image to a web page

We are now going to add some content to the middle Column of Table 2 – an image and some text.

If you need an image for your website, you can't just copy one from another website and use it on yours. Not without the risk of breaching copyright laws anyway (this goes for text too). If you do copy an image without permission and you tred on the wrong toes it can cost you dearly.

Getty Images, for example, are notorious for invoicing those who use their images without permission. They use a company called PicScout to scan the web for unauthorised and unlicensed use of its images and then send demands for payment, often running into thousands of pounds, based on Getty's highest possible price for unlimited use rights.

Fortunately there are plenty of sources of free or very cheap images for you to use legally:

• Use images supplied to you by the merchant you are promoting

• Take photos of products yourself for use on your website

• A lot of companies make stock promotional images available on their website for use by the media and for those promoting their products and services

• Most people have heard of Wikipedia, the free online encyclopedia that has reduced homework time to minutes thanks to the wonders of cut and paste (http://en.wikipedia.org). Fewer folk are aware of its sister project, Wikimedia Commons, home to a database of almost eight million (and counting) freely usable media files including images, video, sounds and more (you can find it at http://commons.wikimedia.org).

• Stock photo websites like Fotolia (http://www.fotolia.com), iStockphoto (http://ww.istockphoto.com), and Shutterstock (http://www.shutterstock.com) offer a huge selection of professional photos and images that you can use for either small one-off fees or as part of a subscription deal.

• For photos of pop stars, sports stars and other celebrities that you can use on your websites, try PR Photos (http://www.prphotos.com).

The various websites that sell Sea Monkeys use the same images as each other and it is safe to assume that they are stock images intended for the promotion of the Sea Monkeys product. I am going to use one from Amazon for the Ocean Zoo. To copy it I click on it with the right button of my mouse, choose COPY from the menu that appears, and then paste it into my image editing program. I can then resize it, crop it, or make any other necessary changes, before saving it as a .jpg file to my Sea Monkeys website Folder.

It is not always possible to copy an image using standard copy and paste techniques. In situations like this you need software that will capture or grab an image. I use the free version of Screenhunter by Wisdom Soft which allows you to capture a full screen, an active window, or a designated rectangle (http://wisdom-soft.com/products/screenhunter_free.htm).

To insert an image into my web page, I first click in the Cell in which I want the image to appear and then click the IMAGE icon on the middle toolbar, just as we did when inserting the logo earlier (you can also click INSERT on the top toolbar and then select IMAGE from the dropdown menu).

When the dialog box opens, I navigate to where the image is on my computer, add the alternate text, make sure the dimensions are set to actual size, and then click the APPEARANCE tab. Unlike with the logo, there will be text in this cell as well as an image and I want to make sure both look good together. This time I will have spacing to the left and right (5 pixels) and top and bottom (5 pixels) of the image, but will still have no border (0 pixels). I also want the text to flow around the image so will set Align Text To Image to "wrap to the right". All done, I can click OK and the image will appear on the web page.

I still want to link the image to the Amazon page so that if anyone clicks on it (as people tend to do) it will take them straight through to Amazon.co.uk. I only need the link and not the full HTML code to do this and there is an easy way of extracting that from the longer code we got earlier.

In Normal view mode, double click on the blue link in the first column for the Ocean Zoo from Amazon. A link dialog box will open and will display just the tracking link from the HTML code we inserted into the code earlier (the rest of the code is mainly for Amazon's own use and not strictly required).

Copy the link from the dialog box, then double click the image to open another dialog box, this time an Image Properties one. The fourth tab at the top of the box is marked LINK. Paste the link into the space and then click OK. The image will now link through to the relevant page on Amazon.co.uk.

How to add text so that it goes round an image

We have already aligned the text to our image and have said that we want the text to wrap to the right of the image. If you click anywhere inside the middle Cell of Table 2, away from the image, the mouse cursor will appear to the top right of the image. Start typing and you will soon see that the text will wrap around the image as required.

I can use information from Amazon's product description on my web page, but it is essential that I don't just copy it word for word. If I did just copy it, my web page would not rank well and would instead jockey for position on the pages that nobody ever sees, including those of affiliates who do just copy and paste and then wonder why they aren't generating many sales. When people say content is king they really mean good original content so bring some originality to the table and there is every chance you will rank in one or more of the search engines. Ranking means traffic and traffic means sales.

Where possible I like to inject a personal touch into my pages. I find website visitors warm to a conversational style of writing (hence the meteoric rise of the blog). Bottom line, I'm selling stuff, not reading the news. Identifying with the reader also helps engender trust so imagine you are writing for your visitors one at a time.

Again, I changed the font from default to Helvetica / Arial and I used the BOLD icon to add emphasis to the opening paragraph. I have also used the HIGHLIGHT icon on the text toolbar to highlight a few sentences to make them stand out. I also changed the text in the first Cell in Table 2, making it smaller and all bold to differentiate it from the text in Cell 2.

How to give a column (Cell) a background colour

To differentiate Cell 3 even further we could give it a background colour. Click anywhere inside the Cell and then click the TABLE icon on the toolbar. A Table Properties dialog box will open, giving the properties of the Cell we are working with.

One of the options is Background Colour and by clicking on the box next to it another dialog box will open, this time giving you a choice of colours. Choose one that is suitable for your design and then click OK. You will return to the first dialog box where you can click either APPLY or OK and the colour change will take effect. I have opted for a pale yellow as black text will contrast well with it (avoid dark text on dark backgrounds as it is difficult to read – sounds obvious, but I see it used almost daily).

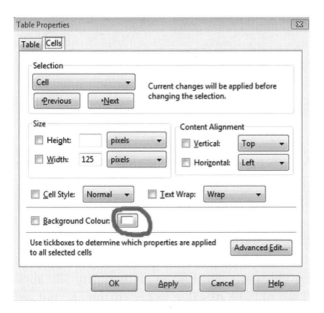

Above: dialog box that opens when you click inside a Cell showing the Cell's properties. Circled is the box you click to change the Cell's background colour.

Now we have a third column that is a different colour to the other two columns. I am going to click inside it again so that I can start adding content. What I want to add here is some navigation links to other (yet to be created) pages on the Sea Monkeys website and for inspiration I will refer back to the list of search terms provided by the Google AdWords Keyword Tool.

I have decided to pose a few questions that people might be looking for answers to – remember to make money from a niche market we have to satisfy its needs and wants. So in this instance I have opted for:

- What are Sea Monkeys?
This will answer one of the most commonly asked questions

- What are Triops?
This allows me to create a page relating to the search keyword "Triops" as discussed earlier

- Where can I buy Sea Monkey food?
Anyone who already has Sea Monkeys will inevitably run out of food for them one day – and will be frantically searching the Web for more

I will also create a page entitled "The man who discovered Sea Monkeys". I told you about Harold von Braunhut earlier. It's information that I have to hand from when I did the research for this book and can now use it again on a website. It means an extra page for very little work.

The other thing I will do is include a link to the Official Sea Monkeys website. This outbound link to an authority site about Sea Monkeys will not only be of value to my customers, but will help my search engine ranking too because I am associating my website with an authoritative one in the same field.

Normally, I wouldn't link to what could be a competitor in terms of sales, but I am counting on the fact that very few people in the UK will order something from the USA when it is available here. Looking at the Official Sea Monkeys website, it doesn't exactly fill me with dread as far as competition goes anyway. At the time of writing, it doesn't even accept online orders – you have to fill in a form and post it in with your "check, money order or cash" (US Dollars only too). This takes me back to the days of mail order bookselling in the late Seventies and early Eighties. As does the "allow about 28-35 days for delivery". My humble website allows visitors to pay online using a credit or debit card and they can have their Sea Monkeys by the following day.

Add a footer Table with copyright information

I want to quickly add Table 3 before going any further. Table 3 is basically the page's footer and can include the stuff normally found at the bottom of a web page. To keep it simple, I am only going to include copyright information, but it could include other links and information if required (web pages are automatically protected by copyright laws, but it is convention to add this information).

Insert a Table as before:

1. Use your mouse to click below Table 2 so that the cursor flashes where we want Table 3 to be

2. Click the TABLE icon on the middle toolbar at the top of the page

3. In the dialog box, set Rows to 1, Columns to 1, Width to 900 pixels, Border to 0 and then click OK.

4. Either double click inside the new Table or click inside it to select it and then choose TABLE from the top toolbar and then TABLE PROPERTIES from the dropdown menu

5. Make sure the tab at the top of the dialog box is set to Table

6. Set Table Alignment to Centre and then click OK

Table created, we just need to add the copyright information:

```
© Sea Monkeys seamonkeys.co.uk 2010. All right
reserved.
```

There is no Copyright symbol - © - on a standard keyboard, but you can create one using the ALT key and the numeric keypad found on the right of most keyboards. To insert a Copyright symbol hold down the ALT key and then type 0169 on the numeric keypad (ensure that Number Lock is switched on). Don't have a keyboard with a numeric keypad? Find a copyright symbol online and simply copy and paste it onto your web page.

How to add a new page to a website

So far we have been building the homepage (index.html) and now we will create the additional pages required to answer the questions in the third Column. The quickest and easiest way to do that is to use the index.html as a template for all of the other pages. That's why I wanted to get Table 3 done, so that I had a completed page to use as a template.

The first new page that we will create will be the "What are Sea Monkeys?" page. The first step is to save index.html as this new page which we will call What-Are-Sea-Monkeys.html (you can't have spaces in file names so use either the underline or a dash to connect words). We do this by selecting FILE from the top toolbar and then SAVE AS from the dropdown menu.

A dialog box will then open asking for the new file name:

```
What-Are-Sea-Monkeys
```

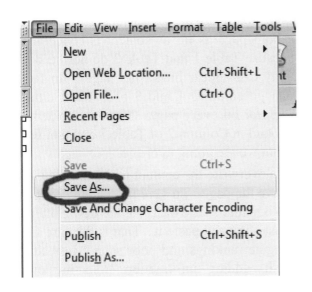

Above: To save a page you have already created as a different page, choose FILE from the top toolbar and then select SAVE AS from the dropdown menu

By default, it should want to save this file into the Folder I created for the Sea Monkeys website. It should also want to save the file as an HTML file.

I might as well add a Title and short Description now too, and I can open the dialog box to do that by first selecting FORMAT on the top toolbar and then selecting Page Title And Properties from the dropdown menu. Where it asks for a Title I enter :

```
What Are Sea Monkeys?
```

I then click SAVE and a second dialog box will open. Where it asks for a Description I enter:

```
Sea Monkeys - everything you ever wanted to
know about the amazing Sea Monkey!
```

Okay, so now I have a page titled, What Are Sea Monkeys?, but it is basically the homepage as far as content is concerned. That's no bad thing because Table 1 and Table 3 do not need to be changed at all. They can appear on all my pages. In fact, there is no need to change columns 1 and 3 of Table 2 either because they too can appear on every page. The only content I have to change is that found in Column 2 of Table 3 and that will be true for every page that we are going to create.

So all I have to do is overwrite the content in the middle Cell with new content and save the page. To save time, I am going to use information from Wikipedia as the basis for the new content, but I am not going to just copy and paste it. That is the sure fire route to poor search engine rankings and poor sales. Instead, I am going to rewrite it, adding information from my own experience of having kept Sea Monkeys as a child, resulting in unique (and hopefully interesting) content for my website. I am also using a copyright free image of Sea Monkeys in a tank from Wiki Commons.

Once completed, I can create the other pages I need using the index.html page as a template. I have three more pages to create:

What are Triops?
Triops.html

Where can I buy Sea Monkey Food?
Buy-Sea-Monkey-Food.html

The man who discovered Sea Monkeys
Harold-von-Braunhut.html

Notice that I name each page so that it is both easily recognisable by me when searching for files (very important on a much bigger site) and so that the file name itself may help with Search Engine Optimisation by the use of keywords and keyword phrases.

How to link your internal pages

I now have a four page website (usually described as a microsite or mini-site) dedicated to Sea Monkeys. At the moment though, those four pages aren't linked in any way so don't really form a website as such. We can put that right very quickly. Returning to our homepage (index.html) and the third column of Table 2, we have the list of questions that will be navigation links to our other pages. To convert each line of text into a link, we highlight it as described before, and once highlighted, click on the LINK icon on the middle toolbar.

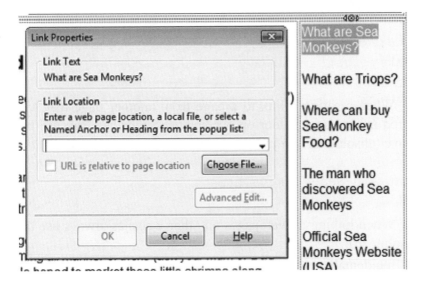

Above: the text "What Are Sea Monkeys?" is highlighted and by clicking the LINK icon on the toolbar, the Link Properties dialog box opens

Where it asks you to enter a Link Location, click CHOOSE FILE, navigate to the Folder containing your website's files and select the appropriate one by clicking on it – in this case the file named What-Are-Sea-Monkeys.html Then click OK.

I then repeat this process to create links to the other pages. I will do the same on the other internal pages because they too require the same navigation links to be added. Rather than do each one again, I can simply copy and paste the completed links from the homepage.

When creating links to pages on the same website, you can either use the full web address or just the file name (providing it is in the same location as the file linking to it) because internet browsers understand both absolute and relative urls. An absolute url is what most people recognise as a web address. Remember to always include the http:// part of the web address. The absolute url to the What Are Sea Monkeys? page would be:

```
http://www.sea-monkeys.co.uk/What-Are-Sea-
Monkeys.html
```

When creating a link to a page from another page that will stored in the same Folder on our hosting Server, we can use the above (absolute url) or just the file name (the relative url):

```
What-Are-Sea-Monkeys.html
```

When linking to web pages on other websites always use the absolute url.

Incidentally, if you want to create a link to an e-mail address you need to place mailto: before it (without a space). For example, to create a link to the e-mail address info@adomainname.co.uk, you would highlight the e-mail address, click on the LINK icon, and enter:

```
mailto:info@adomainname.co.uk
```

Above: The BROWSE icon circled on middle toolbar

To see what web pages will look like once published to the Net, and to check that internal and external links are working, click the BROWSE icon on the middle toolbar. This opens the page I am working on in the SeaMonkey browser and allows me to navigate between the pages that I have created and also access websites that I have linked to. It's a good way of making sure everything is ship-shape before you unleash your latest project on an unsuspecting public.

Publishing your website to the Web

Above: The PUBLISH icon circled on middle toolbar

Unlike with the WordPress website that we built earlier in this book, the Sea Monkeys website has been built on a computer and not on the Web. So for anyone to actually see it, they will have to come round to my house and admire my handiwork or I have to publish it to the Web.

To publish the website to the Web, I will need a domain name, hosting for the website, and a way of getting all of the files from my computer to the hosting server. We covered registering a domain name and buying website hosting in the chapter on building a website using WordPress. Now, all we have to do is get those files to the server. The most common method of doing so is by File Transfer Protocol or FTP.

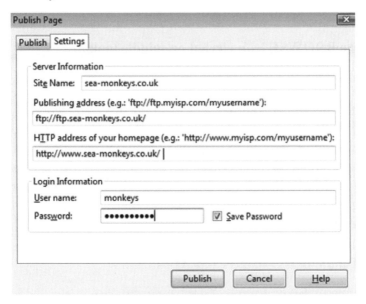

Above: Server Information settings for sea-monkeys.co.uk

SeaMonkey has basic FTP capabilities that can be accessed by clicking the PUBLISH icon on the middle toolbar. When you click on the PUBLISH icon, a Publish Page dialog box will open. The first time you want to publish a website to the internet you will need to input New Site details so that SeaMonkey can communicate with your hosting server. Click the NEW SITE button and another dialog box will open. Fill in the required Server Information and it will be saved for future use:

Site Name: your website's name and really for your own reference eg: Domainname.co.uk

Publishing Address: the address required to transfer files to and from your hosting server eg: ftp://ftp.domainname.co.uk or simply ftp.domainname.co.uk

HTTP Address for your homepage: what most people think of as a web address eg: http://www.domainname.co.uk

Login username: as provided in the welcome e-mail from your hosting company

Login password: as provided in the welcome e-mail from your hosting company

Be sure to check the Save Password box if you don't want to enter your password each and every time you publish anything to your website and then press the PUBLISH button.

That will return you to the first dialog box, with information such as the Site Name, and the Page Name and Filename of the page you want to publish, automatically filled in.

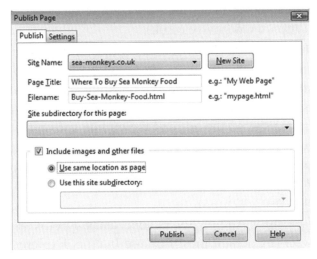

Above: The Publish Page dialog box

When first publishing a page, you will want to include images and any other files, but there is no need to publish the same images every time you update a page so untick and tick the "include images and other files" box as and when necessary.

Unless you are using sub-directories (useful for larger websites), you will want to publish the page to the default "use same location as page".

Now it is just a case of hitting the PUBLISH button (ensure you are online!) and your page and its associated files will be transferred to your hosting server and will be immediately available on the Net.

Good though they are, SeaMonkey's built-in publishing capabilities are basic. The same is true of similar free website editing software packages including KompoZer. One obvious limitation is that you can send files to your hosting server, but can't download files from it.

Full blown FTP software is a much better solution for the long term. I will recommend two free ones quickly here and will provide more information on using both on the Get Out While You Can website (http://www.gowyc.co.uk).

The first is called Filezilla (http://filezilla-project.org). Once downloaded and installed, it allows you to transfer files to and from your computer (the local site) and your hosting server (the remote site). As with most FTP programs, it shows a split window, with the local site on the left and the remote site on the right. Once logged in to the remote site, you can transfer files backwards and forwards simply by clicking and dragging them from one window to the other (other FTP programs have arrows pointing between the two windows).

The second is a nifty Add-on for anyone using Firefox as their internet browser (by default most PCs use Internet Explorer to browse the internet, but it is well worth downloading and using Firefox instead or as well as IE – http://www.getfirefox.net). It is called FireFTP (https://addons.mozilla.org) and once added, it can be accessed from the TOOLS menu on Firefox.

Mission accomplished

Sea Monkeys

Where To Buy Sea Monkeys

Sea Monkeys Ocean Zoo
£7.14
Amazon

Sea Monkeys Ocean Zoo
£7.95
John Lewis

The Amazing Live Sea Monkeys: Grow And Show
£12.99
Play.com

The Amazing Live Sea Monkeys Wrist Aquarium
£12.99
Amazon

The Amazing Live Sea Monkeys: Deluxe Kit (Pirate Gold)
£14.99
Play.com

Sea Monkeys Under The Sea Deluxe Gift Set - Pirate Treasure
£15.00
Amazon

Dogs, cats, rabbits. Parrots that could swear like a trooper. You could keep them all. If you were a kid growing up in the Seventies, there was only one pet you wanted.

Sea Monkeys!

I was one of those kids, totally spellbound by ads in comics that promised a tank full of magical monkey-like creatures that lived in castles and rode bicycles (where were Trading Standards back in the day?).

The truth is that Sea Monkeys don't look anything like monkeys. They don't even live in the sea. They live in a plastic tank in your bedroom.

But strip away all the hype (and, let's be honest here, the bare-faced lies of yesteryear) and what you are left with is something that is still truly miraculous.

By mixing those three sachets together a miracle of nature unfolds before your very eyes.

Just add water and Sea Monkeys really do come to life.

They really are the world's only instant pets

So drag your kids away from the TV or their games console for a moment and introduce them to the magical world of Sea Monkeys.

Let them pour the sachets of what looks like "just powder" into the water and watch their faces light up in amazement as their Sea Monkeys come to life!

The picture above shows the Sea Monkeys Ocean Zoo which is the perfect starter kit at just £7.14 from Amazon.

What are Sea Monkeys?

What are Troops?

Where can I buy Sea Monkey Food?

The man who discovered Sea Monkeys

The Official Sea Monkey Website (USA)

That's the Sea Monkey website complete. Once you are up to speed, it will take maybe two or three hours to build a similar website from scratch. Apart from the updating of prices, checking that links still work, and ensuring that the website is actually live, my Sea Monkeys website can more or less go on autopilot for the foreseeable future.

In terms of earning potential, I stand to make around 50p per Sea Monkeys Ocean Zoo sold. To make £100 in a year, I would therefore need to sell 200 such sets. Supposing one visitor in 100 buys a set, I need it to attract 20,000 visitors in a year or just under 2,000 visitors a month. With a 2% conversion rate, I would need 10,000 visitors a year.

Given the very low commission per sale, it is probably borderline whether it is the sort of site worth investing a few hours in, but in this instance it has also helped me with another revenue stream (this book). Even better, I now have something interesting to say when people ask what I do for a living. I sell Sea Monkeys.

Let Google pay your mortgage

"There is only one success - to be able to spend your life in your own way."
Christopher Morley

When Russian billionaire, Alexander Lebedev, bought a controlling stake in the loss making *London Evening Standard* for a nominal fee of £1 in January, 2009, it not surprisingly hit the headlines. The newspaper industry, a relic of the industrial age, has been severely tested by the advent of the digital age, with the *Standard* one of many loss-making titles currently struggling to secure its future.

This sorry state of affairs is all the more surprising when you consider that its stock in trade has always been information and we now live in the information age, but the *Evening Standard* was perhaps the best example of a newspaper that feared rather than embraced the online opportunities afforded a news orientated business. It was so frightened of losing readers to an internet version of its printed newspaper that it even launched its website under a completely different name, This Is London (http://www.thisislondon.co.uk), to differentiate the online version from the printed one. As if readers wouldn't instantly join the dots.

The circulation of the *Evening Standard* almost halved from more than 400,000 copies a day in 2003 to 236,000 copies a day in 2009. The reason for this decline was partly due to competition from rival (free) newspapers, partly because of the explosion of other sources of news thanks to the internet and mobile phones, and partly because very few people under the age of 25 buy newspapers any more – something that should worry all newspaper publishers.

Lebedev had a bold plan for the *Evening Standard* however. After 150 years of being a newspaper that was sold to its readers, it would be relaunched as a free title. Today, 610,000 copies of the *Standard* are given away each evening, mainly to commuters on their way home from work. The increase in circulation has obviously added to the print bill, but distribution costs per copy have been slashed and the increase in circulation has allowed the newspaper to increase its advertising rates. It's still losing money, but the plan is to be profitable within three years. Time will tell.

There was a time when I would have loved to have done something as bold as Lebedev has with the *Evening Standard*. I could have quite comfortably played the role of media mogul. Those days are behind me now though. Today, I'm far more interested in spending my time more wisely than earning (or losing) more money than I will ever need. It would also be completely hypocritical of me to be ranting and raving about wage slavery while actually employing some wage slaves of my own. But just like Mr Lebedev, I am in the business of giving away information.

Most websites are like the freebie newspapers given away at train stations and shoved through your letterbox. Very few websites charge anyone for reading their content (although if your information is valuable and worth paying for in the eyes of your target market, by all means think along those lines). Just like a free newspaper, a "free" website needs two things to be commercially successful. Readers and revenue (which typically means advertisers). No readers means no revenue, but that doesn't mean any old readers will do. No more than any old visitors will do for your websites either.

The *Evening Standard* isn't given away free at tube stations and train stations by accident. Similarly, its circulation isn't confined to London by accident either. Both are deliberate strategies to help advertisers find the perfect demographic and audience for their products and services. Another deliberate strategy is to always feature property on a Wednesday, motoring on a Friday, and so on.

For someone like me, with no other interest than making enough money to fulfil my Plan B each day, a free to read website beats a free to read newspaper hands down. For starters, no print bills. Distribution costs are far closer to zero too – you are only talking the cost of hosting and bandwidth instead of physically distributing thousands of newspapers. And given the worldwide reach of the Net, getting the audience right – geographical and otherwise – is far easier too.

A web page has another huge advantage over the printed page. Newspapers end up in the recycling bin. As the old saying goes, today's news is tomorrow's fish and chip paper (or at least it was when ink was considered part of a balanced diet). Web pages don't suffer a similar fate. They can be read today, tomorrow, next week, next year. For as long as they remain on a website in fact. Today's news is always news online. That means that a web page that goes live today can earn me or you money well into the foreseeable future.

Of course, you still need revenue from somewhere if you are actually to make money from a website. You could do what the likes of the *Standard* do. Go out and get it. Have rooms full of people hitting the phones all day long. That can be difficult going at the best of times, even when you are representing a big household name like the *Standard*. Trying to sell ad space on a website that hardly anyone has ever heard of is the advertising sales equivalent of working at a Russian Gulag.

The good news is that when it comes to getting advertisers for even the most obscure of websites, there's no need to do a stint of hard labour. Instead, sit back, relax, and let Google sell your ad space for you.

Google wants to pay your mortgage

The success of Google is built on simplicity. When you visit its homepage, you are confronted with little more than a simple search box. No advertising. No nothing. So how exactly does a free to use service like Google make any money?

The first point to make is that Google does indeed make money. Lots of it. In the first three months of 2010, Google earned US$6.77 billion in revenue of which US$1.96 billion was profit. The second point is that its plain Jane exterior hides a whole world of magic that is entered as soon as you type whatever it is you are looking for into that search box.

You see, Google doesn't just display its search results on the pages that follow. You may not even have noticed before, but if you look above and to the right of the search results, you'll find text advertising that is discreetly labelled Sponsored Links. The ads that appear are called Google AdWords and it works like this. Businesses create ads through their Google AdWords account and then choose words or phrases related to their business. When people search on Google using one of those keywords, related ads appear next to the search results.

Advertising space is limited and allocated on a bidding basis whereby the more you are willing to pay per visitor (every time that your ad is clicked in other words), the higher you are likely to appear on the Sponsored Links (Google also rewards advertisers for having quality and relevant landing pages as well as for ads that attract higher click-through rates, so you may bid less than a competitor, but appear above them in the Sponsored

Links). You're charged only if someone clicks your ad, not every time your ad is displayed.

The Google AdWords program is something that you might want to use to promote your own business, but it's not something that I'm going to dwell on here. Creating a Plan B is about making money and I'm more interested in telling you how you can get a piece of this billion dollar action for yourself by allowing Google to place similar ads on your web pages.

It all makes perfect (Ad)sense

Not to be confused with the similarly named Google AdWords, Google AdSense is a program that you can join to generate advertising revenue from each page on your website. That's because as well as displaying those text ads on search result pages, Google has extended the service to what it called the Publisher Network. A network that you can be part of. You simply add snippets of code to your web pages, telling Google where to place ads and what size they can be, and AdSense then delivers relevant text and image ads that are precisely targeted to your site's content. You can even add a Google search box to your site and earn money from the text ads that appear on the Google search results pages generated by your visitors' search requests.

Advertisers that appear on your website are most commonly charged on the same pay per click basis as they would be for appearing in the Sponsored Links on Google itself (the advertiser can also be charged on a pay per impression basis too, when they pay for every time their ad is displayed). Google collects the money and then shares it with you. You don't do anything beyond providing Google with the advertising real estate to sell.

Life just keeps getting better and better. Not only is Google, the biggest search engine in the world, working around the clock to send visitors to your website without asking you for so much as a penny in return. It is also willing to act as your advertising sales department, populating your website with AdSense ads that earn you money every time someone clicks on one.

When I first heard about people making large sums of money by simply placing Google AdSense code on their websites, I was more than sceptical. I had seen some very poor examples of AdSense deployment on web pages and wasn't overly impressed. I didn't for a moment think that these webmasters could be making any real money. I also thought that displaying Google ads on my own pages might look a bit tacky and somehow devalue my content (like it was ever going to win the internet equivalent of the Booker Prize anyway).

Those reservations meant that when I finally did get around to trying Google AdSense for myself in May, 2005, I did so half-heartedly. I placed ads on just one of my websites to begin with, a now defunct reality TV website that was never going to make me a fortune through AdSense simply because of its subject matter. I was setting myself up to fail and that's exactly what happened.

During May, 2005, I earned a grand total of 76c through the Google AdSense program (in those days, all payments were made in dollars, but now you can choose to be paid in pounds and other currencies, including euros, depending on where you live). Four months later and I was fairing little better, earning just US$10.76 during the entire month of August. I just couldn't see how I was ever going to make any serious money doing this and was ready to give it up as a bad idea.

And yet I was still coming across individuals who were making hundreds if not thousands of dollars every month by doing nothing more than allowing Google to display its little ads on their web pages. So on the 11th of September, 2005, I decided to throw caution to the wind and place Google AdSense on what I had previously considered hallowed pages, too good for AdSense. I ended up earning more on that one day than I had during the whole of August. Maybe there was something to this Google AdSense after all.

I started to roll out Google AdSense to other sites and my revenue continued to grow. Not all pages enjoyed a high click-through rate and not all subjects enjoyed the same earnings per click, but my revenue kept on growing month after month. By January, 2008, I was earning US$2,000 a month from Google AdSense alone. In effect, Google was now paying my mortgage.

AdSense for beginners

Here's how it works. You sign up for a Google AdSense account (https://www.google.com/AdSense/login/en_GB/), and once accepted, you paste the snippets of code supplied by Google onto your web pages. Google then uses that code to place relevant ads, that match the content, onto the pages. So a page about boats will show ads relating to boats. A page about horses will show ads relating to horses.

When someone clicks on one of those ads, you earn money. How much money? It obviously depends on what markets you operate in, how many visitors you get to your website, and how many of those visitors click on the ads (the click-through rate – CTR). It can be anything from pennies to pounds per click and you can see what you're earning at any time, day or night, by logging into your Google AdSense account. Typically, I receive 8-10p per click across a wide variety of sites (which is more or less the same Earnings Per Click, or EPC, I enjoy from affiliate marketing).

What's more, there's nothing stopping you from also including other advertising on those pages, providing it doesn't contravene Google AdSense's terms and conditions. Advertising that you have attracted yourself, for example, or you could look for companies willing to pay you a commission on sales via an affiliate marketing program. Google AdSense simply offers you another way of monetising the work you do.

AdSense comes in five flavours that can be accessed via the AdSense Setup tab in your Google AdSense account:

AdSense For Content

AdSense For Content is where Google displays ads on your web pages that are targeted to your site's content or audience. You can customise the ads by type, format (including text or image) and colour, and then it's just a case of copying and pasting the supplied code onto your web pages.

Example of a
Google Adsense ad

As well as the basic Ad Unit, you can also use Link Units which display a list of topics that are relevant to your page – rather like a navigation bar. When users click a topic, they are taken to a page of related ads. Only when they click one of those ads will you make money so a Link Unit is a two step process unlike the basic Ad Unit.

Check first as things may have changed, but you can currently have up to three Ad Units and three Link Units on any one page. How many you use on a page will come down to the page's content and design, but there's usually a happy medium that falls well short of the maximum number allowed. Too much advertising of any variety does not create a good visitor experience.

AdSense For Search

If you've ever seen a search box on a website like the one above, it's not just the webmaster being helpful. He or she hopes you will use the search facility and maybe click on one or more of the Google Ads that appear beside the search results. If you do that, the webmaster earns some money.

Again, adding a Google Search Box to your website is as simple as customising its design via your Google AdSense account and then copying and pasting the code where you want it to appear on your page.

AdSense For Feeds

Without wanting to make things too complicated for anyone new to all of this, it's possible for people to be kept up to date with new content that has been added to a website without actually having to visit the website on a regular basis. This is done via feeds and by something techie called RSS (Real Simple Syndication). Basically, every time something gets added to a website, RSS informs anyone who has subscribed to the website's feed. It's a big deal in the blogging world and comes as standard with blogging software like WordPress. Using AdSense For Feeds, you now have an opportunity to monetise those feeds.

AdSense For Mobile Content

With ever more people accessing the internet via their mobile phone, some webmasters have created mobile friendly versions of their websites. Indeed, according to Morgan Stanley's *Mobile Internet Report 2009*, more people will access the internet using mobile devices than via desktop PCs within five years so it's something that should be on your radar.

AdSense For Mobile Content allows you to place suitably sized Google ads on your mobile website and then reap the rewards. Again, it's just a case of copying and pasting the appropriate code supplied by Google.

AdSense For Domain Names

If you have domain names that have yet to be developed into websites, AdSense For Domains allows you to monetise them. When a visitor goes to an undeveloped domain, they are most often greeted by an error message or an "Under Construction" holding page, neither of which earn you a bean. Domain names that are in the AdSense For Domains program display links, search results, advertisements and other content, all supplied by Google. You earn money when visitors interact with those ads.

Deploying Google AdSense to make you money

The best way to get the most out of Google AdSense is to test, test, and test again. Experiment with the number of ads that you place on any given page and experiment with where you choose to put those ads. A tweak here and there can make a real difference and if that difference is only £3 or £4 a day, that little snowball will turn into a thousand pounds or more over a year.

A good starting point is the Google Heat Map which I've reproduced on the next page (you'll find the full colour version in the Help Section of your Google AdSense account). It illustrates the fact that certain areas of a typical page perform better than others, with the darkest areas performing best and the lightest (white) areas performing worst. Incidentally, this holds true not just for Google AdSense. You can use the Google Heat Map to help position other advertising on a page as well as key content.

Working with the Heat Map, you can use the various Google AdSense formats and sizes to make the most of each page, depending on how you have chosen to lay it out. Always experiment, keeping a close eye on both the click-through rate (CTR) and earnings per click (EPC) across different sites and pages. Google allows you to track the performance of each individual ad unit by the use of Channels. You can use Channels to see how an ad unit at the top of a page performs against an ad unit at the foot of a page as well as between pages and even sites.

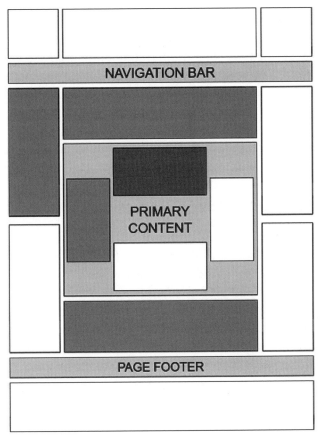

Above: The Google Heat Map shows where ads perform best on a typical web page, with the darker areas typically the most profitable

Bearing in mind that your own experimentation might reap richer rewards and that rules are made to be broken, here are some general guidelines that I have found work for me across a wide range of sites:

• Just because the Google Heat Map tells you that certain areas of a page can perform well, that doesn't mean that all of those areas will perform well at the same time and it certainly isn't an invitation to plaster AdSense ads all over the page. The key to long term success in any business is repeat business. This is as true for Tesco as it is for drug dealers on street corners. It's also true for you. Ideally, you want visitors to come back. At the very least you want them to hang around long enough to see what you have to offer. Fill your pages with ads and most visitors will be reaching for the back button faster than a chameleon's tongue catches its dinner.

• If visitors don't see your Google AdSense ads, it shouldn't surprise you that your Click-Through Rate (CTR) will be low. What might surprise you is that if you make your Google AdSense ads too noticeable (too obviously "adverts") your CTR will be low too. I've found that by blending AdSense into my content, my CTR is at its highest. I do this by making the background and borders of the ads the same colour as the background of the page (almost always white), by making the ad text the same font and size as my main content, and by ensuring that the links are always in blue (blue is the standard colour that everyone associates with links so why anyone uses anything else is a mystery to me). This isn't to fool visitors into thinking that the ads are content per se, but simply to encourage them to subconsciously accept them as part of the content, to hopefully then look at them, and then click on those of interest.

• According to market research experts, Nielsen, website visitors spend 80% of their time looking at content that appears "above the fold" (the area of a web page that appears on a screen without the user having to vertically scroll down to see more). Google AdSense ads (and other forms of advertising) that appear above the fold usually outperform those that appear below the fold.
• I'm hesitant to say what size of ad works best because it really does depend on the type of website, how its pages have been designed, and where on the page ads are placed. Google

themselves state that the 336x280 Large Rectangle, the 300x250 Medium Rectangle, and the 160x600 Wide Skyscraper generally perform best. I do like using the two rectangles mentioned because they can be embedded neatly into content, with text running around them. I'm not really a fan of skyscrapers as far as Google AdSense is concerned. I prefer to use one or two 125x125 Buttons in columns where Skyscrapers would normally be placed (spaced, not together, with text or other content in-between). The 728x90 Leaderboard can also work well for me, either at the top, but also at the bottom of a page.

• I really love Link Units and use them with great success on a number of my content websites. Instead of ads, a Link Unit contains four or five keywords or keyword phrases that match the content of your page and, at first glance, they look like navigation links (one big reason why people click on them). If someone clicks on one of those keywords you don't make money immediately. Instead, your visitor is taken through to a page that shows ads for the keyword that was clicked. When a visitor clicks on one of those ads you will make money. I mainly use the 728x15 Horizontal Link Unit at the top of pages where visitors might expect a navigation bar to be. You can choose to have four or five links in such a Link Unit, with the five link unit using a smaller text size. I like to go for whichever matches the size of my main content text best. A tip I picked up from Jen Slegg (aka Jensense, the Queen of all things AdSense so it's worth hanging on her every word over at her website, http://www.jensense.com) is to use one at the foot of a page too, above the usual copyright notice, where it is unobtrusive, uses up otherwise unused page real estate, but still converts well.

• This point holds true for all advertising, not just AdSense. Some pages will never make you money so don't waste your time putting ads on them. For example, a personal blog with a post about your honeymoon in Hawaii will earn you less money than a commercial blog with a post about Hawaii as a possible honeymoon destination – even if both pages show the same ads to the same number of visitors. That's because of the type of visitors each page is likely to attract. A personal blog is most likely to attract friends, family, and others interested in you. They are likely to be repeat visitors for that very reason. The information they want is primarily about you, not Hawaii. They probably won't even notice the ads.

A page that details Hawaii as a possible honeymoon destination will attract a different audience altogether. An audience of people primarily considering Hawaii as a honeymoon destination. Will they be interested in finding out more by clicking relevant ads? You bet. Why not slap ads on both sites, just in case? Because poorly performing pages can affect how much other pages and even websites in your account earn because of what Google calls Smart Pricing, where advertisers are charged less per click if Google's data shows it is less likely to result in a positive outcome for the advertiser.

• Where you place Google AdSense in relation to your content can have an important influence on CTR. For example, I do well with a rectangle ad block at the end of content – it gives readers something to do when they reach the end of the article, particularly if those ads offer something related to the content such as more information or a fantastic deal.

• By using Section Targeting, you can point Google in the direction of the part of a page's content that you want to emphasise or downplay when it comes to matching ads for a page. This can be very useful when part of a page is about very specific content while the rest is of a more general nature. To use Section Targeting, use one of the following code snippets before and after the relevant content (paste the code directly into your page code):

```
<!-- google_ad_section_start -->
content you want to emphasise on a page
<!-- google_ad_section_end -->
```

or

```
<!-- google_ad_section_start(weight=ignore) -->
content you want to downplay on a page
<!-- google_ad_section_end -->
```

• In common with many other webmasters, I have had little success with Google AdSense on forums. The forums I know that make the most money do so not so much from Google AdSense or any other form of advertising, but from having paid to access private member areas or are large enough to attract sponsorship style advertising.

• One huge advantage Google AdSense has over other forms of advertising is that once you have placed the code on your web pages, you can sit back and relax. From then on in, Google takes over, serving what it believes will be the most relevant and most profitable ads to your visitors. You don't need to update a thing. Google's ad inventory is also so large that there is rarely a shortage of advertisers eager to be seen on relevant pages. This frees you to create even more content for your visitors rather than spend time trying to attract advertisers yourself.

• If you are using WordPress to build your first websites, incorporating Google AdSense is a stroll in the park. There are a number of excellent Plugins designed specifically for this and there are AdSense ready Themes available too that just need your AdSense Publisher ID to be good to go.

Don't kill the goose that lays the golden egg

Given that you are paid every time someone clicks on one of the Google AdSense ads that appear on your pages, you may be tempted to be that someone who clicks on those ads. Don't. Ever. Don't ask friends or family to click on those ads either.

Google takes click fraud very seriously indeed and devotes considerable resources to detecting it. No matter how clever you think you are, assume someone has already been there, done that, and Google has caught them. AdSense related forums are peppered with posts from sorry individuals who have gone down this route and found themselves booted off the program. For the sake of earning a few extra pence (which Google won't pay them anyway once an account is suspended), they are kissing goodbye to potentially years of earning many thousands of pounds. You really have to be short-sighted to even begin going down this road.

I've already talked about my initial poor experiences with AdSense where I was lucky if I earned the price of a cup of coffee in a day. I now know that the website that I chose to test the water with AdSense was so far from the shoreline that I could count myself fortunate that my toes got wet. The content was good for what it was – it just wasn't content that would deliver customers to advertisers.

I regularly see inexperienced webmasters doing much the same thing, with mediocre websites that have been created specifically so that AdSense ads can be plastered all over them. So-called "Made For AdSense" websites very rarely make any real money. It's "Made For Visitors" websites that will ultimately bring home the bacon. Never forget that.

Get out while you can

"Laying eggs all your life and getting plucked, stuffed and eaten - good enough for you is it?"
Ginger, Chicken Run

When the Berlin Wall came a tumbling down in 1989, it heralded the end of Communism. Capitalism had won the Cold War and we could all now live happily ever after in a materialistic world of plenty. Or so the story went anyway.

The truth is that Capitalism didn't emerge victorious over Communism. At best it could be argued that Capitalism has outlived its 20th Century foe, but both ideologies are simply two sides of the same Industrial Age coin. Neither ideology has ever had the answers to all of society's woes. For decades both relied on wage slavery to create the wealth that paid for enough nuclear weapons to destroy life as we know it on this planet we call home. What sort of madness is that? Millions of people spending billions of hours on the hamster wheel of wage slavery so that opposing governments could create stockpiles of nukes? Politicians are probably the last people on Earth you want to put your future in the hands of. Successive governments around the world have shown themselves totally incapable of rising to the enormous challenges that lie ahead.

In his 2001 book, *The Future Of Money*, Bernard Lietaer identified four unavoidable "megatrends" that represent unprecedented challenges for our future: the information revolution, monetary instability, climate change, and what Lietaer calls the "Age Wave".

The eclipsing of the Industrial Age by the Information Age is something that has featured throughout this book. As we mothball steelworks and dismantle heavy industry, as we scramble around for an alternative to oil, it's clear for all to see that we are indeed moving into another age, an age dominated by information. This will inevitably have profound effects on the way we all live our lives. My big hope is that you fully understand the enormous opportunity this affords you to escape the rat race and that you grab it with both hands.

Equally, the recent near total collapse of the banking industry underlines the potentially overwhelming challenges we face from financial and monetary instability. We have now entered a decade or more of austerity that will help pay for some of the mistakes made on our behalf by the powers that be, but the risks we face haven't diminished simply because we have survived one near disaster. Make no mistake about it. Further shocks are on their way. The way the economic cards are so poorly stacked, together with the casino-like nature of much of our financial system, makes this inevitable. In fact, recent events may seem like a sideshow when the full circus comes to town. You need to provide yourself and your family with a financial cushion against such shocks and by developing multiple revenue streams you will do just that.

George Osborne has told us that the Government will have to shed 490,000 public sector jobs over the next four years. The Chartered Institute of Personnel and Development has said that the impact of the Spending Review has been understated and predicts 725,000 public sector jobs will go. Most commentators agree that up to a million private sector jobs will be lost too. Apparently, the same private sector will be responsible for creating one and a half million new jobs over the same period, according to The Office for Budget Responsibility anyway. Who am I to argue, but it begs the question that if job creation is going to come so easily, why isn't the private sector soaking up the current unemployed?

A large proportion of those losing their jobs, particularly in the public sector, will be managers and administrative staff, the very people who will almost certainly have the basic computer skills necessary to start work on a Plan B. The silver lining may well be the opportunity for some of them to redefine how they live their lives and my hope would be that Plan B might be part of the transformation from a life dominated by work to one dominated by living.

Then there's climate change. Whether man is responsible or not, there can be little doubt that the world's climate is changing. We will have to find increasing amounts of money to make good the devastation caused by flooding, droughts and extreme weather: money that we simply don't have. True, we can crank up the presses and print more money, but each freshly printed pound reduces the purchasing power of the pounds already in your pocket. After all, paper money is just that. Pieces of paper. Paradoxically, the more money they print (or create electronically), the poorer you become. That's why "quantitative easing" is no long term solution to our economic woes.

The transition from one economic age to another, the slow onward march of climate change and the frailties of our financial system can take years, decades even, to play out. That's why successive governments have been able to shirk their responsibilities and basically live for the day, spending our future and our children's future to do so. Nowhere is this more evident than with Lietaer's Age Wave.

The simple fact is that we are living longer. In 1984, there were around 660,000 people in the UK aged 85 and over according to the Office Of National Statistics. By 2034, the number of people aged 85 and over is projected to reach 3.5 million. Increasing numbers of us are going to enjoy long retirements, assuming that either we or the generations that follow are able to pay for them. And that's a big assumption.

The bulging baby boomer generation is going to cost this country an arm and a leg in retirement, but that isn't really news, or at least it shouldn't be. From the very moment each baby boomer was born, politicians have known full well what awaited us 65 or so years down the road. Instead of acting on this information, they simply buried their heads in the sand. It's easy to forget for example that we are an oil producing nation. The revenue generated by that oil has been all but squandered, spent largely on bigging up Britain on the world stage.

Not so in Norway, where oil revenue has been ring-fenced for the future prosperity of the Scandinavian country's inhabitants. We too could have done the same, but instead our politicians chose to follow the path of spending it all and then pretending to be wealthy by borrowing more money. Unfortunately, if you borrow a million pounds and live the lifestyle of a millionaire, the reality is that you aren't a millionaire at all: you are a million in debt. Plus interest.

Anyone alive today and living in the UK can expect to pay an increasingly heavy price to provide the pensions, healthcare and the other services that retirees demand, but even that won't be enough. The retirement age will have to be increased and increased again and again so that we work longer and pay taxes longer. A retirement age of 75 is not out of the question, but even that won't end our woes. Those in "retirement" will increasingly have to pay their own way. Vote for whoever you like, but the politicians aren't going to save you. It's every man and woman for him or herself. And I don't mean that in a selfish way. I mean that it's time for each and every one of us to take control of our own lives. You, and you alone, are responsible for your own life, your own destiny.

My advice for what it's worth? Take this as an opportunity to shape your own destiny. Break away from the chains of wage slavery and use financial independence as your passport to a brighter future, anywhere in the world.

Let's start a revolution!

In this day and age, if all you have to sell is your time, you are in big trouble. On a macro level, the challenges that we face can seem overwhelming and they may indeed prove to be so. I don't claim to have all the answers, but I do know this. There has to be a better way forward. Indeed, I believe a better way forward must be found if we are to prosper in the uncertain times we live in. I have said before that creating a Plan B and developing multiple revenue streams won't work for everyone, but if you have read this far I have no doubt that it could work for you.

Declaring financial independence from a system that is crumbling before our very eyes is as good a place to start as any. Even if we were not facing a future of financial instability, climate change, the eclipsing of the industrial age, and an ageing population, I would still question why we devote so much of our waking hours to work.

Given how short our lives are and how priceless our time is, it makes absolutely no sense to me. Running around like a blue-arsed fly in the name of work is quite frankly madness. Escaping the rat race should be a top priority even in so-called good times. Today, it could be your only chance of surviving and prospering in the years ahead.

The way things are shaping up, you need to be looking at alternative ways of making money. Alternative ways that allow you to not only escape the rat race, but that allow you to continue to make money no matter what you are doing and where you are doing it. Alternatives that free your time from a life of wage slavery.

I've been digging a tunnel for the last six or so years that I believe can be used as an escape tunnel for others too. The route I have chosen is to not to sell my time by the hour, but to ensure that the hours that I work make me money via multiple revenue streams for days, weeks, even years, to come. By reading this far, I'm hoping that a revolution has begun in your head. A revolution that is going to take you closer to achieving your full potential than all the years you have spent in education and work to date put together.

Starting in your spare time, you can begin to develop multiple revenue streams that will make you extra money. In time, there is no reason why they shouldn't become a significant proportion of your total earnings, cushioning you against wage cuts, pay freezes and even redundancy. In time, there is no reason why they shouldn't totally eclipse your current income to the point where you are making more money working less hours, doing something that you love. How good would that feel?

We should be doing what movie stars do. Do an hour's work and then allow that hour's work to make us money for days, weeks, months, years to come. We can't all be movie stars unfortunately, but thanks to the Information Age, anyone who can turn on a computer can put their time to work for them, just like those movie stars do. Just like your old mate, David Beckham, does.

We are all on a journey from cradle to grave, but we don't have to walk the path that we have been conditioned to take. In fact the revolution that's starting in your head is going to start asking, then pleading, then demanding, then grabbing you by the scruff of your neck and shaking you, until you give in to its demands for a better life.

Plan A doesn't work. Working longer and longer hours just to make ends meet is a mug's game. How we ever were hoodwinked in believing in Plan A in the first place beggars belief. Marx got it wrong. Religion isn't the opium of the masses. Work is.

In truth, Plan A hasn't really ever worked. Not for the ordinary man in the street who is asked to commit 40 plus years of his life to a system that doesn't value him one iota. A system that values the ordinary woman even less. Plan B gives you an opportunity to reclaim your life. To earn more money working less hours and hours to suit you. What may become of increasing importance is that it also allows you to do it from virtually anywhere in the world. When those megatrends truly collide, you may not want to be stuck in Blighty.

As the years tick by and we come face to face with the unavoidable challenges that lie ahead, Plan A is going to come increasingly off the rails. Don't wait until then. Now is the time to pull the cord, to stop the train. It's time for Plan B. It's time to get out while you can.

Three words

I want to close this book by telling you the secret of unlimited business success. Three words that are worth countless times the cover price of this book. Three words that will serve you time and time again as you fight the good fight towards financial independence and say goodbye to the rat race. Three simple words. Exceed customer expectations.

Exceed customer expectations. Write those three words on a piece of paper, place it in your wallet or purse, and carry them wherever you go.

Exceed customer expectations. In every recipe for making money, the key ingredient has to be customers. No customers, no business. Exceed their expectations in everything you do and they'll keep your tills ringing and your pockets full for many years to come.

I truly hope that this book has exceeded your expectations. My genuine hope is that it offers you a viable blueprint from which to develop your own Plan B. But this book is just the start. The story continues at the *Get Out While You Can* website (http://www.gowyc.co.uk) where escapees just like yourself will be welcomed with open arms and offered further help and support in your bid to escape the rat race.

We have come a long way since I asked you in this book's introduction why you go to work. Now it is time to complete the journey and for you to get out while you can.

Enjoyed this book? Want more? George Marshall is currently working on a follow-up to *Get Out While You Can* called *Why Do Only Fools And Horses Work?*. It will be available in paperback and Kindle format and published around Easter, 2012. See gowyc.co.uk or entrepreneur.co.uk for updates.